THE
U-BOAT
WARS

THE
U-BOAT
WARS

by Edwin P. Hoyt

ARBOR HOUSE : New York

To all men who have ever braved the sea

Manufactured in the United States of America

Design by Stanley S. Drate/Folio Graphics Co. Inc.

And the stately ships go on
To their haven under the hill,
But Oh for the touch of a vanished hand
And the sound of a voice that is still.
—ALFRED, LORD TENNYSON

Map 38
June 1940 – Dec 1941

Principal Atlantic and Home Waters
Convoy Routes showing approximate
zones of close anti-submarine escort

Limit of air cover in July 1941 — — —

60°

C A N A D A

Gulf of
St. Lawrence
NEWFOUND

Sydney

Halifax

40°

NEW YORK

UNITED STATES

· BERMUDA

20°N

JAMAICA
Kingston

Ocean Convoys: Surface Anti-Submarine Escort
(1) ONF   Outward N. American Fast Convoys had continuous escort by Western Approaches, Iceland & Newfoundland Escort
(2) ONS   "   "   Slow   "   "   "   "
(3) OG   "   "   Gibraltar   "   "   " - Liverpool Escort Forces from July 1941
(4) OS   "   "   Southbound   "   "   "   Londonderry   "   "   "   "
  Coastal Convoys:
(5) EC   Outward bound ocean going ships from Southend direct to Loch Ewe, Oban, & Clyde from 31st March – 28th Oct.

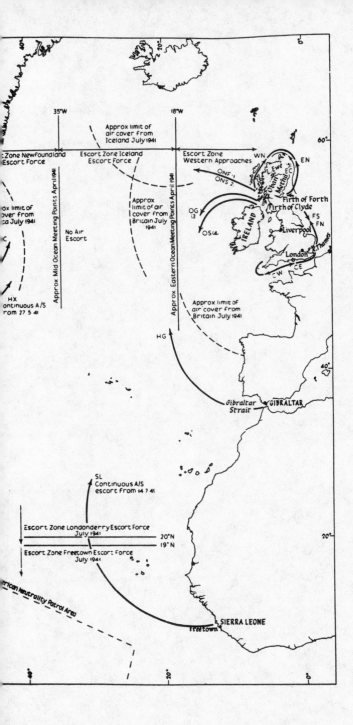

40°

20°W

60°

35°W

18°W

Approx limit of
air cover from
Iceland July 1941

: Zone Newfoundland
Escort Force

Escort Zone Iceland
Escort Force

Escort Zone
Western Approaches

WN

EN

EC

ONF₁
ONS 2.

Oban
Lewis
Mull
Methil

Firth of Forth
Firth of Clyde

ox limit of
cover from
ca July 1941

Approx
limit of air
cover from
Britain July
1941

OG
13

FS

C

No Air
Escort

OS 14.

ICELAND

Liverpool

FN

R.Thames

London

CW

CE

HX
continuous A/S
rom 27 5 41

Approx limit of
air cover from
Britain July 1941

HG

40°

Approx Mid Ocean Meeting Points April 1941

Approx Eastern Ocean Meeting Points April 1941

Gibraltar
Strait

GIBRALTAR

SL
Continuous A/S
escort from 14 7 41

Escort Zone Londonderry Escort Force
July 1941

20°N

20°

19°N

Escort Zone Freetown Escort Force
July 1941

rican Neutrality Patrol Area

SIERRA LEONE

Freetown

40°

20°

0°

Contents

Acknowledgments

I am especially indebted to a number of archivists and librarians at the Office of Public Records in London, and to Dr. Dean Allard and members of his staff in the Operational Archives of the U.S. Navy Historical Division in Washington. Librarians at the Navy library were also very kind. Michael Willis of the Imperial War Museum in London was especially helpful in securing photographs and answering complicated questions about the Royal Navy. And I am most grateful to the management and staff of Durrant's Hotel in London. They said they would take care of us and they did.

EDWIN P. HOYT

Maryland, 1984

1

Beginnings

In the winter of 1938–39, the shadows of Hitler's aggressive ambitions loomed so blackly around Britain that the most optimistic peace lovers had to begin thinking of the practicalities of war.

The Admiralty dusted off the records of the 1914–18 war at sea and began to study its history. It was urgent that someone become familiar with the problems of commercial shipping in 1939, a task that fell largely to the trade division of the Admiralty. At Liverpool, Commander C. J. L. Bittleston began discussions with prominent shippers about the handling of merchant ships in a new war. From A. G. Bates, of Thomas and Brocklebank, Ltd. of Liverpool, Bittleston had a thoughtful letter about the new problems. The Brocklebank firm ran triangular services from Ceylon, India and the United States to the United Kingdom. Obviously in time of war its whole fleet would be at risk.

Bates suggested that in the next war wireless silence would be imperative, but that instant reporting of enemy action had to be arranged. The convoys ought to organize wireless watches to help protect themselves. The implication was that all the ships in a convoy would have some sort of wireless, which was true of only one ship in five during the 1914–18 war. The next step, the immediacy of which was obvious, had to be the training of chief wireless officers for convoys. Brocklebank offered Radio Superintendent W. H. Bailey for such a program.

The convoy system had really been invented by Churchill in 1914 when he was first lord of the Admiralty and the German cruiser *Emden* was scouring the Indian Ocean. Churchill insisted that Australian troops and supplies bound for the western front be convoyed by warships to protect them from the *Emden*. And for a time at the height of the threat, he stopped shipping altogether when armed convoys could not be put together.

Churchill fell from power in 1915, in the wake of the naval and military disaster in the Dardanelles. The convoy system was then developed by the Royal Navy, but at the end of the war it was put in mothballs.

The British governments of the peacetime years represented to Churchill, on the sidelines, "the acme of gullibility" in their dreamy treatment of Germany. Much was made of the Germans' announced willingness to cooperate with Britain in abolishing the submarine. The Germans, even while talking, were building submarines, although not as quickly as they were able. But that was a failure within the German naval hierarchy.

By 1939 Admiral Doenitz had his fifty-six modern U-boats in commission, which represented only half of what he thought he should have. Far more important, in the Type VII, which displaced about 700 tons but was called the 500-ton boat under the formula in use at the London Conference, the Germans had developed the most effective underwater fighting machine of all. Admiral Doenitz, the submarine commander, had laid out plans for the employment of this weapon. It could be modified so that it could travel 13,000 miles. Doenitz also had an entirely new strategy for use in war: the use of the wolf pack. He was held back only by major differences within the German naval high command about the kind of U-boat that was to be built. These differences prevented him from building up the fleet he wanted, with some of the boats fitted out as command boats. For Doenitz expected from the beginning that his operations would be directed largely against armed convoys. His superiors disagreed; some thought he was half-cracked. The U-boat building program was slowed to a walk between 1935 and

1939. Doenitz had to fight to get a communications ship and did not get the *Erwin Wassner,* his flagship, until 1938.

At the conference tables the Germans spoke loftily of restricting the use of submarines in order to prevent them from jeopardizing commerce in the inhumane way of World War I—to return naval warfare to the chivalrous age when ships were stopped and passengers rescued before they were sunk. Certainly the German battleship admirals, such as Erich Raeder, believed in this theory. But not Doenitz.

And across the channel was Winston Churchill, student of naval affairs since the turn of the century, and in the period before World War I one of the leading political figures to shape the nature of the modern British fleet. Many times, almost alone among the politicians, Churchill saw all this talk as hogwash. When push came to shove, he knew the Germans would abandon the sweet talk and once more take up unrestricted submarine warfare. It was the only sensible way to make full use of the underseas weapon; to the pragmatic Churchill it was apparent that this was the way the Germans would go.

In his years as a political outsider, Churchill devoted considerable attention to the development of military scientific research. In 1934 he encouraged Professor Frederick Lindemann in his inquiries into air defenses against the bombers the Air Ministry declared to be invincible. In 1935, although a stout foe of the Baldwin government, Churchill allowed himself to be persuaded to join the Committee of Imperial Defense on Air Defense Research, although his membership was limited to criticism only. His goading in committees had a good deal to do with the rapid progress made in radar.

Churchill kept in touch with naval affairs, through his personal contacts, particularly with Sir Samuel Hoare, who in 1938 was first lord of the Admiralty. Thus he was able to learn about the development of asdic, the sound-ranging device that made it possible to locate a metal object under water. Churchill recognized the vital importance of this antisubmarine weapon, which to him was the supreme development of the Admiralty in the years between the wars.

On March 18, 1939, the British cabinet decided the time had
come for a committee to consider the acceleration of all defense
programs, and Lord Chatfield was given this responsibility.

That was the tentative thinking in Britain in the winter of
1939. Nothing was very definite. The clouds of war were no
more than clouds. As usual, the aggressor would take the initiative.

Soon a whole new set of instructions and rules was established to cover the sailing of ships during a projected war. It
was also planned that most ships would have to sail in convoy,
not individually as many had done in World War I.

When the war actually began in September, the Admiralty
had to relearn all about convoys. They really went back to
basics: someone looked up the word *convoy* in the *Oxford English Dictionary*. The parliamentary secretary of the Admiralty
suggested that the word *convoy* had to be taken in its literal
sense: only ships traveling under armed escort could be considered to be in convoy, for Admiralty purposes. This, of
course, made a difference in the statistical reporting of ships
lost, and that was the point. The process of flocking together
did not make a convoy in the naval sense.

That, however, was precisely what was occurring in these
first days of the war.

* * *

Because of the shortage of convoy escorts, a group of ships
would be given an escort for the first stage of its voyage, travel
without escort in the second stage, and escort again in the final
stage. It was a situation born of necessity.

Churchill addressed himself to that necessity on September
4, the day after the torpedoing of the *Athenia*. He was also
smarting after the sinking of the *Royal Sceptre*, the *Rio Claro*,
and the *Bosnia* only hours after the *Athenia* went down.

Churchill learned that plans were under way in the Admiralty for the development of the convoy escort system. On
paper was a fine scheme to take over eighty-six fast civil trawlers and equip them with asdic. But it had not been done. Nor

had the number of destroyers been increased. And now, with the sinking of the *Athenia*, the Admiralty had to take the position that this aggressive warfare would continue. The Germans were not to be believed no matter what they professed. Convoys—armed convoys—were the only answer, and they would have to be used from the outset of the war, although the Admiralty had not planned it that way.

Churchill came to office planning to equip a thousand ships, each with at least one antisubmarine gun. But at the moment more had to be done.

* * *

Cross-channel convoys had begun with the outbreak of hostilities. These convoys took troops and supplies to the battlefront, and, beginning on September 5, were escorted by destroyers. As a result, there was a shortage of destroyers. The Third Destroyer Flotilla was ordered up from the Mediterranean, and three Polish destroyers were brought down from the Baltic.

The new first lord of the Admiralty had to split his defensive forces between the needs of the fleet and the needs of the merchant shipping. Two flotillas were allocated to the Home Fleet, four flotillas were based at Plymouth and Milford Haven for convoy, and Humber and Channel forces were assembled for general antisubmarine work.

There were still not enough destroyers or armed trawlers to provide escort service for the outbound ships from the Western Approaches. The immediate answer was to assemble homeward bound ships in the Western Approaches at dawn each day. There they followed a controlled route which was patrolled by groups of antisubmarine vessels.

Outward bound convoys were escorted by two or three destroyers from their assembly points to about 12° 30′ west; then the convoys dispersed (and the danger began). It was not much of a system, but it was all that was available on September 4. Churchill decided that aircraft carriers, as well as cruisers, would have to be used to augment the antisubmarine forces.

There would be more trawlers coming. An order to buy sixty-seven trawlers had been signed in June, but was held up by Admiralty red tape. Churchill started cutting. The first trawler had to be ready by September 18, he said, and the first hundred should be in commission by the end of October. Another seventy had to be built with all celerity.

Immediately, the Admiralty requisitioned thirty-one pleasure yachts, including the Duke of Westminster's, and put them to work on antisubmarine patrol; it also took over a number of small whalers, fast ships of about a thousand tons. If they could catch whales they ought to be able to catch submarines.

The other defense was in the air. The RAF Coastal Command was charged with antisubmarine patrol, and the aircraft were flying whenever weather permitted. In September they flew 100,000 miles and attacked thirty submarines. They were not very effective; captured submarine crews indicated they had no fear of aircraft, but the planes, at this stage at least, forced the submarines to dive, thus reducing the effectiveness of the Doenitz blockade.

Admiral Doenitz at the moment was in a difficult situation. He felt so strongly that the submarine building program had to be vastly increased that he had requested a transfer from operations to take over the building program. His request was denied by Admiral Erich Raeder, commander of the navy. And now, in September, when he was supposed to operate against the enemy, Doenitz's hands were tied by Hitler's politics. Hitler had not really expected the British to go to war, or the French either. The German navy would not be prepared for war with England until 1945. The word was out to go slow on attacks on merchant shipping, to obey all the rules, and to hope for a quick negotiated peace.

On September 6 a new restriction came from the Fuehrer. Doenitz was ordered to leave French vessels alone in the hope that France would not work up enthusiasm for the war. The stricture was most annoying. Now his captains had to stop virtually every vessel, make sure it was not French, then decide what was to be done. Meanwhile the British were taking their antisubmarine warfare far more seriously.

*   *   *

Two days after the sinking of the *Athenia*, Doenitz learned from several of his U-boat captains that when they attacked British ships, they heard them signaling—not the usual SOS but a new SSS—and they had deduced (quite rightly) that this was a signal calling defensive forces to come and attack the submarines. This was a violation of the London Submarine Agreement of 1936, which specifically forbade merchant captains from participating in war operations. By transmitting information about the attack—the coordinates, the course and speed—the merchant ships were indeed participating in attempts to destroy the submarines.

Churchill had not only the constant worry of feeding England on his mind, but in the early days of the war he had to settle on a base for the Home Fleet. On September 14 he traveled north to look over Scapa Flow in northern Scotland's Orkney Islands, which had been selected by the Admiralty as the new fleet base. He noted then the terrible paucity of destroyers, so great that the battleship *Nelson* came out of Loch Ewe without a destroyer escort, something Churchill had never seen before. And when Churchill returned to London, he was met by Admiral Pound with grave news.

*   *   *

Lieutenant Commander Otto Schuhart in the *U-29* had been assigned a patrol area in the shipping lane west of the English Channel. On September 17 he sighted what he believed to be a 10,000-ton merchant ship, flying the British red ensign, but before he could make an attack he was driven down by aircraft. At 6 p.m. Schuhart saw an aircraft carrier. It was the *Courageous*, Britain's oldest carrier, and she had been assigned to the Western Approaches on antisubmarine patrol. The aircraft that had driven Schuhart down had been one of hers.

The *Courageous* was escorted by four destroyers, but later that day two of them were detached to assist a merchant ship under submarine attack; only two were left to guard the carrier. Here was a submarine commander's dream: a major warship with virtually no escort.

Schuhart managed to work the *U-29* in close to the carrier, so close that the on-side destroyer was only 500 yards from him when he made his firing plot. The range to the carrier was less than 2 miles. At 7:50 Schuhart fired three torpedoes from his bow tubes, two of which hit the carrier. Schuhart took his submarine deep, deeper than he had ever gone before. Following a prewar submarine disaster, the maximum depth for the 500-ton class boat had been set at 150 feet, but Schuhart would rather brave the depth than stay shallow for what he expected to happen.

And he was right. The British destroyers were on to him, guided by their asdic, and they came running in, dropping patterns of depth charges all around the boat. He could hear secondary explosions as he went down to 180 and then 250 feet. Above, the carrier was breaking up. The destroyers stayed with the job for hours, and the *U-29* was thoroughly shaken up by midnight, when the destroyers finally lost its trail and went away.

The *Courageous* had sunk, taking down 519 members of her crew, including Captain W. T. Makeig-Jones.

On September 17, the day of the sinking of the *Courageous*, the merchant ship *Kafiristan* was attacked by Lieutenant Commander Ernst-Guenter Heinicke in *U-53* while in the eastern Atlantic en route to Liverpool with a cargo of sugar. Captain J. Busby was in his cabin and the second mate was on watch when the submarine surfaced and put three shots across the bow of the ship, all quite in order. The ship was zigzagging, which the Germans regarded as a breach of the London Agreement. But the second mate rang down to the engine room to stand by. And when the captain came to the bridge, he ordered the ship to stop. But he also ordered the wireless officer to send the SSS message as well as the SOS. Such use of the wireless was also regarded by the Germans as warlike, since it could bring down the wrath of the enemy's military.

While the captain was checking his position in the wireless room, the engine room crew panicked, came up out of the hole, put the starboard lifeboat over and tried to get in. The ship was still making way and the boat swamped; six men were lost. The boat dragged along behind the ship, mostly under water. One of the engineers was routed out, and managed to stop the engines by use of an emergency throttle on the boat deck.

Half an hour after the first shot was fired, the captain ordered the ship abandoned. All this while she had been traveling in a great circle, and the submarine making no attempt to fire more shots or to close.

The captain got into the starboard jolly boat while the men got into the two other boats, and pulled away from the ship. The submarine then fired a torpedo which struck under the No. 2 hold on the port side. The ship began to sink. Thirty minutes later the submarine fired another torpedo. This struck in the boiler room and the ship broke in two and sank immediately.

The submarine then came alongside the boats; Commander Heinicke informed the captain that he had called for help. If help did not come, he would tow them toward the Irish coast, or until they met another ship.

Soon the *American Farmer* appeared. And just then came what must have been a response to the captain's call for help. A plane flew over and attacked the submarine with machine guns. The crew dropped down the conning tower, but not all of them made it. The submarine went down, leaving men in the water. Two bombs were dropped where the submarine had dived.

The captain of the *American Farmer* was so upset about the plane attacking the submarine that Captain Busby decided he must be pro-German. He gave the American captain little information, and said no more until they were landed, safe and sound.

Once again the Germans had behaved properly throughout their attack on the enemy ship. But they were less than satisfied

with the behavior of the British. Doenitz made his representa-
tions to Admiral Raeder. On September 23 Admiral Raeder
persuaded Hitler to agree that all merchant ships making use of
their wireless could be sunk or taken as prizes.

On the following day Hitler was also persuaded to end his
restrictions on stopping French ships. On September 30 the
Germans no longer observed the old Prize Regulations (rules of
war) in the North Sea, and early in October permission was
given to attack any darkened ships in British and French waters. Week by week the London Agreement of 1936 was being
whittled down by both sides until, by the beginning of the
second month of the war, it was honored as much in the breach
as in the observance.

The British had lost forty-one ships that September, or a
total of 153,000 tons of shipping. Winston Churchill was anything but dismayed, for in the sinkings he thought he saw a
pattern: the loss the first week had been greatest, at 65,000 tons.
The loss in the fourth week had been slightest, less than 5,000
tons. He was able to go before the House of Commons in his
maiden address as first lord of the Admiralty and promise that
"the British attack upon the U-boats is only just beginning."
The antisubmarine effort was growing stronger every day, he
said, and by the end of October he promised a force three times
as strong as that operating at the beginning of the war.

Always the optimist, Churchill believed then that the Germans had already lost half a dozen submarines. The fact was
that they had lost only two, the *U-27* and the *U-39*; Admiral
Doenitz's efforts, like his own, were only just beginning.

2

The First Gray Wolf

At 6:45 A.M. on October 13, 1939, the sky above the Orkney Islands at the northeast tip of Britain was somber. The heavy rain clouds scudded at a thousand feet before a twenty-five knot wind, and seemed ready to drop at any moment and erase the gray surface of the sea from visibility in another squall.

But for the men of one lone craft off the Orkneys that morning the weather was "perfect," nor did they pay the slightest attention to reports from Weather Station Berlin that the blow was likely to grow worse in the next twenty-four hours. These were the forty-two officers and men of the *U-47*, one of Admiral Doenitz's fifty-six submarines, poised to conduct a war of attrition against their British enemy.

After the sinking of the *Athenia* the Fuehrer's order put a stop to effective U-boat action. As Doenitz and every U-boat captain knew, it was impossible for a submarine commander in darkness and heavy seas to distinguish between a freighter and a passenger liner. Under the circumstances, Doenitz insisted that no ship be sunk unless she was clearly identified as a warship or a vessel carrying the supplies of war, and so the U-boat captains virtually stopped sinking anything at all. Thus they avoided a court-martial, but at the same time the German naval effort was brought almost to a standstill.

In his headquarters aboard the communications ship *Wechsel* in Wilhelmshaven harbor, Admiral Doenitz fumed as hotly as the Fuehrer himself, but not for the same reason. He cursed the stupidity of his superiors who did not seem to understand that if his U-boats were unleashed he could win the war for Germany.

But instead of relenting, the Fuehrer had grown more venomous in his attitude to the U-boat force. The crew of Lemp's U-boat had been broken up, the commander disavowed by Hitler himself, and the gentlemanly conduct—or the promises of it—by the German navy reaffirmed in toasts and speeches in the embassies of Berlin. Admiral Doenitz, fretting in his cabin aboard the *Wechsel*, concluded that only a master military stroke against an undeniable naval target could rescue his U-boats from ignominy. But how was this to be done?

The answer lay on the bottom of the North Sea in 150 feet of water, 3 miles off the entry to Scapa Flow, the giant naval base where the British Home Fleet was stationed in the early months of the war. It lay in the hands of a twenty-four-year-old U-boat commander, Lieutenant Commander Guenther Prien, and the forty-one members of his crew in their Type VII U-boat, 180 feet of steel mechanism, 18 feet wide and weighing 517 tons, or less than many trawlers.

Guenther Prien was an instrument of Admiral Doenitz, a human weapon designed for but one task: to perform the deed that would restore Doenitz and the U-boats to official favor and allow the submarine admiral to begin the effort that would bring victory to the Third Reich.

By October 1 Doenitz had known the worst: he was to be ignored by the OKW in its list of priorities for naval replacements and new construction. He did not need an announcement from the Fuehrer or from Raeder to tell him. It was enough that Captain Godt, his chief of staff, reported that requests to higher headquarters for increased U-boat production disappeared on some desk, that demands for spare parts and even mechanics got lost in the logistics and personnel departments. The number of operational U-boats was down to less than twenty; the others were laid up with shortages. The handful of U-boats was performing as well as Doenitz could expect, sinking warships, even a carrier, but Hitler did not seem to see or hear such reports. Doenitz continued in the deep freeze of the Nazi hierarchy.

As a submarine commander in World War I, Admiral Doenitz had long nurtured a particular dream: to get inside the British naval base at Scapa Flow and wreak havoc there. It was the kind of mission for which a submarine was invented, and two brave German U-boat commanders had made the attempt. Korvettenkapitan von Hennig and Kapitanleutnant Ensmann had each managed, on separate occasions, to move through the antisubmarine defenses and enter the anchorage; but both had aroused the British and both submarines had been lost.

For twenty years Doenitz nurtured the memory of these heroes and during those two decades he had collected every available scrap of information about Scapa Flow, from newspapers, magazines, naval intelligence, and the OKW. In 1939 the admiral knew more about that one fleet anchorage than any but the most senior members of the British naval establishment.

In mid-September, Captain Godt had given Admiral Doenitz a brief memo that excited him out of his depression. Korvettenkapitan Wellner, commander of the coastal submarine *U-16*, so small that the U-boat men referred to the type as canoes, had come home with a report of a strange experience in the area around Scapa Flow.

Wellner had been sent north with little hope that he could destroy anything more significant than a ferry, so small was his U-boat. He had approached the Pentland Firth, the passage that runs between the Scottish mainland and the Orkney Islands. It was the first such voyage of *U-16* and Wellner was unprepared for the vicious current that runs deep in the firth there. The U-boat was caught in the pull and had been unable to escape, in spite of the overheating of the electric engines. Finally Wellner realized that he was in no immediate danger from an attack; no enemy ships appeared, and the current was carrying him directly to Scapa Flow. He relaxed, surfaced when he could, and began to make notes for a thorough report to be delivered to Doenitz.

Wellner's U-boat remained on the edge of Scapa Flow for

more than a day. He wrote down the times of arrival and departure of British patrols, and all ship movements he could observe. He studied the lighting of the harbor and drew a map of it. He drew charts showing the strength and direction of currents. As he left he brought up the periscope and took a good look at the harbor entrance, and as he headed home he sent a radio message to the *Wechsel*, announcing that he had vital information about Scapa Flow.

When Commander Wellner arrived at Wilhelmshaven he was ordered to appear at once aboard the flagship. He revealed all his treasures to the fascinated U-boat chief. Doenitz got out his file and ordered (requested was a more suitable word when one dealt with Goering's Luftwaffe) a new aerial survey of Scapa Flow. Within a week he had it and could sit down to dream. If a small "canoe" could manage to do what Wellner had done and remain undiscovered, what could a Type VII U-boat do in those waters? Wellner had been emphatic: it would be no trick to wait until the submarine nets were open to let a large vessel through. Wellner had noticed that the patrol vessels were slow in getting in and out, and that the interval while the nets and booms were opened was much longer than the Germans ever tolerated in home waters. He was sure a submarine, or even a patrol craft, could pass in after a large ship had entered. And he had noticed that the patrol craft seemed remarkably unalert just outside the fleet anchorage.

For several days Admiral Doenitz's quarters were turned into a clutter of maps, charts, photographs, and reports. He had new aerial views made of Hoxa Sound, Swith Sound, and Clestrom Sound, all of which led into the fleet anchorage. And then there was Holm Sound, which soon attracted Doenitz's attention. Holm Sound had been deliberately blocked by the British, who had sunk two merchant ships diagonally across the channel, and, to make sure that no enemy could pass, had then sunk a third ship north of the two. But Wellner and the charts indicated that there were two other narrow channels that were not blocked. One of these, south of the blockships, was fifty feet wide and thirty feet deep. The other, north of the ships and close to shore, was even narrower and shallower. This last was enormously risky; even submerged a U-boat's conning tower would make a discernible wake or, even worse, its periscope shears would rise completely out of the water.

Doenitz decided it could be done. All that remained was to choose the man to do it.

On October 13, at 6:45 A.M. the man Admiral Doenitz had chosen to breach the British defenses at Scapa Flow assembled the crew of the *U-47* in the forward torpedo room. The silence below was unearthly. The boat rocked a little on the soft bottom of the sea, and they had been down long enough that it was hot in the glare of the greenish lamps behind their metal grills. The boat was sweating inside its pressure hull, as were the men. The narrow upper and lower bunks (never enough for the entire crew) were folded back against the bulkhead and the men were clustered amid the maze of pipes and ladders and the shiny brass of the torpedoes.

When the executive officer, Lieutenant Endrass, announced that all the men were assembled, Captain Prien made his way forward from his tiny stateroom to the compartment. After he had clanged the watertight door behind him, to shut off the noise of the compressors aft, he stood up and looked around.

"Tomorrow," he said laconically, his clear, precise voice enunciating every syllable, "we will enter an English shipping lane." He paused. "The Scapa Flow," he added, and then he turned, unlatched the door and went out.

Behind him the men looked at each other and began to react. Scapa Flow, the Wilhelmshaven of the British fleet. The very heart of the enemy navy.

Someone whistled. That was how they all felt.

3

Scapa Flow

Lieutenant Commander Guenther Prien was not feeling at that moment nearly so self-assured as he had indicated to his crew. He was still in a state of shock from his meeting a week before, when he had been summoned to the *Wechsel*, after returning from leave following his first war patrol. The patrol had not been successful and Prien was expecting a reprimand as he went aboard the flagship and reported to the officer of the watch. But he was ushered into the wardroom with the courtesy he knew was not reserved for wrongdoers. Commander Oehrn, the operations officer, waved at him and smiled. He was asked to sit down at a table with Captain Godt and Commander Wellner. The talk had immediately turned to Scapa Flow and Wellner's adventures there. Then Godt had been summoned by Doenitz. Wellner had followed him. Finally Prien was asked to join them. Doenitz, in his black navy uniform with the submarine insignia and swastika on the breast, stood up behind the desk as Prien entered, and, with an unusually friendly air, motioned the younger man to a chair. Then he began to talk about Scapa Flow; Captain Godt, with pointer in hand, went to the map board and indicated the channel openings into the British base.

When the explanation ended, Doenitz turned to Prien.

"Do you think you can do it?"

Doenitz had chosen Prien from among half a dozen captains of Type VII boats, partly because Prien's boat was provisioned, refitted and ready for its next war patrol, partly because among his U-boat captains only Lieutenant Commander Kretschmer and Lieutenant Commander Schepke ranked with Prien at that point in the war.

Prien, although young, was one of Doenitz's most experienced captains. He had started as an ordinary seaman in 1933 at the age of eighteen and had worked his way up to submarine officers' school, a feat in itself. During the Spanish civil war he had served on *U-26* under Lieutenant Werner Hartmann. He had come home in 1938 to submarine commanders' school and then had commissioned the new *U-47*.

Now Prien hesitated, searching for the right answer. Doenitz sensed the hesitation and hurried on. "Don't answer now. Here, take this"—he thrust a thick folder of papers at Prien. "Study it for the next forty-eight hours and then come back. Be prepared to let me know your answer then."

Prien, making his way to his tiny cabin amidships on *U-47*, on this night and day of waiting, recalled how he had pored over the papers, the charts and photographs, most of them annotated in Doenitz's inimitable scrawl. He took only eight hours to familiarize himself with each detail, and to weigh his chances of success and survival. He had sensed how important the mission was to Doenitz; there was no alternative if he wished to remain in the U-boat force, no matter that Doenitz had said there was no obligation. He sensed the need to comply even more strongly the next morning when he stood before Admiral Doenitz in the commander's cabin. Doenitz would not look at him; his eyes were riveted on a folder on his desk and two large veins pulsed under the skin of his forehead.

"Well?" demanded the submarine chief. "Is the answer yes or no?"

"Yes, sir," said Prien.

Doenitz rose from the desk and crossed around to stand directly before Prien.

"You're sure?"

"Yes, sir."

The admiral smiled for the first time. He clasped the hand of the young U-boat commander, an action so out of character that Prien knew he had made the only decision.

"Prepare to get your boat under way," Doenitz said. Then he turned, and by the time he was back at his desk, Prien had left the cabin and closed the door.

That day and the next the *U-47* was made ready for sea. Prien did not appear, but Lieutenant Endrass ordered the men to remove stores and fresh water from the boat. No one could understand why, but they dared not ask.

At 4 A.M. on October 8, Prien returned to the ship and immediately ordered the submarine to make ready to cast off. The engines had been started and running for an hour.

"Ready to cast off, sir."

"Good," said Prien, as he took over the conning of the U-boat.

"Cast off."

The little submarine (American fleet class submarines were twice as large) began to move through the waters of the Wilhelmshaven base, past the oil tanks and the Kaiser Wilhelm bridge.

Outside Prien heaved a sigh of relief. The weather was dirty and seemed prepared to grow worse. That meant the danger from the British patrol craft in the North Sea would be minimal. As the gray submarine slid through the oily waters of the estuary the four lookouts on deck were fully alert, training their night glasses this way and that, searching for shapes. When they moved into the darker waters of the North Sea, the lookouts began to peer, hoping for merchant ships, but when they saw a tanker and gave the alarm, Prien told them to ignore it. Surprised again, the crew looked at one another uneasily. What sort of nonsense was their captain up to, avoiding battle?

* * *

Prien's laconic announcement to the crew told the men all they were to learn about their captain's plans until they became action. All they knew was that they were to wear felt-soled shoes from that point on.

Prien kept the *U-47* on the bottom all day. At 4 P.M. he went to the galley and ordered the cooks to feed the men the holiday menu for the evening meal. That meant double rations of sausage, eggs, bread, jam, cabbage, cheese, and fruit.

An hour after supper it was time, and Prien gave the order. "Battle stations."

The word was passed through the boat, but no klaxon sounded to alert the enemy. In their felt shoes the men moved to their posts. Prien gave the order to rise to periscope depth and the electric engines started up and began to whir. The boat shuddered as the ballast tanks were blown, and, bow first, she began to rise. At forty-five feet she stopped.

"Periscope depth, captain," the diving officer announced.

Prien stepped to the shears and raised them. With an oily smell the periscopes rose out of their bed and broke the surface of British water.

Prien moved the handles and his body around in the narrow circle of the conning tower. The sea was clear and he adjusted the mirror. The sky in the evening light was empty. He smiled.

"Prepare to surface," he said.

The four men selected as lookouts lined up next to the steel ladder of the conning tower, opened and closed their eyes several times, and put on the infrared glasses that increased their night vision. As the submarine surfaced and the tanks were blown, Prien opened the hatch and went up to the bridge. Next came Lieutenant von Varrendorf, the watch officer, and following him the lookouts, who moved forward and aft of the captain.

It was completely dark by this time, and yet it was not dark. Prien cursed the aurora borealis which lighted up the northern sky and occasionally flashed to light the water around him. He felt as if he were naked on Berlin's Friedrichstrasse at high noon. But no light showed anywhere ashore nor was there any movement. Incredible, Prien thought, the British enemies were sound asleep at their posts.

He gave an order:

"Start engines."

There was a sputtering noise as the starters turned on the diesels, and then a roar, which subsided in seconds, until it was overborne by the sound of the wind and the lapping of the waves around the U-boat. From the bridge the noise seemed so incredibly loud that Prien started, but then as the submarine moved forward, buffeted by the waves, he felt more comfortable. It was a filthy night, and except for the flashes from the aurora borealis, it no longer seemed worrisome.

But where were the British patrols?

* * *

Captain Prien was correct in his deduction that the British had left their fleet anchorage less than safely guarded. What he did not know, however, was that the vast bulk of the fleet was not in the Scapa Flow anchorage that night. On October 8, Admiral Hermann Boehm of the German navy had made a sortie into the North Sea with the battleship *Gneisenau*, the cruiser *Koln*, and nine destroyers. They were discovered off the Utsire light by a British reconnaissance plane. To meet the challenge, Admiral Sir Charles Forbes, commander of the Home Fleet, steamed out of Scapa Flow with his fleet of battleships and cruisers, and the Germans, having enticed the British fleet out, retired back through the Skagerrak and the Kattegat to the Baltic. They had accomplished their aim, which was to bring the Home Fleet within range of Goering's Luftwaffe. That day and the next the German air force flew hundreds of sorties of Heinkel 111 and Junkers 88 bombers to strike the fleet, but the British antiaircraft and fighter protection was so successful that the Germans achieved nothing.

Also, with all that Admiral Doenitz had learned about the Scapa Flow anchorage, he had no way of knowing how completely Admiral Forbes distrusted Scapa Flow. Even more than the Germans, Admiral Forbes knew how badly defended were the approaches, how inadequate were the patrols and the air coverage to prevent submarine incursion into the many channels.

So when the fleet action was ended Admiral Forbes withdrew, not back to Scapa Flow, but to the alternative base at Loch Ewe on the west coast of Scotland, where he felt far more secure. His decision was prescient; on this night he had left only the battleship *Royal Oak* at Scapa Flow to guard the narrows between the Shetland Islands and the Orkneys against the possibility of breakthrough by the German battleship fleet.

*   *   *

As the night wore on, and the U-boat moved toward Holm Sound, Captain Prien grew more tense. The weather was worsening, the seas had grown stronger and the waves slapped the U-boat five to ten degrees off course with every blow. The diesels churned and sometimes the propellers came out of the water to race with a terrifyingly loud noise, then were sucked back under the surface; even the wake seemed noisy to Captain Prien. At half speed the boat lurched and tossed in the sea, and the northern lights kept flashing on to silhouette the gray shape against the foam.

Suddenly Prien's eye caught a shadow. He turned fiercely. A ship? Almost involuntarily his hand pressed the alarm. The lookouts heard the klaxon, and scurried back to the bridge and down the conning tower hatch. Prien followed and dogged down the doors as the submarine dived, and the water came up to the coaming.

"Periscope depth," he ordered. When the boat had leveled off he raised the scopes and looked.

He was fortunate: the shadow was indeed a ship, a destroyer, coming out of the British base on a patrol mission. The British were not completely asleep after all.

Moments went by as he tracked the destroyer to make sure he was not seen. She charged forth into the northern sea and then was gone. The raging wind across the water was the only sound to be heard now.

Soon the U-boat reached the edge of Holm Sound, where the channels narrowed around two tiny dots of land that blocked the waterway above Burray Island. Here was the current that Wellner had specifically warned about; it pulled them inward so fiercely that Prien felt almost as if the sea controlled his actions. He had already decided to use the smaller, narrower channel; in the darkness he could count on the overhang of the shore to conceal the U-boat's upper works from observation on land or in the anchorage. If only those northern lights would stay low . . .

The current caught the U-boat and the helmsman struggled to keep her course. Another man came to help him fight the wheel. For a few moments they headed steadily toward one of the sunken block ships and it seemed inevitable that they would collide with her. But the captain shouted and the men responded; just in time, the submarine veered away. They moved down past Glimp's Holm and by the headland that hangs down from the north, and suddenly they were inside Scapa Flow, the most celebrated of all enemy naval bases. They had penetrated the heart of the British fleet.

In the dirty weather Prien could see little more than the shadows of ships; it was impossible to ascertain their character. To the south there was nothing (that was where the fleet should have been). To the north he saw shadows and identified "two battleships." He was half right. One was indeed the battleship *Royal Oak*; the other was the superannuated seaplane carrier *Pegasus*.

On sighting targets Prien suddenly regained caution. He pressed the diving alarm again, and the deck force trooped down. Then he took the U-boat to periscope depth and began stalking the sitting enemy ships.

"Ready the tubes . . ."

"Tubes all clear."

"Ready tubes one, two, three, four . . ."

"Tubes ready."

Lieutenant Endrass had the duty of pressing the keys that fired the torpedoes.

"Fire!" shouted Prien.

Endrass pressed the keys.

4

Wild Night

Aboard the *Royal Oak*:

It was one o'clock in the morning. For October 14 in this latitude, the weather was good indeed; a clear night and the bright stars above the harbor blinked cheerily. The land was dark but the northern lights were playing above His Majesty's battleship *Royal Oak*.

The ship was lying at single anchor. Virtually all the men aboard were asleep; inside the naval base only the most fragmentary security precautions seemed necessary. Why should it be otherwise? Scapa Flow was safe. Early in the 1930s it had been decided that in the event of a war with Germany, Scapa Flow would become a major fleet anchorage. In 1939, Sir Charles Forbes, commander of the Home Fleet, had decided that Scapa ought to be the main base of the fleet. A survey carried out at the orders of the Admiralty by the survey vessel H.M.S. *Scott* had declared the anchorage suitable.

Based on the survey, the Admiralty had declared: "It is therefore considered that entry of any submarine submerged is impossible, and on the surface would be extremely hazardous."

Blockships had been sunk, and Scapa Flow replaced Rosyth, where enormous sums of money had already been spent to provide antisubmarine booms, nets, and other protection. The orders had been issued to bring Scapa up to this same condition of readiness, but in the summer of 1939 the fleet, as noted previously, was moved before this had been done. The

Admiralty had rejected the idea of sinking more blockships, suggesting instead that safety should be guaranteed by active patrols around the anchorage. By October 14 the three patrol vessels requested by the fleet had still not been provided. The fleet would have to do its own patrolling, said the Admiralty. When the officer commanding the defenses of the coast of Scotland heard this decision, he hit the ceiling. He sent Admiral French, who was in charge of defense of the Orkney and Shetland Islands, to Scapa Flow for his own survey; French recommended more blockships for Kirk and Skerry Sounds. The Admiralty agreed, but the project got buried in the Admiralty's pile of paperwork, and so the blockship destined for Kirk Sound was somewhere down south, waiting to be brought up, as Commander Prien conned the U-47 through that body of water and brought the Royal Oak into view.

Nor was there any patrol vessel to replace the blockship. Orders on October 1 had not mentioned a need for patrols. But nobody was worried. A group of admirals, convening in Scapa Flow on September 13, had congratulated one another on the condition of the fleet; there were no complaints about the safety factor at Scapa.

So all was serene and relaxed aboard the Royal Oak, all the more so because the bulk of the fleet was at Rosyth, Loch Ewe, at the moment.

Then, at 1:04 A.M. everything changed. An underwater explosion occurred on the forward starboard side of the ship. This was Prien's first torpedo. The effect was to break off all the slips to the starboard anchor. The chain went rattling out and the anchor dropped to the bottom. If the explosion didn't wake up everybody aboard the ship, then the rattling of the anchor chain did. The explosion shook the ship from stem to stern and the chain rattling seemed to go on and on and on. Rear Admiral H. E. C. Blagrove, commander of the Second Battle Squadron, put on his trousers and a shirt and hurried on deck. So did Captain W. G. Benn, the commander, the engineer commander, and a dozen other officers. Some appeared in nightclothes.

The skeleton watch on the bridge reported that a column of

water had shot up the starboard side of the ship to drench the forecastle. The captain went up there, looked at the cables, then sent the first lieutenant down to inspect the forward compartments. It was, he said, obviously an internal explosion in the inflammable store, where such items as paint were kept. Fortunately it did not seem to have done much damage. The ship was not listing or settling by the bows.

The assistant torpedo officer went to the main switchboard and then to the No. 3 and No. 4 dynamo rooms. He reported that all was normal.

The captain then went down the forecastle hatch to the cable locker flat for a look. Here he heard a different story. Several officers reported that the inflammable store area was venting through the breather pipe. That meant water was coming in. But fortunately there was no fire.

The captain ordered the damage control party to start salvage pumps, but did not mention closing off the bow's watertight doors and compartments.

All this was relayed to the admiral, who did not appear upset. Nor did the ship's company. Some men turned out of their bunks, came up on deck, looked around and, since they were not called to duty, went back to their bunks and turned in again.

Others went back below because that was what they had been taught to do. The real fear at Scapa was air raids. Many of the men thought the column of water had been caused by a bomb. So they followed the procedure laid out by higher authority.

*   *   *

The captain was still looking around at 1:16 A.M. when a second explosion struck the ship, then a third, and a fourth. (These had to be more of Prien's torpedoes. Although the *U-47*'s log times do not match up with the British times, Prien's log-keeping at the moment was obviously sketchy. He had fired at what he perceived to be two battleships: his first salvo of three torpedoes from the bow tubes; then he had spun the *U-47*

around and fired from the stern; then around once more to fire
three torpedoes from the bow. He believed he had sunk one
battleship and damaged a second. Actually four of the torpedoes had struck the *Royal Oak*.)*

The later explosions hit the ship between the big gun tur-
rets; the effect at this point was "immediate and catastrophic,"
as the captain put it. The *Royal Oak* began to heel to starboard.

Orange-colored flames began to appear at the top of the dynamo room hatch. The forward bulkhead of the dynamo room
bulged forward and steam began to escape. The assistant torpedo officer and the warrant electrician made their way up the
ladder through the flames and reached the marines' messdeck.
By this time the ship had developed a twenty-five-degree list to
starboard, and the messdeck was filled with choking fumes
from burning hammocks.

A sliding horizontal hatch abaft A turret jammed in a closed
position and trapped a number of men. Someone had forgotten
to secure the wire strap that held it open.

There were incidents of heroism. One radio operator stood
at the bottom of a ladder, lighting matches to show men the way
to the deck. A marine corporal supported a hatch on his shoul-
ders so that other men could pass by and go on up to the main
deck. Another rating made his way to the cell flat and released
two prisoners who would otherwise have drowned. Another
jumped overboard three times with a rope in hand to save
others.

The rescue work was begun by trawlers in the harbor, slow-
moving civil ships which had been converted to naval use. The
Daisy II had been lying along the port side of the battleship, and
she began picking men out of the water. Some men were kept
afloat by the Carley floats that had been thrown over by the
captain or that had drifted off the sinking ship. Some clung to

*The sinking of the *Royal Oak* by the *U-47* still raises questions among students
of British naval history. Some hold with the internal explosion theory, some
with the theory that the *Royal Oak* was sabotaged. One reason is the paucity of
information and the incorrect figures in some of Prien's log observations as to
time, latitude and longitude. But to this author the evidence seems incon-
trovertible that the *U-47* did in fact sink the *Royal Oak*.

empty drums, to pieces of wood. A picket boat came alongside and picked up men. Twice it capsized from overloading. The captain's gig was of no use at all; the cover was strapped on and it turned over when men tried to climb aboard. Boats from the cruiser *Pegasus* came up shortly after the sinking and began helping with the rescue. Finally more trawlers came along.

Some men were blown through doors, up hatches and out of scuttles by the force of the explosions. But in the engine and boiler rooms few men got out.

The admiral had gone to the boat deck after the first explosion. Later he moved up to the quarter deck. He was seen after the second group of explosions by the captain's steward, who had gone there to pick up a life ring from the guardrail. The steward saw the admiral and heard him warning the men on the port side who were jumping over to watch out for the propellers. The steward climbed up the slanting deck to the admiral and offered him the life ring.

"Don't worry about me," said the admiral. "Try to save yourself."

The steward was not loath to move then, and he went overboard with his life ring. The admiral stayed on deck, helping the men. He was not seen again.

A launch was fixed to the starboard lower boom. Several men tried to man it, but the ship turned over, and metal from the foretop fell into the launch and sank it; the funnel came crashing down between the launch and the ship's side. One man was sucked into the funnel and then spat out again like a piece of cork.

The *Royal Oak* hung on the line of stability for perhaps four minutes, then began to heel faster and faster. Captain and officers stood stupefied. There was nothing to be done to save the ship. They could not even broadcast an order to abandon; the explosions had knocked out the ship's power and all lights were out.

The captain was still in the cable locker flat. He ordered his officers and men to clear out and walked aft to the messdeck. It was in total darkness. He sent all the men he saw up to the

forecastle and followed them up. When he got on deck he could
sense that the ship was about to go. The commander came up
and he and the captain began throwing over Carley floats and
bits of wood. Some men turned to help them. But they had
precious little time. The deck was slippery and the angle became impossible. The captain and the others climbed up on the
port guardrails and hung there until 1:29 A.M. At that moment
the *Royal Oak* gave a last convulsive heave, her masts went
down and, as the big guns splashed and the ship capsized, all
aboard were thrown into the sea.

Some officers and men managed to climb up over the bilge
keel and onto the bottom as the ship was going down. But most
of the survivors were thrown clear of the ship and struggled in
the water. The ship righted a little, bottom up, and then settled
to an angle of about forty degrees from the vertical. Anybody
down there was certain to drown or to die of asphyxiation even
if he had an air pocket. Down there rested Admiral Blagrove
and 785 other officers and men of His Majesty's Navy.

* * *

When the lights began to flash in the anchorage, and signals
were passed, searchlights probed out; one caught the *U-47*,
went on, stabbed back and caught her again, but then moved
away. Ashore, lights came on along the roads as military vehi-
cles raced this way and that. One driver turned his headlights
out to sea and they caught the *U-47* squarely but then also
moved on. The driver had simply been turning his vehicle
around.

It was time for Captain Prien to get out if he could. The
flashing of the destroyer searchlights continued but, by hugging
the coast again, Prien managed to avoid them. The current had
the U-boat as it moved toward the entrance to Holm Sound, and
behind him Prien thought he saw a destroyer turning his way.

"Give me full power. Everything you've got," he shouted
while he watched the destroyer. She *was* coming up, and she
was signaling.

The U-boat moved jerkily against the current toward the

narrows, and the destroyer seemed to be bound directly after it, but suddenly it veered away, and at that moment, the *U-47* surged through the narrows, so close that Prien could see the wooden pier dangerously near to the starboard bow. Suddenly there came a scraping noise; the U-boat was sideswiping an object to port. Prien jumped. It was a wooden pontoon that had come loose somewhere ashore in the heavy seas. As the boat lurched and shuddered he sent the lookouts below. If he had to go down there would be no time to spare, and in these close quarters lookouts did not help.

As the U-boat cleared the narrows, and the current released its grip, the boat surged forward so quickly that Prien was thrown against the periscope and injured his back. Below, men were tossed to the deck. The submarine seemed to slow.

"Maintain full revolutions," Prien shouted into the speaking tube.

And then the U-boat began to slide easily through the water, and the lights, flame and smoke of Scapa Flow were behind it. The *U-47* had reached the safety of the open sea.

In the confusion of the first hours after the sinking, all sorts of reports emerged. One concerned strange movements ashore, which some officers thought indicated a spy was signaling the submarine. Others concerned possible sabotage. Marine Bandmaster Owens, who was thrown over the side of the *Royal Oak*, swam aft, alongside an officer in his night clothes. Three hundred yards astern of the *Royal Oak* the officer swore he saw a submarine periscope, and called it to Owens' attention.

Right guess, wrong place. The *U-47* had not approached closer than 3,000 yards, and there was no way Owens and his companion could have seen the submarine from their position. What they saw was obviously a floating spar or stick.

Actually, at the moment, no one was even certain that a submarine had done the job, and even after Radio Berlin began trumpeting the news of Prien's exploit, the doubts remained.

The loss of a major warship in a major naval base that had been declared by the Admiralty to be safe for the fleet created an enormous scandal in Britain. Writing about it later, Winston

Churchill said that if he had not been new on the job it might have meant his political ruin. But his opposite number, shadow cabinet (Labor) member A. V. Alexander took the broad view that this was a national disaster, not a political opportunity. Still, questions had to be answered.

The pressure was eased slightly during the next three days when German aircraft raided a number of bases and did considerable damage to other ships. An official inquiry was held between October 18 and October 24 under Admiral R. E. E. Drax.

The board investigation showed that the antisubmarine defenses of Scapa Flow were totally inadequate. All the wrong measures had been taken aboard the ship. Riding lights were showing, which gave Commander Prien a nice point of aim. The sliding hatches of the ship operated athwartships, and several of them had jammed; they should have worked from stem to stern. There were no life belts for the men except life rings along the upper decks, useful only for a "man overboard" situation. No signal was sent by the *Royal Oak* to indicate that she was under attack. The hatches and ports were not closed up after the first explosion, which hastened the sinking of the ship.

As for the Scapa Flow defenses, it was immediately obvious that there were not enough patrol craft to do the job. And none of those carried asdic, the submarine listening device.

Several gaps existed in the four partially blocked exits to Scapa Flow. There were no lookouts around the gaps, no searchlights to cover them. There should have been minefields laid down. The ship had been alert, but not very alert, to air attack. And much was made of this, although it was hardly at issue, since even the board agreed that the ship must have been sunk by a submarine.

Much more telling was a memorandum, written by Admiral Dudley Pound, the first sea lord, for the eyes of Winston Churchill. In this document Pound tried to exculpate himself and all others. The key paragraph was:

> There is no evidence that the defenses of Scapa received inadequate consideration, either in the Admiralty

or by the other officers concerned, namely, the commander in chief himself, the commanding officer, coast of Scotland, whose base was at Rosyth, and later the admiral Orkneys and Shetlands, whose appointment was made on the 25th August, 1939 but who in fact carried out some investigations before that date.

When this draft was received by Winston Churchill he exploded. As to that paragraph above, he responded with one of his earthy marginal comments: "What utter rubbish!"

So the memorandum was redrafted, and this time the blame was thrown largely on the low man on the totem pole. Admiral Burroughs, the assistant chief of the naval staff, and Sir Roger Forbes, the commander in chief of the Home Fleet, came in for a few unkind cuts, but most of the blame was reserved for the junior admiral in the line, Rear Admiral French:

> The admiral commanding the Orkneys and Shetlands, Admiral French, had however a more direct responsibility. He also had opportunities of imparting any misgivings he felt about the details of the defenses for which he was daily and hourly responsible. He did not do so. Being left when the fleet was away with only five trawlers, of which two were resting and one refitting, he should have endeavored to supplement this force by using some of the civil drifters and trawlers which were in the harbor, taking them over and manning them with naval ratings of which he had plenty in the Iron Duke and ashore. The concurrence of the commander in chief, who was often away with the fleet, in no way justified him in being content with possessing only two patrolling craft on duty, and with having in consequence left the eastern entrances, including the known gap at Kirk Sound, for which a blockship was daily expected, utterly unguarded.
>
> Officers of flag rank are expected to be active initiators in all matters affecting the safety of H.M. ships and the vigorous prosecution of the war. They are not

necessarily covered by general or formal approval from higher authorities. These authorities are involved, but their subordinates are not excused, unless the issue has been directly or specifically raised, and they are over-ruled.

That memorandum would most certainly have ended Admiral French's career had it been circulated officially through the fleet. But it was so apparent that everyone concerned was at fault that the memorandum was never distributed. The fact was, as Churchill recognized immediately, that those deadly paragraphs could have referred to Admiral Pound and all the others down the line as well as to Admiral French.

French had taken office knowing that the defense system was inadequate, and he had said so. His chief of staff had only arrived at his headquarters the day before the disaster. French had been working with a handful of officers, virtually all of whom were retired sea dogs, some of them dating back to the 1914-18 navy. *He had not even been assigned an antisubmarine officer for the defense command.*

So to heap the blame on French's head was a particularly obnoxious reaction of the peace-oriented, spit-and-polish navy. If no one else could see that, at least Winston Churchill, with his vast experience in naval affairs, could.

The memorandum was junked and the question of blame rested, as it ought, on the naval establishment which had been caught with its trousers at half mast.

What had to be done immediately was to move the fleet anchorage back to Rosyth, and also to use the base in the Clyde River until the defenses of Scapa Flow could be tightened up. On October 31 Churchill and Admiral Pound went to Scapa Flow for meetings with Admiral Forbes aboard his flagship. Scapa would be reduced temporarily to the position of destroyer refueling base.

5

Doenitz Unleashed

At 2:30 P.M. on October 17 the *U-47*, escorted by two destroyers, slowly moved into the Wilhelmshaven naval base. As the submarine passed the anchored vessels of the fleet a cacophony of sirens, whistles and horns rose up across the water, and men stood at the rails of their vessels and cheered. When Captain Prien had cleared English waters, he had radioed to Admiral Doenitz that he had penetrated the Scapa Flow base and sunk one battleship and damaged another.

Admiral Raeder, who was just then suffering one of Hitler's tantrums ("Why doesn't the navy do something but spend money?") saw that here was an opportunity to regain grace, and no time was lost in informing the world of the magnificent achievement of German arms. At sea, a proud Lieutenant Endrass painted a picture of a red bull on the conning tower of the *U-47*, and the men pleaded with Prien to let the boat be known thenceforth as the Bull of Scapa Flow.

As the *U-47* glided up to the submarine pier, Admiral Doenitz, dressed in a black leather coat, was waiting, surrounded by high officers of the Kriegsmarine, including no less a figure than Admiral Raeder himself.

The submarine stopped. Prien stepped off the boat and saluted Admiral Doenitz smartly. Doenitz gave one of his rare smiles and introduced Prien to Grand Admiral Raeder, who pumped his hand, then insisted on going aboard the *U-47*. He clambered down the conning tower ladder and insisted on

shaking hands with every man of the crew. Then he announced
that by order of the Fuehrer he was conferring on every man the
Iron Cross, second class. The honor was a great one for the
enlisted men, who almost never won so prestigious a medal,
but Germany's gratitude was immense that day, and Raeder's
perhaps greatest of all, because Prien had rescued the navy
from the Fuehrer's wrath.

Raeder announced that each officer would receive the Iron
Cross, first class, and that officers and crew would be flown to
Berlin to be greeted by the Fuehrer at the chancellery. They
were given new uniforms and housed at the Kaiserhof, Berlin's
most luxurious hotel. That night the crewmen went out and
celebrated and the next morning they were driven through the
streets of Berlin in convertible Mercedes limousines, past
crowds of thousands, through triumphal floral arches. They
were saluted at the chancellery by the fuehrer's personal guard
of black-clad SS troops, and received in the Grand Salon by
Admiral Doenitz, Captain Godt, Grand Admiral Raeder, as well
as by General Keitel, the army chief of staff, Reichsmarschall
Hermann Goering, and Josef Goebbels, the minister of propaganda. The presence of the last two figures indicated how tran-
scendentally important this affair was regarded to be by the
powers of the Third Reich.

After a few minutes two tall, carved wooden doors at the
end of the reception hall opened and the Fuehrer himself entered to inspect the crew of the U-47. He shook hands with
every man and smiled. His aides relaxed for the first time in
days.

After the inspection Hitler stopped to chat. Admiral Doenitz
took this opportunity to speak his prepared piece. Since 1935
he had been trying, with only limited success, to secure full
backing for the navy. With 300 submarines, he had said over
and over again, he could dominate the Atlantic and bring Britain to its knees.

Hitler listened and smiled thinly. He then announced the
promotion of Doenitz to the rank of vice admiral, and bestowed
the Knight's Cross of the Iron Cross, with palms, on Com-

mander Prien. Then he took Prien and Doenitz off to his private office for more details about the thrilling exploit. In the office Doenitz again asked the Fuehrer to increase the number of U-boats and explained his desperate situation. At that moment, he told Hitler, only six of his submarines were operational.

Hitler was not pleased to be bearded on such a strictly ceremonial occasion, but he swallowed his irritation and promised Doenitz he would have his submarine building program. In the anteroom, Raeder warned Doenitz that he had come far too close to overstepping the bounds with the Fuehrer, but Doenitz went away from the meeting content. His plan had worked perfectly; he had brought forth the miracle and in its wake the submarine force was to be unleashed. Now in spite of the doubts of Raeder and the high command, and the constant sniping of the battleship men and the Luftwaffe, Doenitz was confident that he could win the war against England.

6

Sparring

From the outset of the war Admiral Doenitz had planned to use the wolf pack technique to attack British convoys. When the U-boats had set out for their war stations on August 19, 1939, he had sent the commanders of the second and sixth U-boat flotillas to sea with them, so that he would have subordinate leaders for the wolf packs if an opportunity came to use them. But two factors militated against the employment of the wolf pack in the early weeks of the war.

First of all, Doenitz did not have enough U-boats. Of the twenty-odd Type VII boats, some came back damaged and others in need of overhaul after the first flush of action. Doenitz knew he could count on only half a dozen boats for service at any one time. He was expecting another nine U-boats to go into commission early in October, but this did not happen.

During the first half of October Admiral Doenitz had to continue to operate as he had in the beginning, sending out individual U-boats to patrol the most likely areas of British shipping. Since Doenitz had now received the promise that he would get his U-boat fleet, that meant what he had proposed to Admiral Raeder in the first three days of the war: thirty U-boats a month. But Hitler was already dragging his heels about allocation of steel. It would take time to change that. Meanwhile, Doenitz must make do with what he had.

Hitler was stalling Doenitz because the naval war was not high on his list of priorities. He still hoped that with the early fall of Poland, the French and the British would lose their taste for the war and that a negotiated peace could be arranged to give Hitler more time to build for his conquest of Europe.

Second, within the naval establishment the battleship men were having their day. On September 26 the pocket battleships *Deutschland* and *Graf Spee* were sent out to raid the enemy on the high seas. The *Graf Spee* turned south toward Latin America, and on September 30 sank the 5,000-ton British freighter *Clement*. By mid-October, with the two pocket battleships freed, Admiral Raeder was also planning to use the *Gneisenau* and *Scharnhorst* to strike terror into British hearts in a raiding campaign. They would threaten the British sea lanes to the west, as the *Graf Spee* was threatening the south.

* * *

In London, Churchill was setting in motion the machinery to counteract Doenitz's U-boat building program. The Royal Navy had entered the war badly equipped to face a major U-boat threat. The fast procurement of antisubmarine vessels was the top item on Churchill's agenda. He was appalled when he looked at the record. No destroyers had been ordered in the naval construction bill of 1938. Thirty-two were being constructed in the yards from previous budgets. Only nine would be delivered before the end of 1940. Also, naval architects and operational admirals had discovered all sorts of new developments to add to the destroyers, and the result was that they were beginning to resemble cruisers. What were needed were small, fast vessels to protect the 2,000 British ships at sea each day and to clear the seas of U-boats.

Early in October Churchill called a halt to the prewar naval construction program. The priority had to be what the yards could build and get into operation in the next year. Naval architects had come up with a new concept for a small, fast fighting craft called the corvette. The Admiralty had placed orders for fifty-eight corvettes, but not a single keel had been laid. This had to be fixed in a hurry. Also, a rush order was sent to Canada for small, fast vessels, and plans were made to build a newer type of escort to be called frigates.

Meanwhile the British navy would have to scour the ports, the marinas, and the dockyards for vessels to serve in the anti-submarine warfare. Little wonder, then, that the Royal Navy could not supply escort vessels for ships outward bound or off at sea and far away.

On October 11, RAF and Royal Navy officers met at RAF Fighter Command Headquarters to try to find a way to give more protection to convoys. It was agreed that the navy would provide ten trawlers, spaced at ten-mile intervals, to screen a line fifty miles from the east coast of England, the northernmost trawler to be approximately opposite Newcastle-on-Tyne. The trawlers would be equipped with wireless capable of reaching the RAF shore stations, and were to report all aircraft proceeding west but none moving east. This protection, of course, was almost entirely limited to prevention of air attack. With the exception of the handful of Coastal Command bombers, there was little the RAF could do to help the convoys against submarines.

The navy had already diverted all food ships to Britain's west coast, and the ships traveling up and down the east coast were now limited to 1,600 tons or less and coastal steamers, delivering goods from one east coast port to another. So the Atlantic ocean and the Western Approaches were where the battle would be fought.

The Admiralty was also putting together its complex rules for the operation of convoys in this new war. For one thing, there would be no stopping to help any ship damaged by mine or torpedo. The convoy would maintain course and speed, or continue its zigzag, until the convoy commander changed the orders. The first outward bound overseas convoys (OA and OB) had sailed on September 7, and thereafter, as noted, the individual sailing of ships had been prohibited. The convoys were protected by aircraft as far out as 200 miles west of Ireland. Then the protection ceased and two days later the ships broke off to head for their respective destinations.

By October 1 Doenitz had decided that the convoys offered too many difficulties. He would have to disperse his handful of

oceangoing submarines over too wide an area for effective results, he said, ignoring the work of Captains Lemp, Prien,
Schultze, Lieb, Rollmann, Schuhart, and Von Dresky, all of
whom had sunk at least two ships on their first patrol.

The fact was that Admiral Doenitz was eager to try out in
action the wolf pack technique he had perfected in training
between 1935 and 1939. So he rationalized in his war diary that
he had to move his U-boats to where they could be concentrated against enemy shipping in a small geographical area.
Looking at his charts he found the area: the Gibraltar run. He
chose one of his flotilla leaders, Commander Werner Hartmann,
to lead the pack in *U-37*. The U-boats in the pack would go to
sea on different days and assemble southwest of Ireland. Then
they would attack convoys heading south toward Gibraltar. If
that area did not prove satisfactory, Hartmann had the authority to change, to move anywhere along the Spanish-Portuguese
coast.

Doenitz's plan, ratified on October 1, depended on the delivery of the new U-boats promised him in October. But by mid-
October only three of the nine boats had arrived. He would
have to make do with what he had. The first wolf pack would
consist of Hartmann's *U-37*, Herbert Sohler's *U-46*, Herbert
Schultze's *U-48*, and Gelhaar's *U-45*. Before mid-month the
boats assembled southwest of Ireland and headed for Gibraltar.

Meanwhile at Gibraltar, Convoy HG 3 was assembling for
the return voyage to the United Kingdom. It was a mixed bag of
ships, British, Egyptian, and French. Captain Ernest Coultas,
master of the *Clan MacBean*, did not like it at all, particularly
when at the convoy captains' meeting he met the Egyptian and
French captains and distrusted them thoroughly. Also, he was
surprised to see there a woman "of what I would call an extremely flashy appearance" who spoke English with a dis-
tinctly foreign accent. She was interpreting for the French captains.

The captains were given sailing orders and secret instructions for a rendezvous point which they would reach on October 14. They sailed in small groups, and then at the appointed

hour got into formation and met the escorts. Their major protection was to be from the air.

All went well until the morning of October 17, when Convoy HG3 encountered Commander Hartmann's wolf pack. The wolf pack stalked the convoy until evening, and then in swift succession Hartmann sank the 10,000-ton steamer *Yorkshire*, Sohler the 7,000-ton *City of Mandalay*, and Schultze the 7,200-ton *Clan Chisholm*. The *Clan MacBean* was the fourth ship in the fifth column, only three-quarters of a mile away from the *Yorkshire* when she was hit. The captains panicked and the convoy broke up.

The *Clan MacBean* sailed independently northward for the United Kingdom. The U-boat pack was reduced to two when Schultze, who had been out on his second patrol since early October, ran out of torpedoes and had to go home. Hartmann trailed all the next day and at 7 P.M. attacked the *Clan MacBean*. Captain Coultas first knew it when he saw a submarine periscope and then a torpedo coming down its track from three-quarters of a mile off the port bow.

Chief Officer H. N. Croscombe, on the bridge, put the helm over hard and the torpedo missed the bow by what the captain swore was inches. Hartmann then tried to maneuver in close for another shot, following Doenitz's standing order. Captain Coultas maneuvered too and kept him bow on. The distance closed until they were only two hundred feet apart, submarine and quarry. Or was it quarry? The submarine's gun was firing, but the men were obviously nervous as they saw the bow of the merchant ship looming larger every moment. They missed again and again at point-blank range.

The *Clan MacBean* had closed to within a hundred feet of the submarine when the skipper saw the danger he was in and crash-dived. Captain Coultas could hear the cries of despair from the German gun crew as they were left high and then wet on the submerging deck. The ship passed directly over the submarine, but Hartmann had managed to get down far enough to avoid being rammed. Then he surfaced to pick up his gun crew and this time Captain Coultas rang for emergency full power and sped away.

7

Convoys

When the convoys were attacked and ships sunk, the Admiralty made it a point to interview survivors to find out just what had happened, so that if possible the navy could keep it from happening again. In this way the British learned of Admiral Doenitz's preoccupation with Q-ships. Several of the ships attacked in September and October had been painted almost naval gray by their owners or captains; this would make them less subject to attack. Less visible, possibly, but when visible the deep gray color frightened the submarine captains, all of whom had been briefed by Admiral Doenitz on his major worry. At least two U-boat captains told merchant masters that they had nearly sunk their ships without warning, believing they were Q-ships.

In fact, Admiral Doenitz's fears had a solid basis. He knew his British enemy, and he knew that Q-ships had been successful in the 1914–18 war. After the First World War the British Admiralty had made plans to use Q-ships in the next naval war, and eight such vessels were commissioned in the last months of 1939 and the first quarter of 1940. They were powerful decoy ships, with torpedo tubes and depth charges and four-inch guns. One mounted nine four-inch guns. They worked all the major sea lanes—Gibraltar, the Western Approaches, the South Atlantic—and not one of them did a bit of good. Two were sunk by wary U-boat captains who fired first and asked questions afterward. It might be said that what appeared to be Doenitz's paranoia stood his captains in good stead.

The care with which the navy and the British merchant shipping establishment approached the U-boat threat also helped the British in the anti–U-boat war. By November 1939, the convoy system was in full bloom. Given the limited resources of the Royal Navy, as much protection as possible was being given the merchant ships at sea. But there were big holes in the system.

One was intelligence. The Germans maintained close and friendly relations with Franco Spain, and the British knew the Nazis were getting information from Spanish sources about shipping at Gibraltar and in the Mediterranean. Lisbon was a hotbed of spies of all nations. There were plenty of suspicious characters hanging around the Caribbean, and Argentina's tilt toward Germany was known to be pronounced.

When accounts such as those of Captain Ratkins of the unfortunate *Lochavon* reached Whitehall, they were distributed to a select list, which included representatives of the civilian war shipping committee. After reading the reports, the civilians had some good advice for the military.

In the case of the *Lochavon*, there had been at least three major violations of security. On the wharves of San Francisco and Los Angeles, Captain Ratkins had been told that his ship would be convoyed from Kingston. At Kingston he was told in a bar the date of his sailing. He also learned that while ship captains had sealed orders, the contents were known to the local pilots on the day before sailing.

Admiral Doenitz's first wolf pack, which intercepted Convoy HG 3 so successfully, may not have simply come upon the convoy in mid-ocean. Four captains of ships that sailed in that convoy later told naval authorities that they were sure the information about their convoy had been leaked at Gibraltar. Three of those four ships were sunk. That sort of problem could be attacked immediately, but the most serious ground for complaint by the skipper—the matter of escort—could not.

Putting their best face on, the port officers usually indicated to the departing skippers that they would have an escort, but not that they would be deserted by the escort partway along the voyage. The *Lochavon* convoy, for example, was escorted by a Canadian destroyer for eighteen hours, but had to cross the central Atlantic without escort. The submarine caught the convoy twenty miles from the rendezvous where it was to pick up escort in the Western Approaches.

The *City of Mandalay*'s HG 3 convoy was escorted for the first day by two destroyers and a seaplane, but the seaplane left before dark, and the destroyers slipped away during that first night. The strongest complaint was that if the ships were not to have escort all the way, then the captains ought to be informed so they could take extra precautions.

8

The Leisurely War

As 1939 drew to an end Admiral Doenitz's hands were still tied by Hitler. Not in the matter of restrictions: the war was swiftly moving toward unrestricted submarine warfare. Doenitz's problem was that he still did not have enough U-boats; they were not coming out of the yards quickly enough to do what he wanted.

Hitler was preoccupied with the land war, and when he thought of the navy, it was Admiral Raeder's navy, the fleet of battleships, pocket battleships, and heavy cruisers for which that admiral had such high hopes.

Hitler had achieved his aim of conquering Poland, now split between Germany and the USSR. The war in the west had settled down to something reminiscent of 1914, a war of entrenchment along the eastern frontier of France. The French expected a German attempt to invade. That month mines took thirty-three merchant ships, totaling 82,000 tons, while the submarines took twenty-five ships, totaling 81,000 tons.

* * *

As long as matters grew no worse at sea, there was no emergency. But the Chamberlain government had to look to the future, and food loomed large as a vital problem. In late November a special subcommittee of the war cabinet was formed to consider the future problems of food management. The chairman was Sir Samuel Hoare, the Lord Privy Seal; other members included the minister of agriculture and fisheries, the minister of food, the minister of health, the minister of shipping, and the secretary of state for colonies, all of them vitally concerned with the problems of producing, delivering, and allocating food, and of making certain that the island kingdom was fed.

Supplies were getting so tight that plans were made for rationing. W. S. Morrison, the minister of food, said his two anxieties were sugar and cereals, particularly the latter. By the end of 1939 England would have only an eight-week supply. That would mean the closure of some flour mills.

As for sugar, the time for rationing was coming, as with bacon and butter. The hope for the future lay in Cuba, and that meant ships.

The minister of shipping, Sir John Gilmour, was feeling put upon. He was hearing the same thing from the army, navy, and RAF, as well as from the ministry of supply. Only this day he had received an anguished call from the French government to help them out. The French had arranged for a naval escort to accompany a convoy bringing aircraft from New York. But they had not arranged for enough shipping tonnage to carry the planes. They had therefore called on the British. Sir John had been forced to divert a British ship, which was about to sail for Australia, and which now would have to go to Le Havre, then back to New York, and then to Australia to bring back grain and meat.

But what of the future?

The minister of health, Walter E. Elliot, said that the government had already cut food imports from 59 million tons per annum to 47 million tons, and could, if necessary, cut to 19,800 million tons. But of course that depended on the ability of British farmers to produce. The minister of agriculture, Reginald Dorman-Smith, said that was a matter of money. If the government would spend enough money, the farmers would bring in the bacon. So the questions of rationing (which items) and production (which crops) and shipping (how much) were referred back to the war cabinet. Everyone knew that this was just the beginning. At the next meeting early in December, a far more explosive issue was raised. What was to be done about distilling?

Some members of the committee felt it was hard to justify continuation of liquor distilling in the face of the coming shortage of grain.

Complete stoppage of distilling for a year would not affect the export trade materially, said one of the experts from the ministry of agriculture.

But what about the home front?

There was enough stock to last three years.

And then what?

Who could say?

Who, indeed. The delicate matter was tabled.

And what about brewing?

That was not even discussed. The thought of cutting out beer was too dismal to consider.

*　　*　　*

The last month of the year saw a general slackening of U-boat efforts as well as anti–U-boat efforts. The distribution of antisubmarine forces indicated that 100 destroyers were available in British home waters, plus 14 patrol vessels, 10 escorts, 5 motorized antisubmarine boats, 36 armed trawlers, and 15 yachts. But in fact, as Admiral Forbes reported, at any given moment perhaps only 45 percent of these vessels were fit for service; the others were laid up for repairs. But the good news was that another 100 trawlers were about to be delivered for antisubmarine work. That would mean more escorts for convoys; and by December it was apparent that escort was the key to everything. During the month only 3 ships in escorted convoys had been sunk.

This was the month in which the British submarines won their first victory over their opposite numbers. On December 4, H.M.S. *Salmon* encountered another submarine eighty-five miles southwest of Lindesnes and sank her. This was Lieutenant Wilhelm Froehlich's *U-36*, out on her second war patrol. On the first patrol, in September, Froehlich had sunk two ships.

But this time he had been careless, caught on the surface by the enemy. He and a crew of twenty-nine men went to the bottom.

British submarines were not basically part of the antisubmarine force, although their record during the war was an admirable one. But other, more traditional antisubmarine measures were also being taken. A new school of antisubmarine tactics was set up to train asdic operators. The larger merchant ships, which could stand the recoil of a deck gun, were rapidly being armed. About 23 percent of those that would be armed received their guns by the end of October. And the RAF Coastal Command was increasing its searches, escorts and patrols.

In October the British began paying special attention to the North Sea. Norway was a principal supplier of iron ore for the furnaces of Britain—and for Germany. From the beginning of the war, the Admiralty went out to stop the German ore import and, by submarine attack and mine fields, had done such an effective job that by the end of 1939 Winston Churchill was concerned lest the Germans invade Norway and secure her raw materials. He was talking of invading Narvik and Bergen to keep those two ports open for the British trade. So far he had been unable to convince the rest of the war cabinet. Across the North Sea the Germans were also talking of invading Norway, using the same line of reasoning.

After sinkings of some Norwegian ore ships early in the war, the Royal Navy thereafter set up ore ship convoys, with a battleship-covering force in case the German battle fleet chose to try to stop the shipments. After two successful convoys the Germans retaliated by sending the battle cruiser *Scharnhorst* into these waters. She sank the British armed merchant cruiser *Rawalpindi* on November 23. Then came a good deal of activity by major naval units, which emphasized to both sides the importance of control of the Norwegian North Sea ports. On the way home from chasing the Germans, Admiral Forbes' flagship, the battleship *Nelson*, ran into a mine laid by a submarine in Loch Ewe, and was laid up for weeks. It was another small triumph for Admiral Doenitz. The magnetic mines laid by the 250-ton coastal U-boats were doing their work far more effectively than the attack submarines. England was lucky in that the Germans had virtually exhausted their supply of magnetic mines by the end of the year, and had to slow the minelaying. But the five magnetic mine fields laid off the east coast and the Thames estuary, and the mines laid around the entrances to British naval bases, continued to take their toll.

By the beginning of 1940 the London Submarine Agreement was in tatters. The prohibition of attacks on passenger liners had been removed. Neutral ships were not safe east of twenty degrees west longitude, which bisects Iceland down the middle. In November the United States government had declared a war zone that extended from the twenty degrees east longitude, covering all of the British Isles and France. That meant American shipping was forbidden in these waters. It was not a particularly important matter to Britain just then, since American shipping was limited. It was a sign, however, of Germany's steady move toward unrestricted submarine warfare; and American acceptance of the German extension of the sea battle zone was a sign of the low state of relations between the United States and Britain, a matter of serious concern to Churchill, and for which Ambassador Joseph Kennedy was largely responsible.

* * *

The Germans entered 1940 with a vigorous mine-laying campaign around Britain. Some small U-boats were used in this work, but most of it was done by surface vessels. From the beginning of January the Germans concentrated on neutral shipping. Doenitz does not mention this in his autobiography, but the evidence is overwhelming. Of the fifty-four ships sunk by submarines in January, forty-three were neutrals. The idea was obviously to put pressure on neutral shipping to stay away from Britain. At first the pressure was exerted in the North Sea. The attack on the most logical area, the Western Approaches to the British Isles, did not begin again until the middle of January, when half a dozen of Doenitz's Type VII submarines appeared.

As the year opened Churchill continued to be optimistic. At the war cabinet meeting on January 2 he crowed that the previous week had been the best since the beginning of the war insofar as shipping losses were concerned. He was not looking at the neutral ship records.

Two weeks later Churchill had to report to the cabinet that U-boat activity had increased seriously. Also, he had to take note of German broadcasts denying a British claim to have sunk seventy submarines since the war began. The Germans said the figure was closer to thirty-five. The actual figure was eleven; the German announcement duped Churchill into believing that the figure was around forty. But Churchill was sure of the figures for delivery of German U-boats to Doenitz, and in this he was much closer to the facts: he claimed that up to Christmas only eight new boats had been added to the fleet. It was more, but not many more. However, by now there were enough boats that Admiral Doenitz felt confident in renewing the open sea campaign in the west. The U-boats went out, not to attack convoys in packs but to attack individual ships. During January only nine ships out of fifty-four were sunk in convoys; three of these were the work of Lieutenant Lemp, who may have been doing penance for the *Athenia*. Lemp's return to grace was complete on this patrol; he was the captain who put the torpedoes into the battleship H.M.S. *Barham* and knocked her out of action for many weeks.

More tragic for the British was the loss of H.M.S. *Exmouth*, a senior destroyer and flotilla command ship in the Moray Firth near Tarbatness on January 21. The *Exmouth* was escorting the merchant ship *Cyprian Prince*, which was carrying valuable materials for the rebuilding of the Scapa Flow defenses. When it was learned that the Danish ship *Tekla* had been torpedoed fifty minutes northeast of Tarbatness at 5 A.M., the *Exmouth* was warned to watch out for that submarine.

There was no need for that; Lieutenant Commander Werner Heidel's *U-55* had already pulled out into the North Sea where, that same day, she sank the Swedish freighter *Andalusia*. But the danger was real nonetheless. Lieutenant Commander Hans

Jenisch's U-22 had moved into *that same North Sea area*. The *Cyprian Prince* was traveling along at a safe distance behind the *Exmouth*; she had been warned that the destroyer was submarine hunting. Night came. The little convoy proceeded north. At about 4:45 A.M. the *Exmouth* was still in sight, but dimly, when the chief officer of the merchant ship heard several explosions in the vicinity of the destroyer. They sounded like depth charges. But four minutes later came another explosion, and the destroyer passed out of sight. The *Cyprian Prince*'s captain altered course and passed through the sea where the *Exmouth* had been. Nothing remained but bits of flotsam. The captain of the *Cyprian Prince* heard voices in the water, and saw some lights flashing. He had stopped his engines and prepared to make rescue attempts. But then he realized that he had a vulnerable cargo aboard and so he started his engines and went on, maintaining radio silence. Only when the merchant ship arrived alone at Kirkwall, just before 6 P.M., did the Admiralty learn of the disaster. Other ships rushed to the area, and they found one life buoy from the *Exmouth*, floating in the water among a handful of orange crates. That was all.

The sinking of the *Exmouth* aroused a debate within the war cabinet. Had the captain of the *Cyprian Prince* done the right thing in abandoning the survivors of the warship when he might have rescued them?

Unfortunately, said the first lord of the Admiralty, the captain had done just the right thing, given his situation with virtually irreplaceable military stores aboard. It was a cruel war.

The *U-9*, a type IIB submarine, saw action early in the war.

Another early sub, *U-25*, type 1A, at the outbreak of war

The sleek silhouette of *U-32*

Achtung! Officers and crew of *U-38* at a ceremonial shapeup

The *U-52*, a type of VII B sub, with its deadly cannon

The launching of a later U-boat, type XXI

Submarines tied up at Kiel, the busy German wartime base

U-boat of type XVII

Subs at the impregnable pens in the Bay of Biscay

Closeup of U-boat trimming panel and hydroplane control

View of the control room of captured *U-532*

The cramped engine room of *U-532*

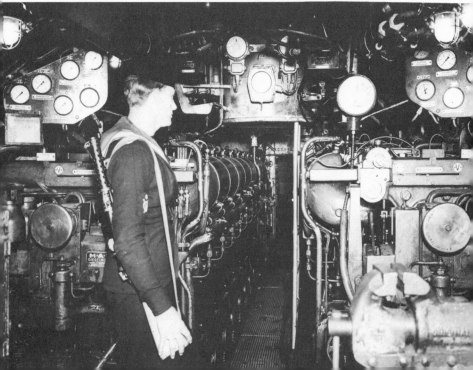

Two-man U-boats called *Seehungs* lying at anchor

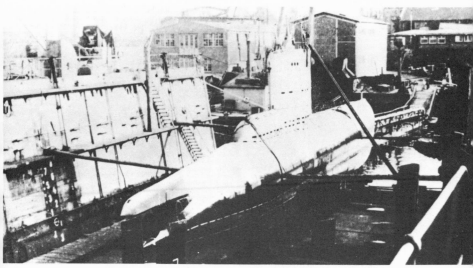

A streamlined, electric underwater boat, type XXIII

U-boats preparing to surrender at Wilhelmshaven

U-boat, with the Union Jack aloft, after surrendering to RAF aircraft

9

The Biggest Bag

On February 18, Lieutenant Commander Otto Kretschmer in the *U-23* sank the British destroyer *Daring*. She was then escorting the first convoy shipment of Norwegian iron ore to England. For a submarine to sink a destroyer was a feat at any time, but for one of the 250-ton "canoes" to sink a destroyer close in by the British coast, in an area infested with enemy aircraft and antisubmarine patrols—that was a feat of enormous daring. But that was Kretschmer. He and Guenther Prien were the lions of the U-boat force. But whereas Prien was a Prussian general in a sailor suit, sarcastic, overbearing, and brilliant in a brittle fashion, Kretschmer was a captain loved by his crew. As Churchill said, a man who loves good cigars can't be all bad; using that rationale under different circumstances he and Kretschmer would have been great friends. Like Churchill, Kretschmer was outgoing, quickwitted and kindly, with a strong sense of humanity. He also shared the Churchillian qualities of patriotism and duty, and a total contempt for weakness. He was, as yet, shaded by the brilliant star of Prien, although his work of laying mines around Scotland in September may have accounted for the sinking and damage of several British warships. But while the mine campaign was enormously effective, it was not the sort of work that brought public acclaim to a U-boat captain. In October, Kretschmer had gone out on his second war patrol and had sunk the small coastal steamer *Glen Farg* off the Orkney Islands, but then he had been warned out of the area after Doenitz had approved Prien's foray into Scapa Flow.

So at the beginning of the new year the score stood Kretschmer two, Prien six, plus the Battleship *Royal Oak*, and an unsuccessful attack on the cruiser *Norfolk*. Sinking a warship gave a captain a special place in the skippers' club, and now Kretschmer had joined up.

10

Norway

The spring of 1940 was an unhappy time for Admiral Doenitz and his U-boat commanders.

It had not begun that way. As March opened, Doenitz was a happy man. His young captains were performing admirably, and in the previous month had set a new record of Allied ship sinkings. He would have eight boats to put into the Atlantic this month and another half dozen "canoes" to continue the highly successful operations in the North Sea. Von Klot-Heydenfeldt was at sea, as was Schuhart, the captain who had sunk the 22,500-ton carrier *Courageous*; the incomparable Schuhart, who in two days in March sank three ships. But March 4, the second day of Schuhart's all-out attack, was the day the roof fell in on Admiral Doenitz. From Berlin came an order: "All further sailings of U-boats to be stopped forthwith. U-boats already at sea will refrain from any operations in the vicinity of the Norwegian coast. . . ."

The struggle for control of Norway was about to begin. The Germans would march into Denmark, a matter over which the English could have no control. But Norway was something else again, for the broad expanse of the North Sea gave the British a battleground on which to conduct the struggle.

Berlin expected the British to act; indeed, they knew they were already acting. The Germans would occupy Narvik, Trondheim and Bergen, but they would not be uncontested. So the U-boats were to help in the great scheme of things, by protecting the German army, navy, and transport forces once they had landed. The U-boats would penetrate the fjords. A line of U-boats would stand sentinel along the coast to attack any British naval or landing forces that appeared. As Berlin warned, the focal point would be Narvik, the central port for iron ore shipments.

If this all seemed a little fuzzy to Doenitz, and beyond the purview of submarine operations, Hitler's will was not to be denied. The U-boats would go to Norway. Doenitz would do something for OKW that he would not do for himself: the submarine school for "canoes" in the Baltic was discontinued, and the six small submarines were brought down for action. Two big boats undergoing trials for sea service were called in and their captains told that they were now operational. By stretching every resource beyond the realm of good sense, Doenitz managed to put together a U-boat fleet for Norway of twelve ocean-going boats and nineteen small ones.

The U-boat fleet set out but accomplished little in trying to meet Hitler's demands. The U-21 ran aground, to the shock and dismay of Admiral Doenitz, who was proud of his captains' navigational record, and the crew was interned by the Norwegians. During March little happened at sea between naval forces; Doenitz had been hamstrung to no purpose at all. U-boat sinkings dropped from the high of February to a new low in March. The mighty Prien went out and had a terrible patrol: a single 1,100-ton steamer was all he could claim. He came back complaining. What was wrong with the torpedoes?

No one could answer that question at the moment. Sour grapes, said many of Prien's contemporaries, sour grapes by an overrated martinet.

Doenitz was not paying too much attention either. His major effort was devoted to the success of Operation Hartmuth, the massing of U-boats to stave off the British.

Norway was a fiasco for Britain. The whole operation was an outgrowth of the ego of Winston Churchill, and so determined was he and so compelling was his presence in the fleet intelligence and operational center that he had his way over the advice of Admiral Pound. The Home Fleet went to sea, marines were landed in Norway, and a number of surface engagements were fought. Submarines played a minor role in the battles, for two reasons.

On April 15 the British destroyers *Fearless* and *Brazen* found the *U-49* in shallow water and sank her. From her papers Naval Intelligence extracted a copy of the Doenitz plan for submarine disposition during the campaign.

More important, in the first week of the campaign, a German torpedo crisis came to a head. In the Norway campaign Doenitz's worst fears were realized. For months his best captains had been complaining that the magnetic exploder of their torpedoes was unreliable. At Narvik it was proved in one situation alone: the German U-boats attacked the British battleship *Warspite* five times under completely favorable conditions, and not one torpedo exploded. Several captains reported premature explosion of torpedoes. *U-25* missed two destroyers; Schultze's *U-48* missed with a salvo of three torpedoes at one cruiser, and another salvo of three against the Cruiser *York*, two other attacks on a destroyer, and the *Warspite*. *U-51* missed with two shots that exploded prematurely against a destroyer.

Faced with this overwhelming evidence of torpedo troubles, Admiral Doenitz withdrew his submarines from the Norway operation on April 17.

The Norway campaign, lasting from early April until the second week of June, resulted in a British withdrawal. Hitler had won another victory, Doenitz had lost five U-boats, and the sinking records of April and May, 1940, together did not match those of the first month of the war. As far as the U-boat force was concerned, Norway was also a disaster.

* * *

Now all the complaints of the U-boat captains were reviewed. Prien's November–December patrol, when he thought his torpedo had hit the *Norfolk* although it had actually exploded in her wake, was reviewed. Prien claimed six misfires, not counting that one. His record in Norway was dismal—one ship—and for the same reasons. Nearly every captain had a similar report to make, so the word was out and U-boat morale was dropping fast.

Doenitz then toured all his U-boat installations. He told the men that a new contact torpedo would soon be perfected, and that they had, after all, the A torpedo driven by compressed air, which had been used almost entirely for night attacks because it left a telltale trail of bubbles. On April 20 Admiral Raeder ordered a complete investigation, which ended in the court-martial of several German naval officers. At the court-martial it was established that 35 percent of what had been blamed on U-boat captains as human error had in fact been due to torpedo failure.

There was no satisfactory solution to the magnetic exploder problem at the moment, but there was an answer. Doenitz gave orders that in the future only contact exploders would be used. This change meant that a submarine captain had to actually hit his target with the torpedo, and that demanded a much greater expertise at shooting. It also, as Doenitz said wryly, put the U-boat force right back where it had been at the end of 1918.

All these problems, coming at the end of a forced campaign involving every U-boat, meant that Doenitz's submarines were virtually out of action during March, April, and May. Many boats needed refits after Norway, the torpedo problem had to be explained, and officers and men needed to become accustomed to the new way. No one understood why the torpedoes still seemed to run deep, even with the use of the contact exploder. The answer was that the captains were to use the shallowest possible setting, which sometimes worked fine. Sometimes the torpedoes ran as set, and then for a large vessel the explosion would be only damaging, not fatal. But that was a matter the U-boat men would have to live with for two more years.

While the U-boats were largely laid up, other events occurred which again changed the nature of the U-boat wars. On the morning of May 10, 1940, the "phony war" came to an abrupt end, when the Germans launched their Panzer forces in a lightning attack around the end of the Maginot line, invading

Holland and Belgium. Britain's major naval and air efforts then had to be concentrated on support of the British Expeditionary Forces in Europe and their allies. On May 15, 1940, Admiral Doenitz had mended his fences and was ready to move back into action in the Atlantic. Those were the orders of Admiral Raeder.

11

The Wolf Packs

From the beginning of the war Churchill had examined the U-boat successes and the anti–U-boat failures in terms of tonnage. So had Admiral Doenitz, although he was constrained by Hitler and Admiral Raeder to paying lip service to the concept of sinking warships. That was the grand concept, but from a sub-mariner's point of view it was better to sink a destroyer than a battleship, even better to sink a freighter. That was what battle-ship men found hard to understand.

In May Churchill left the British Admiralty to become prime minister; his attention was diverted to the immediate problems of survival against a German army that was sweeping across Western Europe. He had little time then to devote to the U-boat wars.

On May 15 Doenitz dispatched the first of the new U-boat operations into the western Atlantic. His purpose was to rees-tablish the confidence of the U-boat crews in their weapons. The first boat out was Lieutenant Commander Victor Oehrn's *U-37*. The past two months spent on the Norway operation had kept Doenitz from keeping abreast of British shipping tactics, so Oehrn went out "blind" to learn what he could and pass it back to the others. It was an indication of the importance Doenitz gave this mission that he entrusted it to the man who had served as his operations officer since the beginning of the war.

Oehrn's boat carried magnetic and contact exploders. He

was instructed to try both; Doenitz hoped that in the open sea the magnetic warheads would function better. Now he would find out.

Oehrn arrived on station northwest of Cape Finisterre on May 18. The next day he fired five magnetic torpedoes, four of which failed; the fifth sank the 5,000-ton Swedish motorship *Erik Frisell*. Doenitz had his answer: 20 percent effectiveness was not enough. The contact exploder had to be the weapon until the experts could arrive at a solution.

Oehrn had the most remarkable cruise of any U-boat commander until that date. On May 22 he damaged the 9,400-ton British motorship *Dunster Grange*. Two days later he sank the 4,000-ton Greek steamer *Kyma*. On May 27 he sank the 5,000-ton British steamer *Sheaf Mead* and the 3,400-ton Argentine freighter *Uruguay*. On the twenty-eighth he torpedoed the French motorship *Brazza*, 10,000 tons, and sank the French trawler *Julien* with gunfire. The next day he torpedoed the 2,500-ton French steamer *Marie Jose*. That exhausted his supply of torpedoes, but he still had time to cruise and he had his deck gun. With that weapon he sank the 7,400-ton British tanker *Telena*, the 950-ton Greek steamer *Ioanna*, and the 2,300-ton Finnish steamer *Snabb*. Then he returned to Wilhelmshaven. The waters around Cape Finisterre were just fine, he said. He had sunk eleven ships, with a total tonnage of 44,463, and had damaged another 10,000-ton vessel, making her useless to the British for a while.

The word of Oehrn's accomplishments quickly filtered through the U-boat establishment and other captains were itching to go out. Doenitz was ready, and they began moving again. They found the pickings far easier than three months earlier; the British were preoccupied with saving their trapped armies at Dunkirk, and with moving them back with the fall of Paris on June 14. Then came the French armistice, and the elimination of the French navy lest it fall into German hands. In June Churchill was preoccupied with the most vital problems of state. Should Britain surrender to the Germans?

Never.

But if Britain was to survive, she must be prepared to defend
herself; already Hitler's planners were working up Operation
Sea Lion, the invasion of the British Isles. The prime minister
had to let others worry about the conduct of the war against the
U-boats. Between June and September the British fought the
battle of Britain, the air struggle in which the RAF decimated
Goering's Luftwaffe, and forced cancellation of the invasion
plans. Then, almost immediately came "the blitz," the German
attempt to force Britain to her knees through saturation bombing.

Churchill was never unaware of the threat of the U-boats.
When, like a jackal, Italy entered the war and brought another
hundred submarines into play for the Axis, Churchill warned
that the next six months of Britain's history would be fateful. In
May the British occupied Iceland (then a Danish colony), and
Churchill asked President Franklin D. Roosevelt, with whom
he had been in constant correspondence for six months, to give
him forty or fifty of the old American four-stack destroyers,
obsolete for fleet work, but which would be invaluable for antisubmarine warfare.

Roosevelt was sympathetic, but there were many in America who did not share the president's belief that the Nazi cancer
must be eradicated, and that the United States was now under
threat. It was not as if Roosevelt could wave his hand and
produce the destroyers. Not during an American election year.
The discussions dragged on, even as Admiral Doenitz's efforts
to increase production and delivery of new U-boats began to
bear fruit.

With the fall of France the Germans now had control of the
Bay of Biscay ports and the French Channel ports. Plans had to
be made to switch British shipping convoys from the route
south of Ireland to the route north of Ireland and into the North
Channel.

That spring and summer of 1940 there were few destroyers
or aircraft available in Britain for escort of convoys. Many ships
were sailing alone. Doenitz knew that his boys were going out
for a happy and productive time so he now moved into an

entirely new mode of submarine operation. From the communications center at Wilhelmshaven he ran his U-boat force like an orchestra:

> If even two days passed without my receiving reports of ships having been sighted by U-boats I at once ordered a redistribution of my forces. As it became more and more evident that we stood an excellent chance of achieving really great successes, I was most anxious that not one single day should pass without the sinking somewhere or other of a ship by one of the boats at sea.

In June Doenitz's boys disappointed him only four times: there were no sinkings on the fourth, fifth, tenth, and twenty-third of the month. But the total for the month was sixty-four ships totaling 260,478 tons—by far the highest tonnage sunk in one month since the beginning of the war. All but one ship were sunk in the Atlantic, one in the North Sea. It was a holiday for the U-boats, and if anyone needed it, a lesson in the necessity of convoys: only eight ships in convoy were sunk, the other fifty-six being unescorted vessels.

New names began to emerge in the list of captains vying for glory and tonnage: Lieutenant Englebert Endrass in *U-46* sank six merchant ships and had a shot at the carrier *Ark Royal*. Lieutenant Hans Jenisch in *U-32* sank five ships on his June cruise. Out in *U-22* in November he had sunk one ship, in December he had sunk two, in January he had sunk the destroyer *Exmouth*, which is what got him promoted to the command of the Type VII boat. On his first patrol in *U-32* in March he had sunk two ships and attacked another unsuccessfully. He was getting up there with the leading U-boat captains.

But the ace of aces, Guenther Prien, was having a heyday. On June 10 he sailed in the *U-47* and four days later sank the 5,800-ton British steamer *Balmoralwood* in the Atlantic. He went on to sink ten ships on this cruise, including one he could not have been very happy about, the *Arandora Star*, a 15,000-ton British liner carrying German and Italian internees from

Britain to a neutral port. In the new German fashion, Prien gave
no warning before he launched his torpedoes and the loss of
life among his countrymen and allies was very heavy.

July brought another change, a most unwelcome one to Britain. The Germans lost little time in taking advantage of their
new empire: the port of Lorient, southeast of Brest, became a
new U-boat base. At the moment it was no more than a staging
base. The U-boats pulled in there to top off their fuel before
going out, and to pick up torpedoes if they ran out during a
patrol. Yet the value to Doenitz was obvious: possession of a
staging base increased the striking power of his U-boats, as the
British defensive power was more or less static.

British and neutral ship losses in August fell from 267,000
to 214,000 tons, still a heavy burden. Admiral Forbes was so
concerned that he addressed a cautionary letter to the Admiralty. Too many antisubmarine vessels had been removed
from escort work to form striking forces. He demurred; escorts
and convoys were the answer to the submarine. He also called
attention to another problem: the fall of France had given the
Germans a new network of airfields closer to British waters.
The British now had to expect combined operation of German
aircraft and submarines. The enemy would also be able to operate their submarines from French bases. All this demanded
more vigilance, better escorts, more escorts, and escorts to take
the convoys farther west.

The Admiralty knew all this. The trouble was that the escorts still were not available, and although some trawlers could
be substituted for patrol work in the north, thus freeing ocean-
going vessels, the solution had to be more escorts; nothing less
would do.

Admiral Doenitz was well aware of the British difficulties,
and was experimenting with ways to capitalize on them. He
was still eager to put his wolf pack theory to a major test. The
chances seemed much better now that Italy had entered the
war. That gave the Axis another one hundred submarines, and
in Atlantic waters, Mussolini's force could be used to augment
the growing U-boat list. The first Italian boats to go out were

Commander Mario Leoni's *Malaspina*, Lieutenant Commander Giulio Ghiglieri's *Barbarigo*, and Lieutenant Commander Riccardo Boris's *Dandolo*. In August they had done quite well for themselves, considering the difference in training and experience. The *Malaspina* had sunk one 8,000-ton British tanker and attacked another. The *Barbarigo* had attacked another freighter, but had had torpedo trouble. The *Dandolo* had sunk two freighters.

The opportunity came in the summer of 1940 when German surface raiders captured several British merchant ships and managed to get possession of copies of the merchant ship signal codes and instructions to merchant shipping. These were made to order for Admiral Doenitz. In July and August he tried to set up several traps but failed, largely because of communications problems. It took too long for the cryptographic section of the OKW to decipher, and inform Doenitz of, changes in convoy planning.

But in September Doenitz got a four-day warning of a big convoy (fifty-one ships) coming to the Clyde River from Cape Breton on the Canadian coast. The convoy had a Canadian escort at the beginning of the voyage. Then the Canadians had to turn back and the convoy went its lonely way across the mid-Atlantic until it was met by British escorts. The trouble for Convoy SC 2 lay in the fact that Admiral Doenitz knew where they were going and when they would arrive, and he had four U-boats to assign to intercept them. Since the British escorts were to meet the convoy at about 12 west longitude, the U-boats would meet them at about 19 west longitude. The chief of the reception committee was to be Prien's *U-47*.

Prien had already spent a few busy days. On September 2 he met the 6,000-ton Belgian steamer *Ville de Mons*, which was traveling unescorted from New York to Belfast. At 1:40 P.M., the ship was on the edge of the "safety" zone, at 12° west longitude, 158° 20′ north latitude. She was heading southeast at thirteen knots and zigzagging. The captain of the vessel was on the bridge when he saw and felt a tremendous explosion at the No. 1 hatch on the port side. He ordered the ship abandoned, and the three lifeboats were lowered. The captain and crew got into them. The captain did not believe the torpedo had done too much damage. He was hoping to lie off for a while and then, when the submarine had gone away, to regain possession of his ship and steam her into Belfast. But fifteen minutes after the first torpedoing a submarine surfaced within a hundred yards of the boats and put another torpedo into the *Ville de Mons*. She sank in ten minutes.

The three lifeboats kept together until 8 P.M., then they got separated. The next day the fourth officer's boat with twenty men aboard sighted a submarine 500 yards off, on the surface, heading southeast. That same day the captain's boat encountered two submarines, which came alongside and asked what ship they were from, and a second which passed them the next day about 2 miles off. On September 7 the fourth officer's boat was picked up by the trawler *Ben Aden* of Aberdeen.

On September 8 the captain's boat with fourteen men made landfall in Britain at Lewis. One member of the crew died from exposure just before the landing. The third lifeboat, manned by the first officer and sixteen men, was picked up by the trawler *Quercia* near Cape Wrath. So all but one of the crew of the *Ville de Mons* were saved. Lucky men. When the captain of the *Ville de Mons* was interviewed at Stornoway naval base, the officer in charge must have thought the entire Atlantic was alive with U-boats.

That officer's report also indicated one of the serious weaknesses of the British anti–U-boat command's thinking: overconfidence in the security of communications. The British officer made much of the amount of smoke the *Ville de Mons* was making at the time, a sore point between Gallic skipper and Gallic engineer. The captain complained that the engineer was polluting the heavens and leaving a track that could be seen for fifty miles. The engineer rejoined that if the cheap owners and skipper had been about their business the boilers would have been properly cleaned in New York.

But at this point Admiral Doenitz did not need smoke to find ships. He was reading the British mail, and passing the word along to Prien and his other boys at sea.

On September 4 Prien attacked Convoy OA 207, outbound from Southend to North America, and sank the 9,000-ton British steamer *Titan* and damaged another ship. Once again, he had known where to look.

Then Prien was ordered to intercept SC 2.

On the night of September 7 the convoy had reached a point about a hundred miles northeast of Malin Head. The weather was overcast, the wind force 5, the swell heavy, visibility was three miles and there was no moon. It was an ideal setup for a U-boat. The convoy was also ideal, consisting of nine columns of ships. At 2:30 P.M. a submarine contact was made by the convoy and the escorts *Skeena* and *Periwinkle* were sent off to chase it. That left the destroyers *Lowestoft* and *Scarborough* with the trawlers *Apollo*, *Berkshire*, and *Westcott* to guard the convoy.

Prien tracked the convoy and at 11:30 P.M. he attacked. The first the British knew of it was when the destroyer *Lowestoft* heard two explosions that came in quick succession. A few minutes later a light was seen on the starboard side of the convoy. Commander A. M. Knapp, captain of *Lowestoft* and commander of the convoy escort, ordered the destroyer *Scarborough* to take charge of the convoy. The *Lowestoft* moved swiftly across the front and swept along the starboard side, then around the stern and up the port side of the convoy. The captain was eager to get rid of the U-boat before the convoy changed course at midnight. If he could break off contact, they might be safe.

The *Lowestoft* made no contact.

The *Scarborough* had remained out in front of the convoy, about 2 miles ahead of the lead starboard ship. At 12:10 A.M. she made contact with a submarine. She moved to attack and when she was 400 yards from the contact a dark shape appeared and then disappeared in a swirl of foam at 300 yards off. The *Scarborough* attacked with one depth charge set at 150 feet. The explosion threw her asdic off, which remained out of order for fifteen minutes. When it was working again, there was no contact.

It took the *Lowestoft* nearly two hours to move completely

around the large convoy. When she was back on station, the *Scarborough* informed her of the activity against the U-boat. So much time had elapsed that the only sensible thing for Commander Knapp to do was to resume his station.

At 3:45 A.M., the convoy had reached a position eighty minutes west of Malin Head when the convoy commander heard another explosion, again with no flash. This time it was on the port side of the convoy. The *Lowestoft* made a swift turn and swept out, but made no contact. It was a difficult time. No merchant ship made any signal. No escort made any signal. No torpedo tracks were seen. The commodore of the convoy ordered an emergency turn to starboard, and ten minutes later another to port.

Nothing more was known within the convoy until morning. Then a ship count indicated that two merchant ships had been sunk. Actually there were three: the *Neptunian*, *Jose de Larrinaga*, and *Gro*, all about 5,000 tons, and all sunk by Prien. Next day Prien got the *Passidon* out of this convoy and Guenter Kuhnke in *U-28* sank the *Mardinian*.

Out of this attack came a strong recommendation from the commander of the escorts for better communications. The convoy should of course maintain radio silence, but if a ship was attacked, then the convoy commander and the convoy commodore should be informed, either by Aldis lamp, flag or, if necessary, by radio.

The fact was that the men on the bridge of the ship *Sherbrooke* had seen the *Passidon* hit, and had not reported it because they had not been told to. Two other ships had seen the *Mardinian* fall out of the column; one captain thought she had been hit, the other not. The fact was that she had been, and thirty-one survivors picked up later by chance by the *Apollo* reported that she had been torpedoed. The survivors were lucky; no one would have thought to search for them.

Commander Knapp's report found its way to the Admiralty and pens began to scratch. It was a complex war, growing ever more so, but the British were learning what they must do.

12

The Convoy Trade

After the attack on Convoy SC 2 Prien's *U-47* reported back to Wilhelmshaven by radio that she was down to her last torpedo. Admiral Doenitz could not have been more delighted. His theory of the wolf pack had been justified, and now he had word of several other convoys coming along to these waters, and a highly experienced captain on the scene to find convoys for him. If he needed any justification, OKW had asked for a submarine to be detailed to give weather reports to guide the Luftwaffe's attacks on Britain. Doenitz did not even have to waste a boat.

Along came convoy OA 210 bound outward from Southend to North America, which gave Kuhnke two ships. Then came convoy after convoy. The proof of Doenitz's "system" was irrefutable (see Table 1).

Then came Convoy HX 72, thirty-seven ships bound from Halifax to England, a slow convoy making eight knots. At 8

TABLE 1
Wolf Pack Sinkings, September 1940

Date	Convoy	Ships Sunk
9/15	SC 3	4
9/17	HX 71	2
9/20	OB 216	4

P.M. on September 21, the commodore of the convoy signaled that zigzagging was to stop at 9:20. Once again the convoy's escorts were commanded by Commander Knapp in the destroyer *Lowestoft*. He had two other destroyers and three armed trawlers to patrol the waters around the convoy. Because of Knapp's bad experience with Convoy SC 2 he had laid down new rules. Any escort that saw an attack was immediately to fire a gun and send up a rocket, then carry out a sweep, firing star shells away from the convoy.

For Commander Knapp the weather was terrible. The moon shone brightly down on the convoy. But at last some relief came in the form of rainsqualls.

At about 10:30 P.M. one of the submarines in Doenitz's wolf pack fired off a star shell over the starboard side of the convoy. At the same time Knapp saw a ship hoist the red light ("have been torpedoed"). Again no explosions were seen and nothing was heard. The *Lowestoft* was on the port side of the convoy, and Commander Knapp tried to find out what was going on. He signaled the commodore but got no reply. He swung out and around and finally saw the torpedoed ship near the center of the convoy.

In rapid succession two more ships were torpedoed, one near the front, the other near the back. Several captains panicked, and the convoy split in two. Ships then began scattering in all directions, which made Commander Knapp's job impossible.

At midnight he saw a ship go up in flames. He rushed to that side and fired star shells out beyond, but found nothing. Then he lost track of what was left of the convoy.

Someone reported a submarine on the surface four miles to his northwest. Knapp went after it, did not find it and realized that he had best try to assemble the convoy and hold it together if possible. There was no way to pull the scattered ships together. They were like sheep flying off in all directions to the joy of the wolves.

At 6:50 p.m. he saw lights ahead and hurried that way. The lights came from S.S. *Collegian* which just then was being shelled by Lieutenant Jenisch's *U-32*. It took *Lowestoft* nearly two hours to reach the scene of this attack. When he arrived the water was empty. No ship, no submarine. Knapp began to search, aided by two other destroyers. He found a contact, and dropped a full pattern of depth charges set to explode at 500, 350, and 200 feet. Then the asdic was knocked out by the explosions, and the contact was lost. The action ended.

Commander Knapp had no way of reading Admiral Doenitz's mind, and the concept of the "wolf pack" was still unknown in London, but the British officer sensed that more than one submarine must have been involved in this night's work. He also sensed something entirely new: the operation of the U-boats on the surface, coming close in to attack. The answer, said Commander Knapp, had to be to turn night into day, to use star shells to light up the U-boats and increase the number of escorts to attack them on the surface or as soon as they were forced to dive.

How right he was. Doenitz's new technique did not involve only the wolf pack, but the change in attack pattern, occasioned by the necessity of using contact exploders on the torpedoes. Five U-boats had made the attack, and they were among Doenitz's brightest stars. Prien was there with his one torpedo, and he sank the 5,000-ton freighter *Elmbank*. Otto Kretschmer was there; he had been rewarded by Doenitz with the brand new *U-99*, and he sank three ships. Lieutenant Heinrich Bleichrodt in *U-48* was a newcomer to the gang, but on this patrol he had already sunk seven merchant ships and a patrol craft and tonight he got two more ships. Joachim Schepke also had a brand new boat, the *U-100*, and he got eight ships out of the convoy. Jenisch took the last one, the *Collegian*.

So of the thirty-seven ships of Convoy HX 72, Doenitz's boys got fourteen, or more than a third, in two nights' work. Nor was that the end of it for the month. On September 25, Jenisch, Oehrn, and Schuhart were directed by Admiral Doenitz to Convoy OB 217D, outward bound from Liverpool, and in two more nights got six more ships. Jenisch went on to sink eight more ships on this patrol, and put himself right up there with the leading U-boat captains.

What a different war it was now from those days only a year

ago when Schultze had stood on his bridge and shared a drink with a merchant captain, then sent him off with sailing directions and a salute.

One of the vessels Jenisch sank late in the month was the 6,700-ton British steamer *Mabriton,* sailing alone from America to Britain. The *Mabriton* had reached a point southeast of Iceland just outside the westernmost limit of protection by British forces. She was steaming steadily before midnight when she was attacked without warning. A torpedo struck near the No. 4 hold on the starboard side.

Chief Officer Embley, who was fifty-seven years old and blind in his left eye, came stumbling up out of his cabin without his glasses, still in his pajamas. He asked the wireless officer if he had sent off an SOS and was told that the aerial had been carried away. Embley went up to the wireless office, but could not get the set to work. As he was sitting there, along came the captain.

"Come on, Mr. Embley," he said. "Get into the boats. She's going fast."

The chief officer then hurried back to his cabin and gathered a few clothes. He could not find his glasses. He then got into the starboard boat, because his own boat had already pulled away. They left the ship's side and then saw there were too many men in the boat. After fifteen minutes they found the port boat, and Embley took over, equalizing the crews until he had nineteen men in his boat. He then hung on to see if the ship would float. But in fifteen minutes more she went down.

Here is Mr. Embley's story of the next six days in an open boat:

25 September, 1940

I suggested to the captain that we should make all the way possible and remain together if we could, steering ESE. The compasses of the two boats were compared and a difference of two points was discovered. Both boats then made sail.

The boats were in sight of each other during most of the day and towards dark the wind was becoming very strong, and the sea high, so I decided to furl the sail and lay to the sea anchor. The other boat tried to follow my example, and in doing so collided with us, causing the boat to leak considerably. We spent a terrible night, having only six blankets between nineteen men. Spray was sweeping the boat the whole night.

26 September, 1940

At daybreak there was no sign of the other boat so we made sail, and after about an hour we sighted her. We ranged alongside and I asked the captain why he had left me. He did not reply, but the other members of the boat stated that they had been pulling all night.

In about two hours the other boat was out of sight astern so I decided to separate as our speed was much greater than theirs. We carried on until dark, when the sea again became very rough and we resorted to the sea anchor and furled the sail. Oil was used during the night. An oar was used to keep the boat head to sea.

Everyone in the boat was very exhausted so I opened a bottle of brandy with a penknife and issued all hands with a tot.

27 September, 1940

In the early hours of the morning I issued the remainder of the bottle of brandy as I was unable to replace the cork (it had gone inside the bottle).

At about 0300 [3 A.M.] I decided the conditions were unbearable so made sail. We had a very fair day but at about 1700 [5 P.M.] the upper gudgeon and the lower pintle of the rudder carried away. We close-reefed the sail and hove to for the night. This night was one of the best we spent.

28 September, 1940

At daybreak we lashed the rudder, the lower part
with a clove hitch brought in taut to the after thwart and
the upper part lashed through the upper gudgeon. This
was quite effective and the rudder gave no further
trouble. Previous to this an attempt had been made to
steer with an oar but was not successful.

We then made sail and carried on throughout the day.
Morale was getting low, with the notable exception of
the men who were eventually saved.

At about 1700 the breeze dropped to a flat calm and
the sea became smooth. We lowered the sail and had a
fairly good night.

29 September, 1940

At 0330 [3:30 A.M.] light breeze stirred. Immediately
hoisted sail on the starboard tack and made our course
within a point, the boat making very little way. We then
decided to put two weather oars out to help the boat
along. In about two hours the wind freshened and we
took the oars in. The wind remained fresh throughout
the day and we decided to carry on during the night.

30 September, 1940

At 0000 [midnight] masses of low cloud passed over
the boat and dense cloud banks were seen on the horizon. These we almost mistook for land.

I thought by this time we must be getting in the vicinity of shipping, so decided to burn a red flare (this took
place at 0525 BST [5:25 A.M. British Standard Time] ac-
cording to the warship's log). Shortly afterwards we observed a low grey shape flashed a torch. The oncoming
ship appeared to be about four cables [cable = 100
fathoms or 600 feet] distant. As my view was obscured
by the sail, I had to be conned by the men in the boat.

The next thing I knew we were across the bows of the

approaching ship and we were struck on the port quarter. . . .

They were struck by the destroyer *Rochester*. Immediately Commander G. F. Renwick ordered engines stopped. Lifeboats were put into the water and life buoys were thrown out. Seven men were picked up: Mr. Embley, the third officer, four seamen, and one black fireman, all wearing life jackets. The rest had been asleep. Besides, as Chief Officer Embley said, they had given up hope anyhow, and he doubted if any of them were wearing their life jackets.

The third officer and the seamen then told Commander Renwick how Chief Officer Embley had held the boat together for six long days, not once leaving the tiller, and not sleeping a wink. He had had a great deal of difficulty with the men who had not survived, they said, and had been able to control the boat only with the help of the survivors. As for the captain's boat, it was never seen again.

That nightmare adventure represented Doenitz's new war.

* * *

By the end of the month Doenitz could report that he had tried his new technique and that it had lived up to his proudest dreams. His captains had sunk fifty-nine ships for a total of 295,000 tons. The U-boat war would never be the same again.

Doenitz was now able to keep more U-boats at sea for longer periods of time, although he still was not getting the sort of building program that he had been promised. His total U-boat force was remarkably small, about thirty operational boats at any one time, with about half that force out. The new French base at Lorient helped a great deal—it cut 450 miles off the distance the boats had to travel from base to zone of operations. Negotiations were also in progress to bring Italian boats up to help out in the north.

Hitler had finally begun to think seriously about the U-boats. In August he had declared a blockade of the British Isles, and made formal what Doenitz had been doing for months:

neutral ships in the area would be sunk on sight. By fall
Doenitz's area of operations was much increased. From Lorient,
La Pallice, and Brest, he could cover the Bay of Biscay nicely,
and could extend his patrols out to twenty-five west longitude,
which was well beyond the range of the British air and sea
escorts. The Admiralty was trying to get some air cover established in Iceland, but the government had to reject the plea;
there were not enough aircraft available to do the job. The Admiralty had been pleading with the RAF to begin using air-
dropped depth charges, but the RAF had dragged its heels for
months. Now, in the fall of 1940, the leaders were beginning to
realize they had to change their ways.

The summer and fall of 1940 were dark days for Britain. It
would be a little while yet before any substantial number of the
new, small, fast antisubmarine vessels could get to work. It
would be a while yet before the Coastal Command could increase its number of aircraft to add to the pool of escorts. But in
late August the British and American governments reached
agreement on the delivery of fifty of the old four-stack destroyers to Britain in exchange for the right to establish U.S. naval
and air bases in British possessions in the western Atlantic and
Caribbean. It was the best thing that had happened in the antisubmarine war yet. It was followed by more good news: after
his reelection, Franklin Roosevelt announced that the weapons
production of the United States would be divided roughly fifty-
fifty between the American forces and the British and Canadians. The decision was enormously important to Britain; had
the United States not decided to continue military support,
Britain could not long have endured in the war.

But the destroyers had to get to Britain. The 23,000 aircraft
ordered from the United States had to be delivered. In the
meantime, the British had to work with what antisubmarine
weapons they had. And that meant Doenitz had the upper
hand.

* * *

If September was a dreadful month for ship sinkings, October was worse. On October 9 Convoy SC 6 from America was

attacked by *U-103* and *U-123*; three ships were lost. In the next six days, three more convoys were hit and lost ten more ships. Then came the four terrible days of SC 7, east bound, loaded with supplies for England.

Once again Doenitz obviously had advance warning from radio intelligence (although in his memoirs his admission is oblique). Knowing the course, speed and time of departure of the convoy, Doenitz had time to assemble a seven-boat wolf pack to attack. There remained a problem: the convoy commodore had the right to vary the course, depending on circumstances. This meant that although Doenitz could look at his superb chart on which all the world was divided into numbered squares on a grid, and tell within a few miles where the convoy ought to be, still somebody had to actually find it. In the case of SC 7 the task was given to Lieutenant Bleichrodt in *U-48*.

Once Bleichrodt made contact with the convoy, he would radio the information back to Wilhelmshaven. Doenitz would then triangulate the source of that radio emission, using another U-boat transmission and a shore station. Now that Doenitz had France at his disposal it was ridiculously easy. There was no reliance on the possibly faulty navigation of a U-boat captain. Doenitz would *know* where the convoy was. Radio and knowing the British code made Doenitz's wolf packs more formidable than he had right to hope at the outbreak of the war. With the system, Doenitz could triangulate the position of a convoy once one U-boat found the quarry.

While Bleichrodt was searching, before dawn on the morning of October 15, Lieutenant Wilhelm Schultze's *U-124* picked up a straggler from the convoy, some twenty miles back, and sank her. She was the Canadian steamer *Trevisa*.

The next day Bleichrodt found the convoy just south of Iceland. In quick order he sank the British tanker *Languedoc*, and the British steamers *Scoresby* and *Haspenden*. The convoy's escorts came after him and forced him down. They lingered around the area for hours, while the convoy went on. So Doenitz lost touch. The only way to regain it was to form a skirmish line with the available boats: Liebe's *U-38*, Mohle's *U-123*, Endrass' *U-46*, and Frauenheim's *U-101*.

Bleichrodt never did get back into this action—he was too far west—but he did sink the steamer *Sandsend*, a straggler from another convoy.

Four hours after Bleichrodt lost touch, Liebe found convoy SC 7; when he reported, Doenitz also sent in Kretschmer's *U-99* and Schepke's *U-100*. In the next two days these six U-boats sank twenty-three ships. That number added to the scores of *U-124* and *U-48* meant this convoy lost twenty-seven ships in all, or a total of 105,000 tons! In terms of the sinews of war that meant:

    200 tanks
    30 8-inch howitzers
    440 25-pound guns
    200 2-pound guns
    120 armored cars
    250 Bren carriers
    26,000 tons of ammunition
    3,000 rifles
    2,100 tons of tank supplies
    10,000 tons of rations
    5,000 tanks of gasoline

Or, to put it in terms of a single ship: one 5,000-ton freighter was carrying 3,000 tons of grain, 5,000 tons of timber, and 300 tons of lead when she was sunk.

Not a bad haul for eight submarines in two days, and that was not the end of it. On October 19, Prien found Convoy HX 79 farther to the west, bound from Halifax to England. Kretschmer, Moehle, Schultzein, and Frauenheim had exhausted their torpedo supplies, but not Bleichrodt, Liebe, Endrass, and Schepke. Together with Prien they made ready to assault the convoy on the night of October 19.

At 8 P.M. it started to rain over the convoy. The wind was light, coming from the southeast, and the sea was relatively calm with only a moderate swell. The submarines surrounded the convoy and watched and waited. At 9:45 P.M. *U-38* fired the first torpedo. It sank the British steamer *Matheran*, in the rear of the sixth column. No explosion was heard, but flames shot up.

Aboard the 5,000-ton British steamer *Whitford Point* here was the reaction: "Our captain immediately ordered extra lookouts, one seaman on the fo'castle head and another on the bridge along with the captain, chief, second and third officers; the gun was also kept manned."

The *Uganda* went next, and then the Dutch steamer *Bilderdijk*. Next came the *Shirak*, a tanker loaded with kerosene. She was the rear ship in the third column. Prien had been waiting, and now he fired. His torpedo struck the *Shirak* on the starboard side amidships. The explosion was violent, the main deck burst, the pumproom flooded, the main steam pipe split, and the top of the funnel blew off. The tanker crew took to the three boats immediately, and all thirty-seven men were picked up only ten minutes later by the trawler H.M.S. *Blackfly*. But the ship did not sink. The convoy went on by. Bleichrodt then came up in *U-48* and put a second torpedo into her. The *Shirak* burst into flame and all tank sections burned, making an enormous beacon on the sea. But the convoy was long gone.

Lieutenant Commander Prien was already turning his attention to the rear ship in the other columns.

The convoy made an emergency forty-degree turn to try to throw the submarines off. After steering that course for an hour, the commodore ordered the ships back to the original course of eighty degrees.

Prien was not thrown off. He tracked the convoy steadily and just before 11 P.M. he fired another torpedo. This struck the steamer *Wandby*, the rear ship in the second column. The ship immediately listed to port as she took water below. Captain J. Kenny fired off two white flares and a red one to indicate that he had been torpedoed and needed assistance. The port bridge lifeboat was wrecked, and the engine room bulkhead split. The fuel oil pipes to the donkey boiler were fractured, but it looked as though the ship might be saved. She could still move slowly

ahead, but that would not last because the engine room was
flooding. The chief engineer tried to start the pumps, but they
worked off the donkey boiler. So the captain decided to leave
the ship for the night and try to salvage her the next day. None
of the merchant vessels in the convoy stopped; they were not
supposed to. But the trawler H.M.S. *Angle* came up for a look.
The convoy escort commander ordered the *Angle* to go to the
assistance of the *Wandby*. Her first lieutenant was sent in the
boat. As he came up, he saw another enormous explosion and
fire off to the north, and then the same pyrotechnics to the
south. The convoy had loosened up and the U-boats were now
inside it, firing.

Their barrage was extremely effective. Working in close to
the convoy and close to each other as they did on the surface,
they could move fast.

Just before 2 A.M. Prien put a torpedo into the *Whitford
Point*. It struck amidships on the port side. All the hatches from
the No. 2 and No. 3 holds went high in the air, and when they
came down they crushed some of the crewmen.

There was absolutely no time to spare. The *Whitford Point*
was carrying eight thousand tons of steel. The captain gave the
"abandon ship" order and ran to his cabin to destroy his secret
papers. Chief Officer J. Marcombe rushed down to the lower
bridge and grabbed an axe to release the boat there. But before
he could swing it the ship broke in half and sank. It had been
less than thirty seconds since she was hit. The captain was
caught in his cabin and drowned. The chief officer was sucked
down with the stern, but the sea spat him forth and he came up
sputtering, struck out and found his hand clutching a hatch
board.

Marcombe got out his whistle and started blowing. One ship
of the convoy, altering course to avoid the wreckage, nearly ran
him down, and then went on. After minutes he found himself
alone, all ships gone. Sixty feet away he could see two other
members of the crew on a raft. They were calling, but since he
could not swim he had to stay with his hatch cover.

He was in the water, blowing his whistle occasionally, in

case someone should come along, when the H.M.S. *Sturdee* came by at 3:30 A.M., on a sweep among the wrecks behind the convoy. The *Sturdee* picked up Chief Officer Marcombe, the ship's bosun, and a fireman. As far as they knew they were the only survivors of the *Whitford Point*.

The convoy went on, the *Angle*'s boat returned with eleven survivors of the *Wandby* and the rest came along in the ship's remaining lifeboats. The *Angle* was detailed to stay behind and watch over the *Wandby* and several other abandoned ships, with the idea that they would be salvaged in the morning.

At 8:30 A.M. the chief officer and the chief engineer re-boarded the *Wandby* to examine her prospects. They did not seem promising; the engine room was nearly flooded, the decks split across the foreside of the saloon, and it looked as though she would soon break in two. The decision was made to abandon her.

The *Angle* wandered among the derelicts. She found the bow and stern of the tanker *Caprella* floating separately, and the tanker *Sitala*, badly holed by a torpedo on the starboard side forward, but otherwise intact.

But the *Angle* was not the only vessel looking over the damaged ships. At 11:15 her asdic operator had an echo, so near and powerful that she had to start a hunt and drop a pattern of depth charges. Finally she dropped twenty-five depth charges in five patterns, and then lost contact. She kept hunting for another twenty-four hours, but there were no more contacts. By perseverance, this little escort had driven away the submarine that was preparing to finish the grisly night's work.

At noon on October 21, a party of volunteers from the *Wandby* offered to try to get the *Sitala* going, and went aboard. Two hours later they had steam up and were ready to set out for England. At first they tried to steam astern, to cut the strain on the damaged bow. But the twisted plates of the damaged section dragged and created vibration, so they turned the ship around and proceeded slowly forward. All went well in moderate sea and wind. But that night the wind freshened, and the seas grew rougher and by midnight they had to reduce speed.

The swell increased. The wind went up from force 2 to force 5 (twenty-four miles per hour). At 4 P.M. on October 22 the chief engineer of the *Wandby*, now salvage captain of the *Sitala*, reported that her plates were beginning to give way. Lieutenant R. Wolfenden, the skipper of the *Angle*, brought his vessel around and looked at the *Sitala*. The forepart of the ship had now bent at a sharp angle. He decided the salvage effort had to end, and took off the crew. In the middle of the transfer, at 7 A.M., the ship split in half and began to settle into the sea. Lieutenant Schepke, in *U-100*, would be credited for another sinking after all.

Altogether the wolf pack took fourteen ships out of Convoy HX 79. Two major wolf pack attacks had been enormously successful, without the loss of a single U-boat. The convoys, and Doenitz's key to them, had given the U-boats sixty ships that month. In addition the Italians had sunk three ships in the south, and Doenitz's lone gray wolves had sunk another fifteen.

13

Stirrings

The carnage among the convoys in October shook Whitehall to the extent that all kinds of new approaches to the U-boat war were considered now, where they had been ignored before.

From merchant seamen came some ideas. The rear admiral of the Third Battle Squadron requested suggestions from the surviving ships of battered convoy HX 79, so heavily worked over by Commander Prien and his colleagues. In a letter to the Admiralty, the radio operator of the Norwegian motorship *Hoyanger* pointed out that in Convoy HX 79 several ships stood out like sore thumbs, especially the Swedish tanker *Janus*, painted white and gray. She seemed almost iridescent in the moonlight. And she had been placed right next to the tanker *Sitala*. They were both sunk the night of October 19. The radio operator had seen a submarine on the surface, inside the convoy, circling around the ships, and firing. The *Hoyanger* had fired her four-inch gun at the submarine, forcing it to dive.

The convoys must be tightened up. The ships in the convoys must not allow themselves to be diverted by watching shows staged by the enemy. While half the convoy was watching events on the starboard side, one or two submarines got in among the ships and wreaked havoc. Had the ships been paying attention, said the Norwegian radio operator, they would have alerted the escorts, and those submarines would have been attended to. Furthermore, said the brash Norwegian, the British simply had to coordinate those convoys better: "For the sake of England, gentlemen, do something about that nest of

subs. . . . Unless this spot is cleaned thoroughly, we may right-
fully expect at least a 25 percent or 130 percent loss in convoys.
Many seamen are asking themselves if the well-known
efficiency of the British Navy is operating with them in
transporting merchandise and especially petroleum products
across the Atlantic. . . ."

The Admiralty was listening. It was not long before new
measures appeared. There were going to be changes in convoy
practices: communications within the convoy, and between the
convoy and the air protection, had to be improved. To do this,
the Admiralty ordered the establishment of one frequency
which would be monitored within the convoy and by the airmen above. There had been much talk about the need for radio
silence. But with half a dozen submarines prowling inside the
convoy, there were things more important that radio silence.

Despite the evidence of first-hand observers, there was still
doubt within the naval establishment that U-boats could actually penetrate the convoys. The monthly review of activity published by the antisubmarine forces suggested in October that
with the exception of Jenisch's attack on Convoy HX 6A, no U-
boat had actually managed to get inside a convoy. There was
still plenty to be learned in high places. But despite a certain
establishment foot-dragging, the lessons were taking hold.

Some of the proposals seemed a little rarified: for example,
the naval liaison officer with the RAF coastal command suggested that tankers be fitted with catapults for launching Hurricanes or Grummans to attack the Focke-Wulff aircraft that
were beginning to appear in numbers over the convoys. Fine.
But where would the land-based planes land? They would not.
They would ditch.

And some better ideas were surfacing, such as an improved
radar for use against U-boats on the surface, to be given to all
escorts, and to the aircraft of Coastal Command and the Fleet
Air Arm. At last the RAF was going to get into the active battle
against the U-boats, and was preparing to air-drop depth
charges, a change pushed by Admiral Forbes for a year.

*   *   *

From the Admiralty came a new directive: a slow convoy, zigzagging by night, had no protection against the new attack, termed "Browning attack" because of the machine gun-like strategy the U-boat commanders were using, surfacing and firing torpedoes at random inside the convoy. (Some did, but the Priens, Schepkes, Kretschmers, and Schultzes certainly did not.)

But if the attribution was sometimes wrong, the reasoning was not. What was needed was more protection. One way to give it, said the Admiralty, was to put two fast ships on the wings of each convoy, which would zigzag at high speed, while the convoy moved along a straight path, but *closed* up *tight*.

An experimental outward bound convoy was arranged to try out this and other new ideas. For it was evident to everyone, from the prime minister down, that a new era had dawned. The use of Lorient and other French bases had greatly increased the range of the U-boats. The new "hunter's moon" attacks on the surface, the wolf packs—all these developments had to be met. If there had been any doubt within the naval establishment of the danger posed by the U-boats, it vanished by the end of October. The Germans were making enormous propaganda capital from the successes of their U-boat captains. The names of Prien, Kretschmer, Schultze, Frauenheim, Schepke, Jenisch and the rest were becoming household words in Germany and beyond. Radio Berlin counted the sinkings (sometimes exaggerated) and informed the world that soon arrogant Britain would be brought down to her knees. The exploits of each captain were accompanied by medals and other honors. Daily the airwaves resounded with Nazi boasts of the U-boat successes.

It was high time for something to happen.

14

Rays of Hope

Not long before Christmas, 1940 Churchill unburdened his soul in a letter to President Franklin Roosevelt:

> The danger of Great Britain being destroyed by a swift, overwhelming blow has for the time very greatly receded. In its place there is a long, gradually maturing danger, less sudden and less spectacular, but equally deadly. This mortal danger is the steady and increasing diminution of sea tonnage. . . . Unless we can establish our ability to feed this island . . . we may fall by the way, and the time needed by the United States to complete her defensive preparations may not be forthcoming. It is, therefore, in shipping and in the power to transport across the oceans, particularly the Atlantic Ocean, that in 1941 the crunch of the whole war will be found.

In the five weeks ending November 3, Britain's sea losses totalled 420,000 tons, a figure comparable to the worst year of the 1914–18 war. The Churchill government estimated that it would take 43 million tons to keep Britain going in 1941, and the losses had cut the incoming tonnage to a rate of 37 million tons. Obviously this loss ratio could not be borne for a year.

What Churchill wanted was American participation in the battle of the Atlantic, plus an increase in shipbuilding and delivery. Britain had to have three million tons of shipping more than she could produce and it could come from only one place, the United States.

Churchill's letter was long and encyclopedic in its attention to the British problems posed by the war. His call was for help. And in Churchill's calm, deliberate way, masked by its clarity and strength, it was a desperate call, and Roosevelt recognized it as such. He also agreed with the logic that if Britain fell, then the Rome–Berlin–Tokyo axis would consider the world to be its oyster. The two great oceans could no longer protect the United States. Roosevelt's problem was to convince an American public heavily laced with isolationist sentiment that isolationism was a thing of the past. Having made the decision that the United States must back Britain to the hilt in this war, Roosevelt set out to do the job.

Lend-lease was the first part of the answer. The United States would produce the sinews of war, and lend them to the British. At the end of the war, the ships, tanks, planes, guns, all military equipment, would be returned—in theory. Anyone who thought about it would realize that not all this equipment could be returned because most of it would be destroyed. But the theory made it possible to persuade a majority of Americans that in becoming "the great arsenal of democracy" they were not becoming "patsies." So the theory enabled Roosevelt to go to the aid of the British in their hour of need, yet preserve an apparent air of disinterest in the struggle that raged across and on the Atlantic.

In fact, America and Americans had been increasingly involved in the war since the first days. Two dozen Americans were killed in the outrageous sinking of the liner *Athenia*. The Germans knew what they had done, but denied it; their denials continued and it took the Department of State an entire year to investigate and conclude that a U-boat had indeed done the job. That delay served the German propaganda purpose of confusing some Americans, but not all. And in the first week of war the U.S. freighter *Wacosta* was stopped by a U-boat off the Irish coast and searched for contraband. Then the American freighter *City of Flint* was captured by the German pocket battleship *Deutschland* and sent to Hamburg under a German prize crew. Americans traveling on other ships of neutral nations had been torpedoed and some had been killed. So the war was not an unknown quantity in America, and the sympathy of most Americans, as well as the administration, rested with Great Britain.

Since September 5, 1939, the United States had maintained a war stance in the Caribbean and the waters of the Atlantic off the East Coast. It was called the Neutrality Patrol. Its purpose was to prevent the belligerents from bringing their war into American waters. The British were not the target, obviously. The ploy was successful; Doenitz dared not send his U-boats across the Atlantic to prey on shipping off the American shore. Thus already the American naval forces were serving a useful purpose in the war against the U-boats simply by limiting their field of activity, out of the area bounded on the east by Halifax, to longitude 60 ° west, then south to latitude 20° north and then to a point sixty miles south of the Cape Verde islands, then parallel to the coast of South America. The German pocket battleships penetrated this area briefly, but the U-boats stayed clear.

In the spring of 1941 the Americans enforced this patrol though the creation of the Atlantic Fleet, under Admiral Ernest J. King. The fleet was based at Norfolk, Virginia, but its major activity was in the Caribbean. The neutrality zone was extended to 26° west, to include the Azores Islands. Doenitz was aghast at the temerity of the Americans to claim suzerainty over 80 percent of the Atlantic; still, for the moment they had read Hitler correctly. He was leery of provoking the United States.

But in the last months of 1940 and the early months of 1941 the British problem did not lie primarily in the Western Hemisphere. The U-boats had not ventured into the Atlantic farther west than in the area of Iceland. Using the German world grid system which divided every ocean into blocks, the action was mostly in the AL, AM and BE sectors.

There the U-boats continued to take a heavy toll, although

the size of the effective U-boat fleet was falling steadily. That fact is an enormous tribute to the tenacity and resilience of Doenitz's men.

In December, 1940, the U-boats were hampered in their operations by some of the roughest weather that had ever hit the Atlantic. That did not keep them from operating successfully. One of the great dramas of the war at sea was played out in the first three days of December southwest of Iceland.

Convoy HX 90 had set out from Canada late in November bound for Liverpool. As was customary in these days following the occupation of France and the refusal of Ireland to grant Britain bases on her soil, the convoys had to steam far north of the Irish isles and down through the Northern Approaches. The advantage was that the weather was usually bad in this area, which was helpful in forestalling air attack and to some extent U-boat attack. The disadvantage was that the convoys and ships clustered in a relatively small section of sea, and were thus more vulnerable to attack than before.

HX 90 had set out with forty-one ships. Two had suffered mechanical failures early out and had returned to North American ports. Nine ships had been separated from the pack by a gale that blew from November 24 to November 26. These included the vice commodore's ship, *Victoria City*. The convoy was then reorganized into nine columns comprising thirty ships in all.

Back in England the Admiralty radio watch intercepted messages between Doenitz and a U-boat in the vicinity of 55 ° north, 23′ west and warned the warships in the vicinity. This U-boat was Lieutenant Ernst Mengerson's *U-101*. He was out on his first patrol as captain.

On December 1 the convoy picked up one of the old four-stack destroyers, now renamed the H.M.S. *Laconia*, as an ocean escort. That afternoon Mengerson came across the steamer *Ville D'Arlon*. She was a part of HX 90, but she had suffered some mechanical difficulties and had fallen behind. Now she caught up with the convoy. What her captain did not know is that she had a companion; *U-101* was trailing her.

The *Laconia* left the convoy at 5 P.M. that same day. The ships were supposed to have three local escorts to take them into the Western Approaches, but the escorts had not shown up by dark. The storm had put the convoy behind schedule and it had not reached the rendezvous point.

The convoy had reached the position 54° 25' north, 20° 25' west and was steering a course of 60° at eight knots at 8:14 P.M. on December 1.

The convoy commodore, riding in the steamer *Botavon*, did not know it but Mengerson was right there and had informed Doenitz, who called in his wolf pack: Commander Prien's *U-47*, Commander Kretschmer's *U-99*, and Lieutenant Otto Salman's *U-52*.

Lieutenant Mengerson was the first to hit the convoy. At 8:14 P.M. he torpedoed the tanker *Appalachee*, leader of the starboard outside column, and immediately afterward put another torpedo into the steamer *Loch Ranza*. He fired a third torpedo that missed another ship.

The *Appalachee* sank immediately, but the *Loch Ranza* was only damaged, and after picking up the survivors of the tanker, the *Loch Ranza* got under way again. But in the interim, three hours had passed and the convoy was long gone.

Two explosions were reported to the convoy commander but when he reached his bridge, he saw only some lights to starboard—not signals. So he concluded that one or two ships had somehow "got tangled up" and went back to his dinner. The convoy proceeded as though nothing had happened.

At 1 A.M. on December 2, the convoy altered course to make the rendezvous point. So did the U-boats.

Half an hour later the *Ville d'Arlon* dropped back, again, hoisting lights to indicate that she was having difficulties. She fell behind the convoy and at 2:10 A.M. Prien found her and put a torpedo into her.

Mengerson was shadowing the convoy closely. He moved around to the port side, and at 3:20 A.M. torpedoed the *Lady Glanely*, the leading ship in the outside column. Meanwhile, Prien had come up to the convoy, moved in close on the surface and approached the tanker *Conch*. The *U-47* was clearly visible to the crew of the tanker as Prien fired his torpedo. The captain tried to maneuver to miss, but failed, and the *Conch* was damaged and fell out of line.

The next ship in the column, the *Dunsley*, turned to starboard to avoid the submarine, and then stopped to rescue the crew. At 4:10 A.M. she was so engaged when Prien's *U-47* came alongside, close by the port beam, and opened fire. The first shell hit the *Dunsley*. Then her deck gun got into action and she began peppering the water around the U-boat. Prien fired ten more rounds of eighty-eight millimeter and a star shell—a group of flares fired simultaneously—to call on any other boat for assistance, and then the *Dunsley* zigzagged away. The U-boat did not follow. Why should a member of the wolf pack go after an armed and vigorous enemy, when there were so many more?

The convoy had made an emergency turn after the last torpedoing, and at 4:15 A.M. resumed its base course of seventy-three degrees. It lost another ship, the *Rajahstan*, which had to drop out because of engine trouble. (She was lucky enough to reach port alone.)

But the U-boats were still out there, right with the convoy.

At 5:15 A.M. Mengerson moved around again and torpedoed the *Kavak*, the last remaining ship in the starboard column. This 2,700-ton ammunition ship then blew up with an enormous roar and flash of light.

By this time Lieutenant Salman was catching up to the convoy. The steamer *Tasso* had lagged back, and was zigzagging independently behind the convoy. Salman torpedoed her and moved up to the convoy. He then torpedoed the steamer *Goodleigh*. So did at least one of the other U-boats, for she was struck by three torpedoes.

At 5:38 A.M. the steamer *Penrose* sighted a U-boat on the surface close on her port beam. The convoy then made an emergency turn to starboard, and a few minutes later, returned to the base course. There were no more U-boat attacks that morning not, as the commodore believed, because of the growing light of day, but because Prien had exhausted his torpedoes. Mengerson had suffered a diesel engine breakdown. Kretschmer had turned to follow *Forfar*, a 16,000-ton armed merchant cruiser. At this point Convoy HX 90 was coming into the Western Approaches, and many ships were to be found. This was particularly true because Convoy OB 251 had just dispersed here.

OB 251 was an outward bound convoy, and the point 56° north, 17° west was the place where the escorts left her. The convoy continued on course until 11 P.M. on the night of December 1 and then the ships broke off to go their own ways. The Admiralty did not yet have the wherewithal to give them proper protection. The three escorts, *Viscount*, *Vanquisher*, and *Gentian*, had brought OB 251 this far; now they were to pick up HX 90 and take it safely back to Britain. They had left OB 251 at 7 P.M. on the previous night and were now looking for their new charges.

* * *

Lieutenant Commander Wolfgang Lueth's *U-43* was not a part of the Prien wolf pack which hit HX 90 the night before, but had just entered the area in response to Doenitz's messages, along with the *U-95*, *U-94*, and *U-140*.

Lueth's first victim was *Pacific President*, followed almost immediately by *Victor Ross*, a 12,000-ton tanker.

Into that same area came the straggler *Victoria City* from Convoy HX 90, which was sunk that day by the *U-140*.

A real saga was occurring not far away. The tanker *Conch*, having been torpedoed by Prien on the night before, was still afloat and still limping toward Britain. She was found again on December 2 by *U-95*, which put three more torpedoes into her. Still she did not sink, and kept moving very slowly homeward.

* * *

The commander of the escort group recognized on the night of December 1 the dangers to both Convoy OB 251 and HX 90 from the number of submarines in the area. His hope was that by steering to a position astern of the HX 90 rendezvous point, he could cover both convoys. In fact, he managed to cover neither. At 4 A.M. on December 2 came word that the *U-99* had attacked the *Forfar*, and all three escorts turned south to that area. They came across several ships but did not find the *Forfar*, the *Victor Ross*, the *Lady Glanely* or the *Loch Ranza*, all of which had sent out distress messages. They did not find them because the three ships were no longer afloat.

This search was particularly fruitless; it caused the *Vanquisher* to run short of fuel and she had to return to Londonderry to replenish; she did not join up with Convoy HX 90 until 7 P.M. on December 4. By that time Doenitz's wolf packs were long gone.

The *Viscount* and the *Gentian* tried to catch up with Convoy HX 90. The *Viscount* was diverted by the distress signal from *Goodleigh*, and arrived on the scene in time to hear the last torpedo fired by Lieutenant Salman strike the ship. From 7:30 until 9:20 P.M. the *Viscount* was picking up survivors from *Tasso*, *Kavak*, and *Goodleigh*.

The escort *St. Laurent* had been traveling in company with the *Forfar* but left her in the night to go to the assistance of another torpedoed ship. She finally came up on the *Conch*, which had been torpedoed one more time, this time by Kretschmer's *U-99*. She spent twenty minutes picking up survivors.

The *Viscount* found one U-boat on the surface, chased her down and put out a pattern of depth charges. No U-boat was sunk.

The *Viscount* then went to the assistance of the S.S. *Dunsely* which had been set afire by Focke-Wulff bombers that day. She was carrying survivors from the *Forfar* and told the *Viscount* captain there were more in the water. The *Viscount* went to the scene and began picking up men. Said her captain: "Condition of survivors was terrible owing to oil fuel and exposure and recovery was difficult. Every live man was picked up. Fourteen hours medical attention was necessary on one man who finally pulled through. The conduct of *Forfar*'s survivors in the face of great danger and discomfort was exemplary."

So by mid-afternoon on December 2, HX 90 still did not

have any real protection. At 4 P.M. the destroyer *Folkestone* made contact, and almost immediately found a U-boat trailing the convoy. The convoy made an emergency turn, and the *Folkestone* went after the U-boat with depth charges. But at 4:25 P.M. the *Stirlingshire* was torpedoed in the convoy by Lieutenant Kuppisch's *U-94*. The boat dived and got away from two escorts, the *Folkestone* and the *Gentian*, which had just joined up.

The two escorts took stations at the front and on the side of the convoy, but at 8:20 P.M. the *Wilhelmina*, now the outside ship in the starboard column, was torpedoed by Kuppisch, and she went up with such a bang that the *W. Hendrik*, immediately to her port side, thought she had also been torpedoed.

The *W. Hendrick* dropped out of line. Almost immediately a Focke-Wulff condor swooped down out of the cloud cover and attacked the convoy. At this moment the *Viscount* was finally coming up and her captain began firing on the plane with his four-inch guns. The condor then veered off and attacked the *W. Hendrik*, which had fallen back about five miles. The *Viscount* put on speed, dashed through the convoy and attacked the plane, which then veered away and was gone.

The convoy then made another emergency turn and managed to throw off the submarine pursuers, which had been forced down by the presence of the three escorts. The enthusiasm of the pack for the chase was gone, and that was the end of the assault on HX 90. The Germans had sunk ten of the thirty ships.

*   *   *

The fate of Convoy HX 90 received more than usual attention at the Admiralty, and out of it came some more conclusions about the best means of increasing the protection of merchant ships. There were still some who believed in the antisubmarine patrol, but the pulling and hauling of the available escorts in the area around 54° north and 18° west in this case had evidently played into the hands of the enemy. The director of the Admiralty trade division called for extended escort to take the ships farther west on their way to North America, and to pick up the homeward bound convoys sooner. The argument could be made, and was, that all this accomplished was to push the U-boat operating area farther west; but it also extended the distance the U-boats would have to travel and made it harder for the growing force of condor bombers.

The RAF began giving more attention to the submarine base at Lorient. New evasive routing measures were put into effect, changing all the old patterns. At the end of December the anti–U-boat forces added up the figures of losses for December, and found that although the figure of tonnage was high, it was almost entirely because of the assault on convoy HX 90. After that, losses to U-boats had fallen quite low. The admirals were not quite sure to which factor they should attribute the change.

The fact was that the losses were low because of weather, the changes in routing and changes in the merchant shipping codes. Admiral Doenitz was the first to admit that his problem continued to be to find the convoys, and the Royal Navy was making this ever more difficult. Only two convoys were found by the U-boats in January, 1941.

The number of ships sunk by the U-boats had averaged eight per boat in the fall of 1940. In January and February it fell to an average of two per boat, twenty-one ships, 127,000 tons. It was an enormous improvement. Another new ingredient had been added to the anti–U-boat mix: radar. The asdic system was useful only against submerged submarines. But submarines on top of the water could be detected by radar, and by January, ships and planes were being fitted out with this apparatus. Also RAF Squadron Commander H. de V. Leigh devised a searchlight for use with aircraft on convoy escort duty. The Leigh light was like a tank's battle light: it could be turned on suddenly to blind the deck crew of a surfaced U-boat and to illuminate it thoroughly for attack. The RAF Coastal Command was coming along in its appreciation of the U-boat menace and in its development of devices to defeat the U-boats. The major problem existing in the winter of 1941 was no longer attitude, but aircraft. It would be months more before the United States could deliver a supply of the proper kind of aircraft, Catalina flying boats, to undertake this work.

And yet another factor was coming into play. At last the Flower class corvettes were becoming available to add to the escort forces of Britain. The ninety trawlers had been delivered, and during the winter the Western Approaches command had the wherewithal to form escort groups. This change meant that a number of ships could work together over a period of time, so that the officers and men knew how to cooperate to the best advantage of their convoy charges.

*   *   *

Just as the British were beginning to congratulate themselves, however, the sinkings in February jumped: thirty-nine ships, nearly 200,000 tons. What the U-boats failed to do, the Luftwaffe succeeded in doing: they sank twenty-seven ships, 90,000 more tons. The rate of sinking was then back to the near disastrous level that could not be allowed if Britain was to survive.

These February figures were all the more worrisome because Churchill and Admiral Pound fully expected a renewed U-boat onslaught on the Western Approaches with the arrival of better weather in the spring. They knew that Doenitz at last was beginning to get new boats, although they were not fooled by the German change in the numbering system. Originally the U-boats had been numbered consecutively; in the early days of the war their numbers were painted. But when the numbers hit the one hundred mark, suddenly they began to increase in numerical power in an unmethodical manner. By September, 1940, *U-138* was at sea, but there were nothing like even a hundred U-boats in existence. In the winter of 1941 U-boats began to emerge with numbers like *U-552*; it was a part of Doenitz's psychological warfare to convince the world that Germany's undersea fleet was unbeatable. Another weapon was the accomplishments of the U-boat captains. By the winter of 1941, Germany boasted sixteen U-boat commanders who had sunk over 100,000 tons of shipping, and had been awarded the

Knight insignia of the Iron Cross. Leading them all was Lieutenant Guenther Prien, who was also awarded the Oak Leaves in October, 1940, although his actual sinkings were a long way behind those of Lieutenant Kretschmer, who claimed more than 200,000 tons by then. Another comer was Joachim Schepke, who was favored by Doenitz even above the other two.

* * *

The Admiralty was particularly upset in reviewing the results of the U-boat offensive for February, because of the evident increased cooperation between Doenitz's U-boats and Goering's Luftwaffe. A study of attacks on Convoy HG 53 from Gibraltar indicated that this cooperation could be fatal.

HG 53 sailed from Gibraltar on January 6 escorted by one sloop and one destroyer. It was attacked by a U-boat on January 9 and two ships were sunk. But the U-boat then shadowed the convoy, and homed six Focke-Wulff condors in on the convoy that day. Five ships were sunk by bombs.

The U-boat continued to shadow and attacked again on January 10, sinking one ship. She then continued to transmit information apparently intended for the *Hipper*, a German cruiser, but the *Hipper* was attacking another convoy.

Identical tales were repeated several times during February. As March began, Churchill and Admiral Pound fully expected the renewed U-boat attack to begin. They could have been reading Admiral Doenitz's mind. He transferred his main area of operation to the *AL* and *AK* grid areas farther west, south of Iceland. The admiral expected his U-boats to show an excellent catch for the month of March.

Churchill was ever watchful of the U-boats, ever conscious that they were his greatest enemy. At the end of February he announced that the battle of the Atlantic was vital, and that it must be won by any and every means. Ships and planes were to be transferred from other duty to this work. To show his concern, the prime minister formed a new Battle of the Atlantic Committee in the cabinet and took personal charge of it. The

Admiralty called for more vigilance, and increased the availability of escorts.

* * *

The U-boats began to go out—Prien, Hardegen, Kretschmer, Clausen, Lemp, Schepke. Lieutenant Prien had one quality that endeared him above all others to Admiral Doenitz: he loved to be at sea, stalking and sinking enemy vessels. Because of this, one Prien patrol followed on the heels of the last with little time off between, and the Prien practice became the practice of the U-boat fleet. Without a real leave, Prien had been on active duty since the summer of 1939, eighteen months of grinding activity and constant tension. His thin face and black-ringed eyes attested to it in February, as he got ready at Lorient to go out on patrol again.

Out he went. On February 26 he sank four merchant ships and the next day another, all from Convoy OB 290. But then came more than a week of failure; no convoys seemed to be on the horizon in Prien's area. Admiral Doenitz grew concerned, and redoubled his demands that the boats search, search, search, until they found the convoys. The spring offensive had to begin with a bang.

15

Admiral Doenitz Moves West

THE PLACE: Ten Downing Street
THE TIME: 5 P.M. March 19, 1941
THE OCCASION: First meeting of the War Cabinet Battle of the Atlantic
Committee

The prime minister, Winston Churchill, took the chair. It was indicative of the vital nature of the business before this new committee that the Labour party's number-two man, Ernest Bevin, was also in attendance. Others were: First Lord of the Admiralty A. V. Alexander; Lord Beaverbrook, the minister of aircraft production; and six other ministers, plus Admiral Pound, the chief of the Coastal Command, Air Vice Marshal A. T. Harris, and half a dozen other high-placed senior officers.

Churchill's timing was perfect. Britain now had some of the sinews of war that she needed to fight the U-boats successfully. As much as technical equipment now, the question of defeat or victory in the eastern Atlantic would depend on the efforts these high officials and their subordinates would make.

They went over the shipping figures for the previous week and the weeks before. They could draw some confidence from the sinking of four U-boats in two weeks (U-551 was not yet sunk) and the performance of the escort service.

The prime minister again emphasized the absolute necessity

of controlling the U-boats and his confidence that this would be done. Absolute priority, he reiterated, was to be given to controlling the U-boats in the Northwestern Approaches to Britain.

The British now had seagoing radar. It was far from perfect, there was trouble with echoes and false images, but they had a way of finding surfaced submarines that were beyond the reach of the asdic.

Also they had new techniques making use of old methods. The illumination of the convoy by star shells was extremely effective in bringing up the escorts to attack a surfaced submarine. And, some merchant vessels now also attacked with their deck guns. Star shells were soon augmented by "snowflakes," an even brighter and longer lasting system of lighting the sky at night. All the old strictures against using radio were thrown off at the moment of attack. Each convoy member was instructed to report any U-boat movement, attack or threat that he saw—*Immediately*. Thus, the escorts were beginning to know what was going on inside their convoys.

Radio was playing a much greater role, as the shipping merchants had predicted at the outset. Lifeboats had recently begun to be equipped with small radio transmitters to assist rescues at sea. The development of radio telephone—talk between ships—made it possible for the escort commander to control his vessels swiftly and move them about. The improvement of depth charge equipment and techniques made it possible in the past few weeks to begin throwing a pattern of ten charges, rather than the former five.

And, finally, antisubmarine warfare had a new priority and a new headquarters at Liverpool, where Admiral Sir Percy Noble was the new commander of Western Approaches. In his headquarters he had an elaborate situation chart which at any time showed the movement of convoys and individual vessels plus the protective and air forces available.

Radio Direction Finding (RDF) was still in its infancy in Britain. The first truly acceptable set would not be ready until July, 1941. Also, a whole new training program for antisubmarine war was in development, which would include a month of intensive work for every new escort vessel before she went into action. The trouble until now had been that so desperate was the need for them that ships had been pushed out to sea almost as they came out of the yards, and the crews had been forced to learn from experience. Britain's push in the shipyards, America's fifty destroyers and new aircraft, and Canada's corvettes had all bought Britain the time she needed.

But the trouble was still shortages, particularly of aircraft and escort vessels to cover the entire transatlantic voyage of the convoys and to bring more ships into convoy. As was agreed, the convoy was indeed the solution to the U-boat. In January, for example, 2,966 ships had been convoyed in all directions, and only 13 had been lost. To be sure, the losses in February and March were much higher, but January showed what could be done.

The percentage of lone ships sunk by U-boats was about four times as high as that of convoy ships sunk, but as yet there were not enough protectors to do the job.

* * *

Admiral Doenitz was looking happily to the future. The U-boat building program was now in full swing and he expected to have 250 U-boats by the end of the year. A full-scale enlistment program was operating in Germany, utilizing the stories of the heroic captains to the hilt. "War correspondents" were now going along on U-boat cruises, to get all the glorious details and write them up for broadcast, newspaper and magazine stories. At the moment Doenitz had only about 30 submarines operational, and of those it was hard for him to keep more than a dozen at sea at one time, but they were doing a great deal of damage. In March 206,000 tons were lost to U-boats. Churchill could take the optimistic view: that the loss was considerably lower than in September and October, 1940, the last period of intensive U-boat activity, and that the highly vaunted "spring offensive" had not really materialized. Still, 200,000 tons in a month meant 1,200,000 tons in a year, or five percent of Britain's registered tonnage at the outbreak of war.

Doenitz's answer to the increasing vigilance of the British in their Northwestern Approaches was to carry the war farther west and south.

On April 2, Lieutenant Engelbert Endrass in U-46 found Convoy SC 26, homebound to England from North America, far to the west of any point at which a convoy had been attacked before: 58° north, 28° west. The Admiralty months earlier had asked for establishment of an air base in Iceland and cover for convoys, but it had not yet been done. The convoys had no destroyer escort as they traveled eastward below Greenland to Iceland, and this is where Lieutenant Endrass found SC 26. The only protection was the armed merchant cruiser *Worcestershire*, traveling between the fifth and sixth columns of the twenty-two-ship convoy.

Endrass began shadowing the convoy, making his reports to Admiral Doenitz. The admiral called up all nine boats that were operating north of 57° and west of 18°. They included Lieutenant Helmut Rosenbaum's *U-73*, Lieutenant Commander Eitel Friedrich Kentrat's *U-74*, Lieutenant Jost Metzler's *U-69*, Lieutenant Commander Robert Gysae's *U-98*, and Lieutenant Herbert Kuppisch's *U-94*.

The Admiralty was keeping track of Doenitz's transmissions back and forth to his U-boats, and at 8:55 P.M. sent a message to the *Worcestershire*, indicating that SC 26 was probably being shadowed by a U-boat. When the message was received, the *Worcestershire's* captain consulted with the captain of the *Magician*, who was commodore of the convoy. They agreed that under the circumstances, without escorts, they had already set up the best possible defense using evasive tactics. The first move was taken at 10:30 P.M., and the convoy turned to course 104 degrees at six knots.

*　*　*

Endrass tracked the ships on the night of April 2. The course change at 10:30 was a signal that the enemy ships knew something was in the air. At midnight he attacked. His first victim was the tanker *British Reliance*, the ship just astern of the commodore's vessel. She was hit by a torpedo on the port side, forward. Thirty second later she was hit by a second torpedo, amidships.

The commodore saw all this, and although the stricken ship did not fire a rocket as ordered, he still made a course change, with an emergency turn of forty degrees to port. This turn faced the convoy directly at the submarine and caused Endrass to miss his next shots at another freighter. He moved around the convoy for nearly an hour. At 1:10 A.M. the convoy resumed its base course. Endrass then fired again, at the steamer *Alderpool*. The torpedo struck her in the port side. The commodore ordered another emergency turn, this time to starboard.

When the *Alderpool* was torpedoed, the captain of the *Thirlby* decided to stop and pick up survivors. He was engaged in this when Endrass' U-boat was sighted on the port bow. The captain turned to put his stern to the U-boat and bring the four-inch deck gun to bear. This maneuver put the *Alderpool* between the *Thirlby* and the submarine, and the U-boat fired a torpedo, which hit the *Alderpool*. Then the U-boat fired two more torpedoes at the *Thirlby;* one missed ahead and the other astern. The *Thirlby* then went off at twelve knots, out of the convoy, on her own.

The steamer *Athenic* made the mistake of turning to port instead of starboard, and got out of line. Ten minutes later her captain broke radio silence: "U-boat in sight, bearing ten degrees."

The commodore made another emergency turn to starboard.

Not all the ships followed. One that did not was the *Athenic*. She was completely out of line and out of the convoy. Her captain watched the U-boat and turned to try to ram. But Endrass was more interested in keeping track of the convoy than in any particular ship, so he moved off to the east to get ahead and wait for the convoy again on the base course.

From various directions other submarines were also trying to close the convoy.

And from the east where they had been escorting outward bound Convoy OB 304, the escorts *Havelock*, *Hesperus* and

Hurricane were ordered to go to the assistance of the *British Reliance*. They put on speed to twenty-four knots and headed west.

The convoy went on, leaving its stragglers. In the next two hours, two more turns brought the convoy back to its base course. There was some confusion but by 4 A.M. the convoy was in good order.

At 4:06 A.M. the convoy was hit again; this time the second ship in the sixth column, the *Leonidas Z. Cambadas*, was torpedoed by Kentrat's *U-74*. Immediately afterward the men on the bridge of the commodore's ship saw a torpedo track crossing from the *Magician's* starboard bow to her port quarter. A few seconds later the leader of the fourth column, the *Westpool*, was hit by two torpedoes on the starboard side and sank immediately. She was the victim of Rosenbaum's *U-73*, which had just joined up.

The commodore decided to turn to starboard and fired off green flares. But he saw that so many ships were already turning to port that he decided to conform, lest he split up the convoy further. In all the confusion, the *Tennessee* turned back to the west to go it alone and avoid the U-boats. While moving westward, her radio operator picked up a distress signal from one of the lifeboats of the *British Reliance*. She went on twenty miles and found the boat and rescued the survivors. It was the first case of the new lifeboat radios being directly responsible for rescue. The *Tennessee* then set a course for Iceland and arrived without incident.

At 4:15 A.M. Kentrat torpedoed the steamer *Indier*.

The commodore looked over his convoy. The moon had set at 3:30 A.M., but the northern lights kept the sky bright and the ships stood out against the clear, quiet sea.

"Do you think it's any use scattering?" he radioed the *Worcestershire*.

"Yes, I think it is," was the reply from the merchant cruiser.

So the commodore gave the order to scatter and meet again at the rendezvous point, where they were to pick up the escort ships that would take them into the Northwestern Approaches. The convoy dispersed at 4:20 A.M.

On receiving the commodore's order to disperse, the steamer *Ethel Radcliffe* turned to port and held that course for fifteen minutes. Then she swung back to her original course, and as she did so, a U-boat appeared on the surface to port. The captain swung the ship around, "hard aport" and tried to ram. The U-boat evaded. The gun crew fired one round from the deck gun and the submarine dived. The *Ethel Radcliffe* then headed home to England, arriving without incident.

* * *

The steamer *Tenax* left the convoy on the orders and steamed due north for an hour and a half. She turned east then and was heading toward England when a U-boat appeared on the surface off her port bow. The captain swung the ship and the crew got off one round from the deck gun before the submarine submerged. *Tenax* then headed for the rendezvous for stragglers and at 4:20 A.M. on April 4 she sighted the H.M.S. *Hesperus*. The escort took her safely to the British shore.

* * *

The tanker *British Viscount* chose to stay on the base course to England. At 4:35 A.M. Rosenbaum torpedoed her on the starboard side and she burst into flames, a beacon lighting the sea for miles around.

* * *

The steamer *Welcombe* altered course to port to put the burning tanker astern. At 4:45 A.M. the captain sighted a U-boat only 200 yards away on the port quarter and the deck gun crew began firing. They claimed a hit, the submarine heeled violently and disappeared. At daylight the ship altered course to seventy degrees and began to zigzag toward England.

* * *

The steamer *Helle* sighted a U-boat just after the convoy scattered, but the submarine did not attack. At dawn she began zigzagging towards the rendezvous point at eight knots.

* * *

The *Worcestershire* increased her speed to fourteen knots, to proceed ahead of the convoy for two more hours. Then the local escorts were expected to show up and the *Worcestershire* could turn about and head back to Halifax.

But Kentrat's *U-74* had moved out ahead to wait for the convoy, and at 4:43 A.M. she was in position to attack the *Worcestershire*. The captain of the merchant cruiser saw the torpedo coming, and ordered the rudder to port, on the starboard side of the forecastle, and jammed the rudder hard aport. All she could do was steam in circles. So the captain stopped her and she lay there dead in the water, lit up by the blazing *British Vicount*. After an hour, the crew managed to get the rudder working and centered. It would move fifteen degrees port and starboard. A course was set to the north, to get out of the submarine operating zone. Messages were sent out about the status of the convoy.

*   *   *

At 9:45 A.M. on April 3 the *Hurricane* was detached from the other escort vessels to escort the *Worcestershire* and took up position. The *Worcestershire* was making seven knots, and *Hurricane* circled her endlessly, at fifteen knots, all the way to Liverpool.

*   *   *

Somewhere north of the convoy the *Thirlby* was moving along at twelve knots, heading for England. From time to time the bridge watch caught sight of a submarine on the surface. At 5:20 A.M. on April 3 a torpedo struck the *Thirlby* a glancing blow on the starboard side. It made a screaming noise, and skidded along the side of the ship, and then bounced off without detonating.

The U-boat appeared again just before 6 A.M. and the gun crew fired a round. The U-boat dived.

*   *   *

After giving the order to scatter, the commodore of the convoy set a course to the east and sped along zigzagging, toward a new rendezvous for stragglers. At dawn on April 3 ships began to come in sight and the commodore ordered them to take station on him.

* * *

The *Havelock* and *Hesperus* continued to steam westward at top speed, until noon on April 3, when they sighted the commodore's ship and five others. They set up a rendezvous with the escorts *Veteran* and *Wolverine* for 4 P.M. and sped on.

* * *

The *Veteran* and the *Wolverine* parted company from Convoy OB 304 at 6:45 A.M., but they were not quite sure where they were supposed to find SC 26. At noon they had a message from the *Worcestershire* giving them the most probable location.

At 4 P.M. they found the convoy. It now consisted of eight ships. They were formed into four columns and the convoy went on under escort (see table below). At 10 P.M. the convoy made a fifty-degree alteration of course to starboard.

* * *

SC 26, April 3, 1941
H.M.S. *Veteran*

Harbledown	*Magician*	*Empire Dew*	*Anacortes*
Eelbeck	*Taygetos*	*Editor*	*Daleby*

H.M.S. *Wolverine*

All day long Lieutenant Gysae's *U-98* had been speeding to catch up with the convoy. At 11:30 P.M. she found the straggler *Helle* and torpedoed her. The *Helle* began sending: SSS SSS SSS SSS . . .

Gysae did not stop but hurried on, and just before 3 A.M. on April 4 came up with the *Welcombe*, which had quit zigzagging at dark. Gysae torpedoed the ship. She began sending SSS SSS SSS SSS . . . and was still sending messages almost until the

moment when she went down fifteen minutes later. While the
boats were assembling, the U-boat turned a searchlight on
them, then switched to the stern of the Welcombe, apparently
checking the name.

* * *

At 2:42 A.M. on April 4, Lieutenant Kuppisch's *U-94* attacked the *Harbledown*, hitting her with two torpedoes on the
port side. The entire bridge collapsed, which meant the
wireless office too, so no signal was sent. But the commodore's
ship *Magician* was right alongside, and he saw. He ordered an
emergency turn to starboard. The convoy turned and steamed
at 143 degrees for twenty-seven minutes, then returned to the
base course.

The *Wolverine* had been off the port beam of the convoy.
She sped up the side but found nothing. She fired two new
experimental rockets of a quarter-million candlepower each.
They lit up the sky brilliantly for half a mile, but seemed to
intensify the darkness beyond that point.

Wolverine continued the search until 4 A.M., when she
rejoined the convoy.

On seeing the rockets fired by *Wolverine*, the *Veteran* came
rushing back to the end of the convoy and saw the *Harbledown*
stopped dead. The *Veteran* prowled around for a while and
then rescued the survivors of the *Harbledown*. She rejoined the
convoy at 6:15 A.M.

The two escorts patrolled restlessly all day long but there
were no more attacks. During the afternoon of April 4 they were
joined by the escorts *Convolvulus*, *Verity*, *Vivien*, and *Chelsea*.

* * *

The *Athenic* steamed on toward England at her own pace
after sighting that periscope early on the morning of April 3.
She made no attempt to rejoin the convoy but moved along
without incident until just before 7 P.M. on April 4, when she
was struck out of the blue by a torpedo on her starboard side.
The SSS message was sent and the crew abandoned ship.

Twenty minutes after they took to the boats a second torpedo struck near the engine room and fifteen minutes later the ship sank. Lieutenant Rosenbaum was given credit for sinking her.

* * *

At 7:25 P.M. on April 24 the *Daleby* broke radio silence to report a periscope between the columns. The escorts made what appeared to them to be doubtful contact, and dropped a few depth charges, to placate the captain. They still did not believe that U-boats got inside convoys.

But the presence of six escorts with seven merchant ships was enough to discourage any U-boat captain, and the convoy—what there was left of it—suffered no more casualties, moving into the north channel on April 8.

* * *

The reports of Doenitz's captains following this convoy attack convinced him that the British had not invented anything new to harry his submarines, and that the loss of his top three U-boat captains in two weeks in March had been little more than coincidence. But there Doenitz erred, for although no spectacular devices (such as sonar) had yet come onto the scene, there had been plenty of change. Most of all, the change had been in the upgrading of attention now given the war against U-boats by the British government.

16

Doenitz Puts on the Pressure

In the spring of 1941 many new devices to protect shipping were under consideration and were being tested. Many of them came down directly through the Battle of the Atlantic Committee which was meeting weekly at Ten Downing Street. They included equipping merchant ships with Bofors antiaircraft guns, outfitting fifty merchant ships with fighter planes, and piggybacking a Hurricane fighter on a B-24 bomber. Those measures were directed primarily against the Focke-Wulff condors that had been taking such a heavy toll on merchant shipping near Britain. By April 1 the first ships were at sea with their fighters, and took credit for driving off at least one German air attack.

But the building of aerodromes in Northern Ireland was to counter submarines, as was the employment by Coastal Command of American PBY flying boats as successor to the cumbersome Sunderlands. The first five PBYs had been handed over to the British in March. Further, with the movement west of the U-boats, there could be no further delay in securing the sea lanes around Iceland. After the SC 26 convoy disaster the Admiralty assigned four escort groups to work the Western Approaches as far west as thirty-five degrees, which meant the water south of Greenland. Also, ten Hudson bombers of the

269th Squadron were transferred to Iceland in April, as was a squadron of Sunderlands, which had a depot ship moored in Reykjavik harbor.

Shipping losses were continuing to escalate so drastically that Draconian measures were in order. The war committee was moving toward prohibiting the sailing of any ship that made less than fifteen knots except in convoy. The figures showed that fast ships could outrun U-boats, but slow ones had little chance. But the problem, as before, was the shortage of escorts, so the prime minister decided to let the present unhappy situation continue a while longer, on the principle that at least most of the ships were getting through.

The concentration of Prien, Kretschmer, and other U-boat commanders on tankers had created serious fuel shortages. At the outbreak of war rationing had reduced the average Briton's mileage ration to thirty-five miles per week. If anything more was to be done, it meant the abolition of the ration altogether. But savings of 100 million gallons a year was needed on the basis of current projections. How were they going to achieve it?

By such measures as cutting out supplementary rations except in the most important cases, by cutting 10 percent arbitrarily out of industrial allocations, by cutting farmers' allocations subject to appeal, and the same for fishermen.

When a government had to consider such measures, it was indicative of desperate conditions, and as the prime minister had already told Roosevelt, this was precisely the situation in Britain that spring. The sinkings were not decreasing, because while the British were sending more escorts and planes into the battle, Doenitz was attacking with more U-boats and Goering was sending more bombers.

Yet despite the apparently gloomy outlook, there was a new element of hope that could not be evaluated by any normal standard. It was the growing commitment of the United States to the British war effort.

In March, W. Averill Harriman arrived in London as the special representative of President Roosevelt. At the second meeting of the Battle of the Atlantic Committee, Churchill sug-

gested that the minister for shipping take up the matter of better
repair facilities in U.S. ports with Harriman. In April, Harriman
was deeply involved in finding ways that the Americans could
help without violating provisions of the United States Neutrality Act. He offered to intervene personally to get priority for
British ship repair in American yards; he was discussing
schemes of transshipment that would allow American lines to
carry aircraft and other war materials to the Persian Gulf and
India without violating the letter of the law. He was exploring
ways to turn over thirty fast ships to the British, but cautioned
that this should be done in units of five or six, in order not to
arouse opposition within the United States Congress and from
the isolationists. Harrriman also suggested that wool shipments
from Australia to the United States be cut to free more for
Britain.

By the end of April, Harriman was actually attending the
Battle of the Atlantic Committee meetings at Ten Downing
Street, and for a foreigner had unprecedented entree into the
secrets of the British war effort.

At the meeting on April 23 Harriman offered the information that seventy-seven fast cargo liners would be launched in
the United States in 1941 and another fifty in 1942, and that the
United States government might be persuaded to hand over "a
considerable number" if the British played their cards right.
The best case, he said, was to ask for the ships to carry military
equipment to the Middle East (the point being that the United
States had a vital stake in preserving its interests in Middle
Eastern oil).

Harriman was privy to the most intimate defense secrets at
such meetings: the abandonment of the piggyback B-24 plan
because the B-24 was as fast as the Hurricane, the improvement
of the merchant ship fighter program, the progress of work on
British airfields and ports, and the reports on bombing raids on
German factories. What Harriman heard at these meetings
could have been extremely embarassing if it ever got out. But
Churchill knew he had nothing to fear from Harriman or President Roosevelt. Their problem was to manipulate American

public and Congressional opinion into further support for the British war effort.

In April shipping losses were again high. Doenitz had more than twenty submarines at sea during the month. Most of them worked the North Atlantic, but some had moved south into the waters between eastern Africa and the projecting eastern tip of Brazil. They were working over shipping coming up from South Africa and also from South America. They sank fourteen ships that month. Overall the tonnage was worrisome: 216,000 tons lost in March and 232,000 in April.

May was to be worse.

It began with Doenitz's move of many boats to the South Atlantic, mostly off Freetown on the West African coast. This port was the assembly point for shipping from South America and the Cape of Good Hope. To use the U-boats to Germany's advantage, Doenitz had to arrange for supply ships to sail into the South Atlantic, and this was done in April. In May he was able to take advantage of the changes. *U-38*, *U-69*, *U-97*, *U-103*, *U-105*, *U-106*, and *U-107* worked the South Atlantic successfully, sinking thirty-one ships, most of them lone sailers.

Doenitz knew that the British were strengthening their North Atlantic convoy system. The Canadians announced in May that they would open an escort base at Saint John's, Newfoundland, and that seven corvettes were now ready for duty and fifteen more would join up in June. That meant a vital increase in the western defense forces: the Canadians had eight destroyers and twenty corvettes on escort duty. The increase meant that for the first time a convoy could sail from North America under constant escort protection across the Atlantic. It was a major change and the first convoy to sail under the new conditions was HX 129. The convoy did not lose a ship.

But the same could not be said of two other convoys that crossed the Atlantic that month. The first was the westbound OB 318, which was hit by the U-boats on May 7.

The convoy had been brought west as far as Iceland without incident by H.M.S. *Westcott*, H.M.S. *Newmarket*, and H.M.S. *Campbeltown*. In mid-afternoon the convoy received a signal from the Admiralty announcing that the convoy had probably been spotted by a U-boat which had reported to Admiral Doenitz about an hour earlier. The Admiralty was restrained. "Probably" was the key word. There was no "probably" about it; the Admiralty knew exactly what had happened, because the Admiralty was reading Doenitz's radio messages. But that fact was not to be allowed to get out, or the secret that the British had breached the German codes would be compromised and one of the most valuable war assets in British possession destroyed.

By May the British had two communications successes in the battle of the Atlantic. First was the breach of the German codes by Magic, the superb decoding machine that gave the basis for the ULTRA messages warning of German activity. These had to be used carefully in the naval as well as the land war for fear of German discovery.

The second development was the perfection of land-based HFDF or Huffduff—the radio direction finding system that triangulated the location of radio broadcasts and told the Huffduffers where the U-boats were. The British were still working on their seagoing Huffduff, but with the growing involvement of the Americans since the autumn of 1940 the British took advantage of the American Huffduff system. The United States maintained an arc of land-based radio stations around its perimeters, with headquarters outside Annapolis. Stations in Britain and North America could triangulate almost any North Atlantic broadcast. On the American side, the information was passed along to the United States Navy communications headquarters in Washington, which passed it to the British. But this sort of cooperation was not a one-way street. In return the British gave the Americans new information about their rapid development of radar with such finds as the cavity magnetron, which made it possible for the Americans to modernize their warships. Later, in the battles of the South Pacific, the radar would make all the difference in the war against the Japanese.

But as the British had already discovered to their chagrin, knowing what the Germans were up to and doing something about it were two different matters. The fact was that a wolfpack of U-boats was now assembling to assault Convoy OB 318, and except to warn the escorts on the scene, the Admiralty could do nothing further.

Knowing that the convoy was being trailed, the commodore ordered a change in course, from 290 degrees to 318 degrees, hoping at least to throw off the boats that were moving in following Lieutenant Kuppisch's transmission. These were Lemp's *U-110*, Lieutenant Adelbert Schnee's *U-201*, and Lieutenant Herbert Wohlfarth's *U-556*.

* * *

At 6:30 P.M. May 7 the convoy met H.M.S. *Ranpura*, H.M.S. *Bulldog*, H.M.S. *Amazon*, and H.M.S. *Broadway*, which had come down from the new base at Iceland. A little over an hour later the *Westcott* group turned back for Iceland and then Londonderry. Their fuel was running low.

When the commander of *Bulldog* learned of the course change, he said it was not enough; the course was then set at 318 degrees and the escorts formed up around the thirty-five ships in nine columns.

* * *

Lieutenant Kuppisch had spent the afternoon running up ahead of the convoy. At dark he made sure of its position, then dived and let it go over him, came to periscope depth and prepared to attack.

* * *

Just before 9 P.M. the night of May 7, the *Bulldog* had a radar contact 200 yards ahead. It was lost before it could be classified. The captain of the *Bulldog* was suspicious enough to turn and steam down between the seventh and eighth columns of the convoy.

* * *

Fifteen minutes later Kuppisch surfaced and attacked the steamer *Ixion*, the rear ship in the fifth column. She fired two rockets and they were still in the air when the *Eastern Star* was torpedoed ten seconds later. Kuppisch had used the machine gun approach, firing a spread of three torpedoes into the heart of the convoy. One had struck the *Ixion*, one the *Eastern Star*, and the other had missed. He turned and fired his stern tube, and missed as well.

The *Eastern Star* was loaded with a cargo of Scotch whisky and it went up with a beautiful blue white flame, lighting up the sea around. Two minutes later the commodore ordered an emergency turn to port to get away from that telltale light.

The steamer *Nailsea Manor*, the rear ship in the eighth column, altered course to port, and at great danger to herself stopped to pick up eighty-six men from the *Ixion*, then set out to rejoin the convoy.

* * *

The *Bulldog* was steaming down between the seventh and eighth columns when the torpedoes blew. Her captain realized that she must be very near the submarine, and he dropped a depth charge right there. He then turned up into the convoy, just as it was executing the emergency turn; there was a terrible mess, which kept the helmsman of the *Bulldog* swinging this way and that for fifteen minutes until the ship could get out. Then she joined the U-boat hunt.

H.M.S. *Rochester* began to sweep the starboard quarter of the convoy, and at 9:20 P.M., while turning to port, sighted a periscope on the port beam. An asdic contact came at the same time. She prepared to attack.

The *Amazon*'s captain decided the attack must have come from the rear of the convoy, so he sped down between the third and fourth columns at twenty knots and soon had an asdic contact. He also prepared to attack.

For the next hour and a half the three ships carried out six depth charge attacks. But the U-boat got away.

When the submarine attack began the other escorts moved to cover the convoy. The *Broadway* dropped one depth charge on the port quarter. The *Primrose* hurried up to guard the port flank.

An ammunition ship goes up with a bang in the North Atlantic

A Royal Navy destroyer—an "ocean greyhound"—hot on the trail of a U-boat

The result of a U-boat torpedo on an Allied ship

A British ship, its stern blown off by a torpedo, is towed into Gibralter

Another torpedoed British ship lists heavily to port

Survivors on a raft are rescued following a submarine attack

U-744 enters Brest harbor after a successful "cruise" in the Atlantic.
Several weeks later it was destroyed by a British frigate.

Down, down a U-boat goes, sunk by British fire

Grand Admiral Erich Raeder,
chief of the German naval
forces for most of World War II

Admiral Carl Doenitz, the U-boat
genius, at the head of a naval
inspection force

U-boat Captain Gunther Prien shakes hands with Admiral Schlachtschiffe after sinking the British carrier *Royal Oak* in Scapa Flow. Looking on is Grand Admiral Erich Raeder.

Gunther Prien in full uniform and decorations—one of the superheros of the U-boat forces

First Sea Lord Admiral of the Fleet Sir Dudley Pound on the bridge
of the ship that took Prime Minister Winston Churchill to America
for his last meeting with President Roosevelt

Commander Weir of the Royal Navy giving landing instructions to
captured U-boat commander (in white cap)

Prime Minister Winston Churchill on a morale visit to British naval
forces in Scotland at the height of the U-boat menace

Captain F. J. Walker of the British
navy, the famous U-boat hunter,
who died before the ultimate
victory

The *Angle* took station at the head of the convoy. The *Nasturtium* also moved up to the head of the convoy, though she had a contact and dropped one depth charge.

The *Dianthus* dropped a charge and then took her old station on the side.

The *Auricula* kept her station. The *Daneman* was ordered to stop and pick up survivors from the *Eastern Star* and saved the entire crew.

The *Marigold* screened the torpedoed *Ixion* and picked up six officers and thirteen men. When the *Ixion* and the *Eastern Star* sank, the escorts moved on their way and rejoined the convoy.

At 10 P.M. the commodore decided they had evaded long enough and ordered an emergency turn to starboard to put them back on the base course of 318 degrees. Shortly after this, the escorts *Aubretia*, *Hollyhock*, *Nigella*, and *St. Apollo* joined up with four more merchant ships from Iceland. This was the Seventh Escort Group.

From London came the word that another U-boat was transmitting to Doenitz between 62 and 63 degrees north; the convoy altered course at midnight to 270 degrees.

The convoy now consisted of thirty-seven merchant ships guarded by sixteen escorts, a number that would have been impossible even three months earlier. This state of affairs did not last long; the Seventh Escort Group remained with the convoy for only a couple of hours and by 6 PM on May 8 they were going off to meet Convoy HX 123 and take over its escort.

At this point the escort of Convoy OB 318 was actually reduced, because the *Rochester*, out chasing a submarine, had not been informed of the course change and failed to find the convoy that night. So the convoy now had nine escorts for thirty-seven ships.

The weather that night was fine, with a slight overcast. The sea was calm, with visibility five miles from the convoy. The commodore was in fine spirits, believing that his course changes had outwitted the enemy and that the convoy was free of snoopers.

His dream was brought to an abrupt end just after 9 P.M. when the Admiralty reported that once again the convoy was being trailed by a submarine. The commodore altered course thirty degrees to port, and again was sure he had shaken off the enemy. There were no attacks that night of May 8. The reason was that Kuppisch, who had been out on patrol since April, had fired all his torpedoes.

All went well until noon, when the lead ship in the starboard outside column, the *Esmond*, was hit by two torpedoes on the outward side. Lieutenant Lemp's *U-110* had caught up with the convoy.

* * *

The *Bulldog* was stopped near Lemp's oil slick when the asdic operator had a contact. This must have been Lieutenant Herbert Wohlfarth's *U-556*, since Schnee had moved around to the rear of the convoy. The *Broadway* immediately closed on it, and began dropping depth charges. The two ships made several attacks, and remained in the vicinity for twenty-four hours, watching and waiting.

At 12:20 P.M., when the commodore of the convoy made his second emergency turn to port, the ships went to a course of 140 degrees. The escort *Ranpura* sighted a periscope, 5,000 yards off to the northwest, and the *Amazon* closed on the position.

At 12:28 P.M. the *Empire Cloud* was torpedoed and a few seconds later the *Gregalia*. This was Schnee's work. The *Gregalia* sank but not the *Empire Cloud*. Immediately three escorts were on the submarine, and she went down, with no chance to finish off the *Empire Cloud*. The *Amazon* called for a tug to be sent to the ship's assistance, and eventually the *Empire Cloud* was towed safely into Reykjavik harbor.

For four hours the escorts hung around the place where Schnee had gone down sweeping and dropping depth charges. Some oil came up, but the U-boat survived. Schnee did not, however, take any more ships from Convoy OB 318.

Ranpura, *Hollyhock*, and *Daneman* continued to escort the convoy. The commodore had considered scattering his ships at dusk for better protection, but in view of the fact that he still had three escorts, he decided against the idea, at least until any further attacks.

So OB 318 continued westward, thirty-three ships in nine columns, with three escorts.

At 11:45 P.M. the convoy altered course to 190 degrees and then at 2:20 A.M. on May 10 altered course again to 220 degrees.

* * *

Wohlfarth had finally escaped the attentions of H.M.S. *Broadway* and the *Bulldog*, and was trailing the convoy again.

At 2:50 A.M. the *Aelybryn* was torpedoed on the starboard column of the convoy. The commodore ordered an emergency turn to port, the *Hollyhock* went charging off to find the submarine and failed, and the *Daneman* stood by and picked up ninety-six survivors of the stricken ship.

The presence of the *Hollyhock*, however, did keep Wohlfarth from any further destruction at the moment. For the next two hours he was busy evading the escort.

* * *

When the *Aelybryn* was torpedoed the master of the *Chaucer*, the second ship in the eighth column, looked hard for a torpedo track as he increased his speed and turned to starboard. He was an intelligent man, for another of Wohlfarth's torpedoes missed the ship by a scant few feet.

At 3:11 A.M., the convoy commodore made a difficult decision. He had thirty-two ships to protect. All the escorts were out chasing submarines or picking up survivors. The commodore decided to disperse the convoy. The ships were told that they were now on their own.

It might not have been the wisest decision. Three more ships of OB 318 were lost before they reached North America, two more to Wohlfarth and one to Liebe's *U-38*. But twenty-nine ships of the convoy arrived safely. Nine had been lost, 50,000 more tons of shipping.

In May, then, the war between the U-boats and the anti–U-boat forces did not change as much as the British might have expected, given their increased emphasis on the battle of the Atlantic. To be sure, the British were extending their protection westward, but so were the U-boats now prepared to move west. The last two attacks on Convoy OB 318 had occurred between 32° and 35° west. Just a few weeks earlier the limit of U-boat activity had been 20° west.

The growing strength and range of the U-boat fleet was felt again in the North Atlantic on May 20, when Convoy HX 126 was discovered, again by Kuppisch, who had gone home and come out again on a new patrol.

Kuppisch moved far to the west on this search, past forty-one degrees, due south of Greenland. There he found the convoy without escort. *U-94*, *U-556*, *U-111*, *U-98*, *U-109*, and *U-93* sank nine ships in two nights of battle. At dawn on May 21 the commodore dispersed the convoy and no more ships were sunk. It was re-formed again south of Iceland when the escorts and the escorting aircraft joined up, and made its way safely back to the United Kingdom.

*   *   *

U-boat sinkings of merchant ships were up. To counter the British advances in anti–U-boat warfare, Doenitz had new boats with longer range, capable of carrying more torpedoes, and his fleet was growing. More important than the number was the nature of the fleet. Earlier Doenitz had depended on his 250-ton boats, but now these were almost all retired. Each U-boat that came off the ways had more range and more power than the model before it. The pattern of battle had indeed changed. Where the British could put up enough aircraft and escorts to sea, they could keep the U-boats off balance, and cut losses to a minimum. But too many ships were still sailing independently. Of the sixty-six ships sunk in May, forty-one were traveling alone, and only twenty-five were sunk from convoys. And as the British gained skill in protecting the convoys, the U-boat captains gained skill in avoiding the escorts. If the British were to slow the depradations of the U-boats, they would have to do still better than they had done.

17

Enter America

The month of July was more heartening for Britain. With the establishment of the Canadian escort system in the spring, the British also changed their convoy routings, and it would be a while before the Germans caught up.

In July two dozen U-boats operated in the Atlantic plus half a dozen Italians. The Germans plugged the U-boat war unmercifully in their propaganda, but the fact was that the Axis powers together sank only twenty-four ships in July. Seven of these sinkings were ships of Convoy OG 69, bound from the United Kingdom to Gibraltar. The German propaganda machine claimed twenty-four ships, a destroyer and a corvette from this convoy, but the claim was two-thirds fabrication. The truth was that the Italians were doing better than the Germans: with six boats out they sank seven ships; with twenty-four boats out, the Germans sank seventeen.

Since December, 1940, the war in the Mediterranean had been growing hotter. The Stuka and Heinkel bombers caused an enormous amount of destruction and threatened Britain's lifelines to Gibraltar, Malta, and North Africa, where the desert war surged back and forth. Crete fell to the Germans. Greece was overwhelmed. Rommel moved into Africa and began to drive on Egypt. The Germans took control of the air. In midsummer the key to the desperate struggle in the Mediterranean was supply, which meant ships. The German assault on Convoy OG 69 in July was carried out by a combination of Focke-

Wulff aircraft and U-boats. That it did not succeed was due to the increased number of British escorts. End to end antisubmarine escort had been adopted, another indication of Britain's growing ability to meet the U-boat threat.

A key to this ability was the growth of Coastal Command. In July, Coastal Command aircraft flew 2,100 hours on anti–submarine patrol and 4,300 hours on convoy duty. Coastal Command was a hodgepodge of aircraft: Wellington bombers, Hudsons, Beauforts, Whitleys, Catalinas, Sunderlands, and Ansons. Not all of them, particularly the Anson, were effective. But they flew, they sighted submarines, and when they did not attack successfully, at least they forced them down. Aircraft were also responsible for the sinking of two of the three U-boats destroyed in August.

* * *

The summer air attack on shipping was the major problem in the Mediterranean; the U-boat continued to be the principal menace, particularly on the Atlantic lifeline.

By the end of August, 1941, Churchill and his Battle of the Atlantic Committee had become cautiously optimistic. Their efforts seemed to be paying off in more satisfactory convoy performance.

An assessment of shipping losses since the beginning of the war showed that 1,847 ships had been lost from all causes. That meant 7,459,000 tons of shipping or a third of Britain's prewar tonnage had been sacrificed. Of these ships lost, 818, or 4,034,000 tons, had been lost to U-boats; and 433, or 1,369,000 tons, to aircraft attack. The U-boats were responsible for 54 percent of the sinkings.

There was one nagging figure: between June and the end of August the U-boats had sunk ninety-six ships or 447,000 tons, and the percentage of U-boat sinkings had gone up 72 percent.

Yet the Atlantic War Committee was inclined to look with satisfaction and point with pride.

In the last week of the month a large number of ships passed safely through exceptionally heavy concentrations of U-boats in the North Atlantic. Here is the assessment of the special

Admiralty department set up to deal with the U-boat war for August:

Taken as a whole August was a satisfactory month. Although the increase in U-boat construction begun at the outbreak of war is now being translated into a steady increase in numbers of U-boats operating, our losses are still being kept down to comparatively low figures. This is due partly to the greater efficiency of our A/S escort forces and aircraft against enemy units, the latter reduced in efficiency by a combination of past losses in personnel and the dilution inevitable in a heavy programme of expansion.

Good management has earned good luck and fortune has smiled on us.

One reason for the optimism was a growing sense of the participation of the United States in the Atlantic war. For the first year and a half American warships had carefully avoided the zone blockade declared by Germany around the British Isles, but in the summer of 1941 this was no longer so. The extension of the American zone of neutrality had made the American ships more active. On June 20 the U.S. battleship *Texas* was steaming along, well inside the blockade area, when she came within the periscope view of Lieutenant Rolf Muetzelburg, captain of the *U-203*. Muetzelburg did not wait long to decide what to do: the ship could well have been turned over to the British as had the fifty destroyers and ten Coast Guard Cutters. He attacked. Fortunately his torpedoes missed the *Texas* and the battleship's bridge watch did not even know how close the call had been.

Muetzelburg was as lucky as the battleship; when Doenitz heard what his pugnacious lieutenant had done, the submarine admiral nearly had a heart attack. Out went a general radio message to all U-boats: "American warships, even if met within the blockade area, will not be attacked since . . . to do so does not, in my opinion, coincide with the Fuehrer's political intentions."

How right he was. When Doenitz spoke to Hitler, the latter

put an absolute quash on such attacks in a manner that made
Doenitz's job of convoy assault almost impossible.

Attacks on warships had to be restricted to cruisers, battleships, and aircraft carriers and these could be attacked only
when the submarine commander was certain they were British,
not American. To Doenitz the order meant his captains could
not defend themselves against the British destroyers and corvettes—there was never time to identify an attacking, small
warship. After enormous effort Doenitz received permission
from OKW for the U-boats to defend themselves against actual
attack, but for the next few months their freedom of operation
was sharply limited.

Doenitz was also suffering other troubles that summer. The
shortage of copper reduced U-boat production in July from
twenty-five boats a month to fifteen. Also, Doenitz learned
when some memos annotated by OKW staff officers had been
returned to him in error that Admiral Raeder's staff declared
"we don't want to become a Navy of U-boats."

Doenitz was also troubled that summer by repair problems.
For every one hundred days, the average U-boat was now
spending sixty-five in dockyard and thirty-five days at sea. The
reason: thousands of dockyard workers had been pulled off
submarine work to reconstruct and repair the pocket battleships and cruisers that were the delight of Admiral Raeder's
battleship men.

Then in June came the attack on the USSR and an enormous
amount of pressure on Doenitz to divert at least ten boats to the
arctic, to sink shipping bound for Murmansk. Doenitz resisted
strongly; to take boats out of the Atlantic scene just then, he
said, was to endanger the whole U-boat war against Britain.

So in the summer of 1941 the United States participation in
the battle of the Atlantic became a reality. It had begun with the
transfer of the fifty old destroyers, which were now doing
yeoman service from Iceland to the Western Approaches. Next
had come the Lend Lease Law which was signed by President
Roosevelt on March 11. Then had come the transfer of ten
United States Coast Guard cutters to Britain as escort vessels.

Most of these went south to the Sierra Leone route, where Britain was trying hard to build up a convoy service to stop Doenitz's depradations on lone ships.

In April American naval and air bases were opened in Bermuda and air bases on the east coast of Greenland. On May 15 the Americans took over the naval base at Argentia, Newfoundland, thus freeing British and Canadian forces. Late in May President Roosevelt announced that an unlimited national emergency existed; the only possible reason was the growing threat of Nazi Germany. The Americans replaced the British in Iceland.

But all these measures were what might be called "shoring up" the British effort, without any serious danger of direct American involvement. All that changed on September 1, 1941, when Admiral King ordered American naval forces to convoy merchant ships in the Atlantic. That move was a violation of international law. The Germans protested, but the American course was already set, and had been since the day Averill Harriman began attending the meetings of the Battle of the Atlantic Committee. Admiral King pragmatically referred to the American position as "a realistic attitude toward events in the Atlantic."

The decision to escort convoys put the United States Navy on a collision course with Admiral Doenitz's U-boats, and it was only a matter of time before an incident occurred. It came four days later, when the American destroyer *Greer* was steaming between Iceland and the U.S. coast 180 miles southwest of Reykjavik. A British plane advised that a U-boat was located 10 miles west, on the destroyer's course. The destroyer increased speed and zigzagged to the point mentioned, then began trailing the U-boat and reporting its position for the benefit of any British craft or planes that might happen by. At 10:30 A.M. a British plane answered the informational calls of the *Greer* and dropped four depth charges near the submarine, but did not damage it seriously. The plane went away but the U.S.S. *Greer* remained to harry the submarine. Finally Lieutenant Georg-Werner Fraatz, commander of the *U-652*, turned the tables, ap-

proached the Greer and fired two torpedoes. The Greer
managed to evade both, and then came after the U-652, dropping three depth charges. They also missed. The destroyer and
the U-boat then went their separate ways.

A few days later President Roosevelt told Americans in one
of his "fireside chats" that the Greer had been attacked by a U-
boat but he did not tell the whole story, that the destroyer had
created the incident. His indictment was that the U-boat had
carried out an act of piracy, and he compared the U-boats to
rattlesnakes. As with rattlesnakes, he said, the Americans
would not hesitate to strike the first blow to crush the U-boats.
So, as of September, 1941, the United States was actually at war
with Germany, although at the moment the war was confined to
the high seas.

*   *   *

By September the Canadians were escorting eastbound convoys from the eastern coast of North America to the rendezvous
points south of Newfoundland. The American escorts then took
over, and accompanied the convoys to the meeting point
around 58° north, 22° west, where the British would then take
them back into the Western Approaches. Working farther west
as they were, it was inevitable that the U-boats would soon
come into frequent contact with the American escort service.

In September Doenitz's strength in the mid-Atlantic was at a
new high. Five wolf packs would work those waters that
month. Doenitz had estimated that the British must be taking
their convoys far north of the old routes, and he sent a dozen
boats out to discover where they were going. On September 9,
southeast of Greenland, Lieutenant Friedrich Guggenberger in
the U-81 found a straggler from Convoy SC 42, the 5,000-ton
steamer Empire Springbuck, and torpedoed her. Finding a
straggler and finding the convoy were not the same, and so it
was not Guggenberger who caught up with SC 42 but Lieutenant Eberhard Greger's U-85. He attacked the steamer Jedmoor
and missed.

But the convoy was elusive and it was not until the night of

September 10 that Lieutenant Heinz-Otto Schultze in *U-432* came across the main body of ships. The escorts were inadequate for the large size of the convoy, and they could not deal with the thirteen submarines that moved in to attack, the largest number of U-boats yet to go after a single convoy. On September 10 and 11 the U-boats sank fourteen ships and damaged four; the convoy got away for three days, but was discovered again and the U-boats sank two more ships, one virtually in sight of the British homeland.

On September 19 Kentrat's *U-74* found another homeward bound convoy, SC 44, in the frigid waters east of Greenland, and sank the corvette *Levis*. Four U-boats took five merchant ships from this convoy. There was a difference, however, from the past. The presence of the larger number of escorts that the British could now put to sea meant that the U-boat captains did not have the time to check their results as they had before. Thus many larger claims were coming into Doenitz's headquarters. The British dismissed all these as pure propaganda, but it was not quite that simple. In Convoy SC 44, for example, Kentrat attacked—and missed—three ships he claimed. Topp's *U-552* attacked four, but sank only two. And Lieutenant Hugo Foerster's *U-501* was sunk on its maiden patrol by the Canadian ships *Chambly* and *Moosejaw*.

Still, the British problem was that there were too many U-boats in too many places. Convoy OG 74, bound from England to Gibraltar with supplies for the faltering British forces in Africa, was hit on September 20. Five ships were lost. The eleven-ship convoy SL 87 from Sierra Leone was attacked by six submarines and lost six ships. The convoy had four escorts, but six submarines were too many to keep down.

Convoy HG 73, homeward bound from Gibraltar, was discovered on September 25, and in two days lost nine ships.

When the figures were added up in London, many faces grew long. The shipping loss for September had jumped up to over 212,000 tons. What was more disturbing was the fact that forty of the fifty-three ships had been sunk while in convoy. True, thirteen convoys had arrived in September without losing a single ship, but the convoy sinkings still represented 71 percent of the total, which was a new high.

*   *   *

But matters beyond the control of Admiral Doenitz were intervening at a time when he once again had the British in serious trouble in the battle of the Atlantic. He had been forced to put four submarines on the Arctic run to harry Soviet shipping. Now, in the late summer, Hitler ordained that the effort of the U-boat force must be diverted to the Mediterranean, where the British were playing hob with the Italian shipping supporting Rommel's Afrika Korps.

At the end of September the first six U-boats moved in past Gibraltar. And Doenitz had even worse news from navy headquarters. Orders were being drawn to transfer *the whole force of operational U-boats to the Mediterranean.*

The war had reached a new critical phase in the Mediterranean; Doenitz had just a little longer now to assault the enemy in the North Atlantic, and he had to take advantage of every day, for in his heart Doenitz believed that here was where the decisive war had to be fought. The North Sea, the Arctic, the Mediterranean were all sideshows where the U-boats could not be decisive. But if the U-boats could conquer the North Atlantic, then Britain would be finished.

In October, with few boats left to work the Atlantic, Doenitz had very little luck for the first two weeks. Nine U-boats scored, but none sank more than one ship.

Then, on October 15, Convoy SC 48 was steaming along eastward off southern Greenland when it was discovered by U-553. The fifty-ship convoy had something new: four American destroyers were among the eleven escorts. They were attacked in the next two days by nine U-boats which sank ten ships. The convoy also lost three of its defenders: the destroyer *Broadwater*, the corvette *Gladiolus* were both sunk by U-boats, and the American destroyer *Kearny* was torpedoed, with a loss of life heavy enough to create a *cause celebre* back in America. She did not sink, but was taken back to Iceland by the *Greer*, the veteran of submarine attacks. The convoy went on, reinforced by another seven escorts which, in conjunction with American patrol bombers from Iceland, finally drove the U-boats off. But the attack on the *Kearny* brought the war that much closer in America, as Churchill and Roosevelt knew it would.

And there came one final scene in the North Atlantic drama that fall. On October 31 the American destroyer *Reuben James* was part of the escort of Convoy HX 156, steaming south of Greenland toward England. The *Reuben James* had just made a submarine contact and turned to investigate when she took a torpedo opposite her magazine on the port side. The whole front part of the ship disintegrated as the magazine exploded, and five minutes later the after section sank. Depth charges, not set on safe, exploded amidst the men in the water, and in the end only forty-five men and not a single officer were saved.

By this time orders to Doenitz to move his submarines out of the Atlantic were coming through, and his effort now had to be devoted to the Mediterranean. But the damage of confrontation with the United States had been done in these last hours. Lieutenant Commander Erich Topp had the honor or the ignominy, depending on how one looked at it, of sinking the first American warship in the war. The U-boat war would not be the same again.

18

U-Boats in the Mediterranean

In the summer of 1941 the Mediterranean was to Hitler what the North Atlantic was to Churchill. Hitler was engaged in a bitter struggle to control the North African shores of the Mediterranean; he and Mussolini already controlled the European shores. He had invaded the USSR and in his wildest dreams could look forward to the day when the Middle East would be within the reach of his Nazi legions. But none of this could be accomplished so long as the British controlled Egypt and Gibraltar and maintained the naval and air base at Malta from which they could sting the Axis.

That summer the German and Italian campaign was going badly, not so much on land, where Rommel was in fine fettle, but on the sea. The British in four months of summer had sunk a quarter of a million tons of Italian shipping that was bearing supplies, mostly for Rommel. The British fleet in the Mediterranean posed a constant threat to the air and land power of the Axis. Thus, in August Hitler decided that more power must be exerted in the Mediterranean, and he ordered air and U-boat reinforcement of the area. Doenitz was ordered to send six boats down to the Mediterranean. At the same time Hitler prepared to strengthen the air forces there by bringing in Marshal Kesselring's Air Fleet Two. Doenitz did not like the idea of sacrificing his submarines; he was still certain that the key battlefield was the North Atlantic and that here Britain would stand or fall. The withdrawal of six boats from the North Atlantic perturbed the German admiral.

The six U-boats appeared in the Mediterranean early in October, having passed through the straits of Gibraltar under the noses of the British. But they did not accomplish much. On October 10 Freiherr von Tiesenhausen's *U-331* made the first attack, on a 500-ton freighter, and thought he sank it. He did not even hit it. One reason for the inaccurate reporting was the fact that the Mediterranean was so strictly patrolled by British air and naval forces that once a U-boat captain fired a torpedo his only sensible course of action was to dive down and run. That way he did not have time to observe the results of his shooting.

That was the way it went all month for the six U-boats. The result at the end of the month: six boats, two ships sunk, one patrol boat damaged. Even in the worst of times in the North Atlantic Doenitz's U-boats had been averaging two ships sunk per patrol, and a patrol might last only three weeks; a minimum of ten British merchant ships on the North Atlantic run had been sacrificed in October to cover Hitler's demands.

At the end of October, Hitler ordered Kesselring down to the south, and Doenitz was to send more U-boats. Doenitz took six more boats from bases at Lorient and elsewhere on the Bay of Biscay and sent them through the straits. Two did not make it, and one, the *U-433*, was sunk by the British corvette *Marigold* almost as soon as she completed the passage. In November, then, there were ten U-boats in the Mediterranean. How did they fare?

Their task primarily was to sink British warships, to reduce the British power in the Mediterranean and thus let Kesselring's air forces regain air superiority if Rommel's supply train was to be properly reestablished.

In the first twelve days of November, the ten U-boats did nothing at all. On November 13 Lieutenant Franz-Georg Reschke's *U-205* trailed the British Task Force H and at about 5 A.M. came up to periscope depth, fired a spread of three torpedoes at the carrier *Ark Royal* and a destroyer, put periscope

down and hauled out of the area. As they went, Lieutenant
Reschke heard explosions and assumed that he had put two
torpedoes into the Ark Royal and sunk a destroyer. In fact he
had hit nothing.

The Ark Royal was returning to Gibraltar that day, together
with the Malaya, the cruisers Argus and Hermione and seven
destroyers. The sea was smooth, with a little ripple brought by
the ten-knot wind from the southwest. The day was cloudy
with occasional rainsqualls but visibility was good enough for
flying. The Ark Royal was landing and sending out aircraft all
day long.

Lieutenant Friedrich Guggenberger's U-81 had been stalking
the task force all afternoon. At 3:40 P.M. he fired a spread of
electric torpedoes; one of them struck the Ark Royal on the
starboard beam, abreast the island. A column of water rose fifty-
five feet to the flight deck.

There had been one small warning. A destroyer had
reported a contact fifteen minutes earlier, but it had come to
nothing. There was no torpedo wake (electric torpedoes) and
no sign of a submarine. But at 3:53 P.M. the destroyer Argus
reported a periscope. Even so, many aboard felt that the ship
had been damaged by an internal explosion. In fact the damage
did not seem too great. Nothing much could be observed over
the side, and the crockery was intact, the aircraft were intact,
and not a man was even thrown off his feet.

But flooding began immediately. The ship took a ten-degree
starboard list, and the main switchboard flooded out and communication throughout the ship was lost.

Three minutes after the torpedoing, the list had increased to
twelve degrees, and the boilers had flooded. Eighteen minutes
later the list had gone to eighteen degrees, and the decision was
made to move most of the crew off the ship. The destroyer
Legion came alongside and began taking men off.

At 4:30 P.M. it seemed that the damage had stabilized, and
the captain decided to try to get the Ark Royal going again. The
tug Thames came up and took the carrier under tow at two

knots. There seemed to be every hope that she could get to Gibraltar safely.

But with the order to abandon ship earlier, many key men had already gone, and they had not bothered to close up the watertight doors between compartments. So the flooding continued to increase until at 5 P.M. all steam failed. The destroyer *Laforey* came alongside and ran supply cables across the deck, and an electrical repair party from the *Hermione* came aboard with portable pumps. The captain had ordered counterflooding, so the list was now down to about fourteen degrees. After much hard work, steam was restored to one boiler at 9 P.M., but by this time the list had increased again to eighteen degrees.

By 10 P.M. partial electric power had been restored, and by 10:30 the situation seemed so generally improved that the *Laforey* moved away. But the ship continued to fill with water. What the British did not know then was that the *Ark Royal* had been hit by one of the magnetic torpedoes, which had blown a hole in the bottom, a hole that was not readily visible, but which kept bringing in a steady supply of sea water. Even as things looked better up top, the water had started to come in over the elbow of the uptake in the port boiler room and increased steadily. This reduced the area for the escape of gases, and the boiler casings became red hot and fires broke out in the boiler room. Eventually they got so bad that the boiler room had to be abandoned and then all steam was again lost and the power system shut down.

At 3:40 A.M. on November 14, the salvage crew was again ordered to abandon ship. The list was then twenty-seven degrees. She was abandoned by 4:30 A.M., and at 6:13 A.M. the *Ark Royal* turned turtle and sank.

Score one for Admiral Doenitz's submarines, for the *Ark Royal* had been an enormous thorn in the side of German air power and Italian shipping.

But that was all the nine U-boats accomplished until November 25. On that day the battleship *Barham* was traveling in company with the First Battle Squadron flagship *Queen*

Elizabeth and a number of lesser ships 100 miles northeast of Sollum. Again it was a fine day and the sea was calm. They were moving along at seventeen knots, zigzagging, when the destroyer *Jervis* made an asdic contact on her port side, 1,100 yards off.

At 4:21 P.M. the fleet altered course, and moved into perfect position for Lieutenant von Tiesenhausen's *U-331*, which was lurking around the edges of the force, waiting for a chance to attack. Tiesenhausen fired a spread of torpedoes. At 4:25 P.M. the *Barham* was hit by all three. She listed ten degrees to port, and in a minute, heeled over and lay on her beam ends. In six minutes she sank.

Von Tiesenhausen was a brave man. He surfaced in the middle of the British fleet to see what he had done; the cruiser *Valiant* saw him and tried to ram. But the U-boat was so close that the ship could not turn in time, and so the *U-331* ran right through the British fleet on the surface. Several destroyers saw her and were preparing to attack, but they were all called off to pick up the *Barham*'s survivors. The submarine hunt did not get going for an hour, and by then von Tiesenhausen was clean away.

Score two for Doenitz. The *Barham*, a 31,000-ton ship, was an important part of the British Mediterranean fleet. Her loss was a terrible shock, particularly since she took down Captain G. C. Cooke and 861 officers and men. And score three: on November 27 the *U-559* sank the Australian corvette *Paramatta* off Bardia.

But that was all. Nine of Doenitz's best submarines in the Mediterranean could only manage a score of three warships for a month's work.

Meanwhile, on the North Atlantic run, Doenitz's decimated force of U-boats sank only thirteen merchant ships and the cruiser *Dunedin*. In contrast with the carnage of September and the hard days of October it was almost as though death had declared a holiday in the North Atlantic. And December was even better for the Allies; the U-boats took only four ships out of the North Atlantic's convoys.

So Hitler's diversion of all the available submarines from the North Atlantic to the Mediterranean had been a costly venture, one that had turned the war around for a British government that in the summer had grown ever more worried about its ability to feed its people and keep the military supplied with the materials of war. After a steadily rising level of merchant ship sinkings, it was an enormous relief to have two months of almost uninterrupted, successful sailings. The surcease of sinkings made an enormous difference in Britain's level of supplies. As the year 1941 ended, the picture in the North Atlantic looked brighter than it had for more than a year.

19

Doenitz's War
Against America

General Tojo had said nothing to Hitler about his plans for war in the Far East or about the coming attack on Pearl Harbor. When it came, Admiral Doenitz, like all senior German officials, was caught by surprise.

On December 8 Admiral Raeder informed Admiral Doenitz that Hitler's restrictions on sinking American warships or operating off the American coast were now rescinded. Doenitz then asked for permission to move a dozen boats out of the Mediterranean area where they were doing little good and send them against America. Permission was refused. Hitler would not allow any diminution of the forces in the Mediterranean. Doenitz could send six boats to the American waters. That was all.

Doenitz now had under his command a force of ninety-one U-boats, but given the demands of Hitler, only fifty-five were available. Sixty percent of these were in dock undergoing refits or repairs, which left twenty-five, and of these twenty-two were at sea, leaving three boats available. But the only boats suitable for the long voyage to American waters were the Type IX C boats (740 tons), half again as large as the Type VII. These should be able to stay out for six weeks, with about two weeks on station.

After Germany declared war on the United States on December 11, Doenitz's three U-boats were still not ready to make the long voyage. It would be weeks before even five Type IX C U-boats would be available for the six-week patrol. Doenitz called the five U-boat captains into his office one by one and instructed them: they would have about two weeks on station, with the rest of the time in transit. They were not to attack shipping, no matter how enticing, until they reached their assigned patrol areas, unless the target were more than 10,000 tons. They were to stay out of sight of enemy forces; their attacks had to be a total surprise. Doenitz was sure the American antisubmarine defenses were fragmentary and disorganized and he wanted to take full advantage of the element of shock. The captains grinned when they were told the name of the operation: *Paukenschlag* ("kettledrum beat"). The admiral wanted to open the campaign against America with a loud bang.

The campaign would begin along the American coast between the mouth of the Saint Lawrence River and Cape Hatteras. Thus the United States would get the full impact where it could hurt most: off Boston, New York, the Chesapeake Bay, and the Potomac.

The commanders were to move to their patrol areas and wait for a signal. Doenitz would radio them when they were to start shooting. Weather would play an important role. And not until all the boats were ready for action would the group get orders.

The captains chosen were Lieutenant Heinrich Bleichrodt, Lieutenant Ulrich Folkers, Lieutenant Reinhard Hardegen, Commander Ernst Kals, and Commander Richard Zapp. Bleichrodt had first distinguished himself in September, 1940, when he sank ten ships. Folkers, untried, was on his first patrol as a captain. Hardegen had not done well on his first patrol, but in June he had sunk six ships. Kals, although a commander, had been serving ashore for years; this was his first war patrol. Zapp had done moderately well off the African coast with three ships sunk on one patrol. They were not the cream of the crop— Doenitz's most able captains were in the Mediterranean and the

South Atlantic—but they were the best Doenitz could round up
on short notice.

* * *

It was the third week of December before the first boat sailed
from Lorient for the two-week voyage across the Atlantic.

Almost at the same time, Doenitz had some good news. His
barrage of memos to Admiral Raeder had finally got through to
OKW and the transfer of boats to the Mediterranean would
cease. He was free once again to use his U-boats as he wished.
Four boats of the new Type IX C had been sent to the waters of
Gibraltar earlier when they became operational. These were far
more suitable for the long voyage to the Americas, and were
now available at the Bay of Biscay bases. In addition to the five
boats that would work the North American station, Doenitz
decided to send these four to the western Atlantic, to attack
around the fringes of the Caribbean.

Doenitz's staff had analyzed the logistics sending Type VII
boats 2,000 to 4,000 miles into American waters. The boats
could manage to work off Canada, 2,000 to 2,500 miles, but
even New York was too long a run (3,000 miles) until Doenitz
got his tanker U-boats, which finally were now under construction and the first of which would be delivered in spring, 1942.

Seven more U-boats, Type VII C, were moved up from the
southern Atlantic and ordered to sail into Canadian waters. By
the first week of January, sixteen U-boats were on their way to
begin the new war.

For three years the Americans had kept a close watch on
Britain's naval war through naval attachés in London. For a
year they had been privy to most of Britain's secrets, including
all the developments of the war against the U-boats. And yet
when war came, so secure did the Americans feel behind their
two oceans that virtually no planning had been done for any
large-scale participation in the battle on the Atlantic. The
senior antisubmarine officer in Washington was a chief petty
officer. For three years the British had been building small, fast

vessels to counter the U-boat threat. The United States had not built a single one. The American navy's idea of a sub-chaser was a 2,000-ton destroyer.

* * *

In the third week of December, when the first Type IX C U-boats set out from the pens at Lorient, British agents warned London that they were sailing for America. The message was passed to Rear Admiral Adolphus Andrews, commander of the Eastern Sea Frontier, which was responsible for American coastal defenses from the Canadian border to Cape Hatteras, precisely the waters where Operation Paukenschlag would strike.

The admiral had been rounding up ships since December 7. By early January he had 20 vessels and 103 aircraft to guard a coastline of 1,500 miles. The largest vessel at his disposal was a 165-foot Coast Guard cutter, which could make sixteen knots. Most of the others were tugs, trawlers, and yachts. Some were so small that they could not mount depth charge Y guns; the recoil would pop the guns right through the decks. And the U-boat four-inch gun was larger than anything the admiral had in his arsenal. Nearly all the aircraft were obsolete.

In mid-December Admiral Andrews appealed to Admiral King for help. King was now *the* power of the navy. He had been appointed to overall command after Pearl Harbor with the title Commander in Chief, United States Fleet, even though that title was not strictly legal since the commander in chief, by law, was the President. King responded to Andrews' appeal and sent minelayers to mine the approaches to Portland, Maine; Boston; New York harbor; and the Chesapeake Bay.

December and early January were marked by numerous hysterical "sightings" of periscopes and reports of imminent invasion by the German fleet. But on January 12 Admiral Andrews received a report that the British passenger steamer *Cyclops*, 9,000 tons, and sailing alone, was torpedoed 300 miles off Cape Cod. Lieutenant Hardegen, unable to resist, had done the deed.

Cyclops nearly met Doenitz's specifications but not quite. And her sinking did what Doenitz had feared: it alerted the Americans that U-boats were coming.

But Doenitz did not know then that the American defenses were almost nonexistent.

*   *   *

On the night of January 12 Admiral Doenitz signaled his five Paukenschlag commanders to begin beating the drum. Kals was the first to score. A little after 1 A.M. on January 13 his *U-130* sank the Norwegian steamer *Frisco* in the Gulf of St. Lawrence. Eight hours later he sank the Panamanian *Friar Rock* in the same area.

Hardegen's patrol area was farther south. On the morning of January 14 the *U-123* surfaced sixty miles off Montauk Point, Long Island, and sank the tanker *Norness*. The next day he sank the tanker *Coimbra* and on January 17 the steamer *San Jose*.

On January 18 Zapp's *U-66* sank the tanker *Allan Jackson*; the next day Hardegen sank three ships and damaged another. In the beginning his strategy had been to lie on the bottom during daylight hours, then surface at night and attack ships moving up and down the coast. But he soon found that lying on the bottom was unnecessary since the American defense was nonexistent. Three of the four ships he attacked on January 19 were attacked in broad daylight. This was the beginning of what the U-boat commanders came to call the American Happy Time, when the war was going for them as well as it had in the fall of 1940 off the Western Approaches.

Kals' *U-130* joined the drum beating once more on January 21, sinking the tanker *Alexander Hoegh* south of Cape Breton. Then along came Bleichrodt and Folkers.

Hardegen had used his last torpedo against the tanker *Malay* off Cape May on January 19, but the ship survived despite additional shelling and made it into port. Hardegen was loath to leave the happy hunting ground and, even without torpedoes, he stayed around for several days. On his way home, he surfaced and shelled the 3,000-ton freighter *Culebra* until she sank. Then he returned to Lorient to tell Admiral Doenitz that the American waters were indeed the happy hunting ground and that Doenitz ought to send out mine layers and more U-boats to take full advantage of the unprepared Americans.

Kals continued on the American patrol and sank two freighters and four tankers. When he ran out of torpedoes he surfaced and shelled another tanker, the *Halo*, which did not sink.

After sinking the *Allan Jackson*, Zapp's *U-66* sank another tanker and three freighters. Bleichrodt sank three freighters and the 11,000-ton Canadian tanker *Montrolite*. Only Folker's *U-125* did not perform up to standard: he damaged the tanker *Olney* and sank one steamer. Thus, the first five boats to attack in American waters returned to Germany having sunk over 150,000 tons of shipping.

* * *

As the original five boats left, three more Type IX C boats had arrived off Chesapeake Bay. Admiral Andrews had tried to confuse the enemy by moving the sea lane sixty miles out to sea in the Hatteras area. But the change did not help and the three boats coming in simply met the flow of traffic closer. The *U-106* sank five ships; the *U-103* four; the *U-107* three.

By the end of January it was apparent that the Germans had suddenly turned their major U-boat effort west. Most of the ships sunk were in that area and were traveling alone. With one exception convoys in the Western Approaches to Britain were untouched.

What was happening in American waters was at first unbelievable to the British. They knew by the middle of January that a large number of ships were being sunk. What they did not know was how ill-equipped the Americans were to counter the U-boat threat. The convoy was not in use; the same problem Britain had faced in 1939, but which was far more serious: there were not enough escorts to assist any convoy at this point. Whereas the British as a seafaring nation had many trawlers and other relatively seaworthy craft to call upon, the Ameri-

cans had very few. And as for aircraft, the army air forces,
which had the planes capable of antisubmarine operations but
had neither the skills nor the inclination to use them, while the
navy, with its greater skills, had virtually nothing but float
planes with which to work.

In mid-February Admiral Andrews had available nine vessels that could make fourteen knots or better, and another nineteen vessels that could make between twelve and fourteen
knots. Most of the U-boats off the American shore could make
eighteen knots. Andrews had no aircraft available for air cover.
In other words, as Andrews pointed out, he did not have
enough vessels to make up two convoys and he had no air
cover. The convoy system would have to wait.

* * *

The salvation of shipping along the American coast that
winter was Doenitz's shortage of the eighteen-knot, Type IX C
long range submarines needed for the job. He did send seven
Type VII boats to work off Canada in January, but the conditions were so bad that the smaller U-boats accomplished relatively little. But it was not long before Doenitz discovered that
by adding fuel supplies and cutting some amenities his Type
VII boats could operate off New York, and that was bad news
indeed for Admiral Andrews and the Allied cause.

Hardegen had come home swearing that if Doenitz could
put ten times as many submarines on the American coast he
would find all the targets the admiral desired. There was no
doubt that the Germans had almost full sway. Only one U-boat
was sunk in the Atlantic that month, the U-93 by H.M.S. Hesperus. The Americans neither sank nor damaged any boats. It
was a sign of total inability to cope with the U-boat threat. At
the end of the month, when the figures were added up, 327,000
tons of shipping had been sunk, most of the ships off the
American coast.

Doenitz was delighted. Here was his chance to strike a blow
against Britain. The U-boat force now numbered about 250,
with more coming off the ways nearly every day. He made

plans to send every available U-boat to the ports in the Bay of Biscay, which was closest to the American theatre, to fill up with fuel and head west.

But at the end of January Hitler began to worry about Norway. He had one of his inspirations: Churchill had never given up on Norway and was about to try again to capture it. Hitler demanded that all available U-boats be sent to Norway to form a defense chain there.

Doenitz was nearly beside himself. He managed to get the blanket order cut down; he would send eight boats to Norway. That meant he had about twenty boats to send into the Atlantic.

Bleichrodt, Winter, and Forster went back to the American coast in February and were joined by Bigalk and half a dozen other commanders in early February. Meanwhile another half dozen boats were working the South Atlantic and Caribbean and, as they came off station, were replaced by other boats. And still Doenitz had enough U-boats to attack the convoys crossing the Atlantic. HX 173 lost a merchant ship, ON 63 lost the British corvette *Arbutus*, ON 60 lost the Free French escort *Alysse*, SC 67 lost the Canadian escort *Spikenard* and the motorship *Heina*, and two other convoys lost stragglers.

The major damage done to convoyed ships in February was to Convoy ON 67, outward bound from the United Kingdom to America. ON 67 was escorted by the U.S. destroyers *Bernadou*, *Edison*, *Lea*, and *Nicholson*, and the Canadian *Algoma*. The convoy was taking a more southern routing than usual. Two-thirds of the way across the Atlantic it ran into Lieutenant Adolf Piening's *U-155*, which was moving into the North American zone to raid. Early on the morning of February 22 he attacked three ships and sank two of them, including one tanker.

The convoy went on and almost due east of Cape Breton, it ran into four more submarines: *U-558*, *U-162*, *U-158*, and *U-587*. They sank six ships and damaged two more.

On the morning of February 24 the convoy commander ordered a drastic alteration of course. The escorts patrolled constantly around the edges of the convoy and swept out at night to follow all RDF bearings. The Radio Direction Finding system was now beginning to demonstrate greater accuracy. The escorts made definite contact with five submarines, but did not sink any. Yet, because of this aggressive action, the escorts saved the convoy from further attacks. Or was this altogether true? The Germans knew that there were fat pickings along the American coast, and there were no escorts to trouble about and very few aircraft to disturb them.

Convoy, however, had to be the answer, as the British could show the Americans. Here is a table from the Battle of the Atlantic Anti–U-Boat War Committee's monthly report covering February, 1942 (see Table 2).

The big change in February over January was Doenitz's expansion of the U-boat campaign to the Caribbean. Half a dozen U-boats, plus several Italian submarines, moved in to attack. Their temerity was alarming.

On February 16, Lieutenant Commander Werner Hartenstein's *U-156* entered the important oil port of Aruba, Curacao, in the Dutch West Indies, and attacked three tankers. He sank one and damaged the other two, then went outside and shelled the harbor installations without fear of retaliation. The Caribbean command was spread thin, and besides, the Americans were still thinking in terms of patrol rather than convoy.

TABLE 2

Month	Ships Sunk by U-Boat No.	Tons	In Convoy No.	Tons	Not In Convoy No.	Tons	% In Convoy
September	54	205,000	37	146,000	17	59,000	71
October	31	151,000	15	67,000	16	84,000	44
November	12	62,000	5	23,000	7	39,000	37
December	23	102,000	5	21,000	18	81,000	21
January	50	288,000	2	12,000	48	276,000	4
February	55	326,000*	6	34,000	49	292,000	10

*Revised figures showed even greater losses: seventy-one ships, 384,000 tons overall.

Three days after Hartenstein's bold foray, Lieutenant Albrecht Achilles' *U-161* entered the harbor at Port of Spain, Trinidad, as though it were a cruise liner, and torpedoed an American freighter and British tanker. Both sank at anchor. Other ships, particularly tankers, were sunk in the Gulf of Venezuela. The U-boats also hit shipping off Port of Spain. Between February 19 and 23 two or three U-boats settled down in the strait that runs between Florida and the Bahamas. Altogether there were about forty boats at sea in the Atlantic. It seemed that Doenitz's wildest dreams were about to come true, even though, as he liked to point out, at no time were more than six or eight boats operating in any of these areas.

Churchill watched the growing losses with concern. On February 6 he had warned Harry H. Hopkins, his go-between with Roosevelt, that the heavy losses ought to be drawn to the special attention of the President. Three days later his expression of concern was backed by action. He offered the United States reverse lend-lease: twenty-four antisubmarine trawlers and ten corvettes *with their trained British crews*. The offer was accepted by Roosevelt.

The Americans were having a hard time adapting to the war. One clear danger was the failure of American cities to black out. The lights along the Atlantic coast shone as bright as day, and the glare outlined ships running up and down the shore at night. Andrews recommended to Admiral King that American cities should be forced to black out at night. A roar came up from the chambers of commerce! Atlantic City protested, as did Miami. Blackout? It would be bad for business!

Churchill again brought up the subject of convoys. President Roosevelt turned the idea over to Admiral King, who turned it over to his staff. Convoy? A peculiarly "limey" solution to the problem, said King's staff. Hardly applicable in the United States. Besides, the only way convoys could be managed was to strip the Atlantic fleet of its destroyers, since there were virtually no other ships available. And the fleet must be kept intact! So much for the convoy idea.

The Americans had a lot to learn, Roosevelt admitted in a

letter to Churchill. But by May 1 he hoped to have an adequate patrol system in operation. Churchill was now convinced that the Americans barely understood the problem. Patrol would never solve it. Convoy was the only answer.

On March 11 Churchill told Hopkins that unless the United States could provide escort forces to stop the sinking of tankers in the Caribbean (twenty-three sunk in February), he would have to stop the tankers from sailing, or delay sailings of all convoys until escort vessels could be sent south to fill the gap.

Roosevelt agreed; it was the only way until the ship gap could be filled by July 1, when additional destroyer escort craft and planes would be available to American forces.

Having been given so much advice, the United States Navy felt impelled to offer some to Churchill. It suggested that the British should begin to bomb the submarine facilities. Churchill recognized the irritation.

The American press had been extremely critical of the navy's failure to come to grips with the submarine menace. In his own way, Churchill had kept up the pressure. Convoy . . . convoy . . . convoy . . . Admiral King was finally stung into reply: "Those of us who are directly concerned with the combating of the Atlantic submarine menance are not at all sure that the British are applying sufficient effort to bombing German submarine bases . . . It seems that the RAF is not fully cooperative."

That churlish remark was greeted by Churchill with aplomb—he knew how humiliating it must be for the United States to recognize a deficiency. But there was some truth to what King said: at the time when it counted the RAF Bomber Command had firmly resisted the navy's requests to work over the U-boat bases. Churchill assured Roosevelt that the bases would receive attention. The RAF bombed the shipyards, Kiel, and the U-boat pens at Lorient and elsewhere along the Bay of Biscay. But the bombings were not effective, since Doenitz was expecting them. During the past year the Todt Organization, Germany's superconstruction firm, had been at work building bomb-proof U-boat pens at the bases. Lorient and La Pallice were now complete. They could have been destroyed under construction, as the navy suggested, but now they were bombproof.

At this time, Dr. Karl Silex, editor of the *Deutsche Allgemein Zeitung* and a World War I U-boat officer himself, paid a visit to Doenitz at his command post in Lorient, from which the admiral was now directing the assault on America.

Here is part of Silex's report:

Nowhere in the harbor is a submarine seen. The harbor is dominated by a gigantic building. It squats over the harbor, as it were. Its extent makes one overlook its great height, although it is towering over anything else in the neighborhood. This squatting monster looks like a gigantic block of concrete without doors or windows, but its sharp outline nevertheless makes a surprising architectural impression. . . .

In the interior we see submarines which have just arrived from across the ocean, stabled with many others, like motor cars in a giant garage. This, then, is one of the shelters which were constructed at every one of our bases by the Todt organization. A Faustian work! Along the ceilings of vast hangars cranes are passing overhead. Within the submarines shipyard workers are hammering away while on deck others are busy with the hulls. In another hangar are machines such as are needed by shipyards. Submarines, workers, materials, machines, all are protected by the thickest concrete walls ever seen, while the concrete roofs are thicker still. . . .

The Todt organization had been detailed by Hitler to protect the submarines, and had built walls and roofs of reinforced concrete twenty feet thick, impervious to virtually all bombing, as the Allies discovered at the war's end. Thousands of tons of bombs were dropped on the submarine pens but only one armor-piercing bomb managed to break through. The Allies never wiped out the submarine pens.

Much more effective was another move promised by Churchill, but delivered at this point only in part because of a serious shortage of bombers: the aerial surveillance of the Bay of Biscay. The Admiralty wanted six squadrons; Churchill could not then give them; the solution, he suggested coyly, was increased American plane production.

With the United States now in the war, Britain's problems were America's problems, and vice versa. At the moment the British were more aware of this than the Americans, and generous in overlooking the serious deficiencies of the American naval organization in planning for the U-boat war. What was needed was not quibbling, but strong and immediate action to stop the flow of oil onto the American beaches. So successful were the U-boat captains that the U.S. Atlantic coastal beaches south of Cape May were littered with debris from sunken ships and scummy with black oil from sunken tankers. As March began, even the most ardent "limey haters" in the American navy were beginning to take pause. Something had to be done, and fast.

20

The Tide Slackens

As the third month of Doenitz's campaign against America opened the U-boat situation was worse than ever. The United States government's major contribution to the war against the U-boats was to censor the news about sinkings. Doenitz was not fooled; he had his own sources of information—the captains who returned to take their place on the honor roll of commanders who had sunk more than 100,000 tons. This list was growing longer. By the end of January it included nine holders of the Iron Cross with Knight Insignia and Oak Leaves. The Knight Insignia meant 100,000 tons, the Oak Leaves meant 200,000 tons. Kretschmer, a prisoner of war, still led the list with Swords added to his Oak Leaves. And behind these superheroes were twenty-nine others who had earned the Knight Insignia with 100,000 tons.

In March unlucky was the U-boat captain who did not sink at least three ships on a patrol to America. Several captains could claim four, five, six; Lieutenant Ernst Bauer sank seven ships and damaged three. Hardegen came out late in March and sank seven ships and also damaged three. Commander Fecia di Cossato in the Italian submarine *Tazzoli* sank six ships. From the Allied viewpoint the situation in the Americas grew so desperate that something drastic had to be done. So many survivors of sinkings reported that their ships had been silhouetted against the lights of a city that Lieutenant General Hugh Drum, commander of the Army Eastern Defense Command, finally ordered a blackout. On March 15 Admiral Andrews sent a plea to all commands to beg, borrow, or steal vessels capable of carrying guns and depth charges. He would even take the menhaden (cod) fishing fleet from New England, whose boats could not make more than five knots. He was delighted when five pleasure yachts were found that could be converted to patrol work.

The really good news was that the British trawlers began to arrive in March, with ten corvettes to follow. As of April, Admiral Andrews would have ninety-four ships to patrol from Canada to his new southern border, the Gulf frontier in Florida.

Churchill had convinced Roosevelt that the convoy was an essential, and the president laid down the law to Admiral King. On March 16 Admiral King ordered a meeting in Washington to set up convoys. But how could Andrews set up convoys when he had available to him, on temporary loan, only three destroyers and eight patrol boats? The only sort of convoy he could envision was the type the British had ruled out at the beginning of the war—a convoy without protection, which was no convoy at all.

What happened to that type of convoy was shown on the night of March 17 when the tankers *Papoose*, *W. E. Hutton*, *E. M. Clark*, *Acme*, and *Esso Baltimore* sailed up the coast by Cape Hatteras with a number of merchant ships in an unprotected convoy. In numbers, someone had said, there might be safety.

That was before they ran across the spot off Hatteras where Lieutenant Commander Johann Mohr's *U-124* was lurking. In short order Mohr torpedoed the *Acme*, and then the steamer *Kassandra Louloudi* when she came to the *Acme*'s assistance. Mohr then sank the *E. M. Clark*, the *Papoose*, and the *W. E. Hutton*. He missed the rest of the "convoy"—the *Esso Baltimore*.

By mid-month Admiral Andrews estimated that at this rate of sinkings the U-boats would destroy two million tons of shipping in a year. He went to Washington to plead with Admiral King for help. The tankers were going down so fast that the

Petroleum Industry War Council warned that if the situation did not improve America would be out of oil in six months. Shell Oil Company offered to equip its own tankers with Piper Cub planes that would search ahead to warn the captains of submarines. Indignantly the navy rejected what the oilmen believed was a sensible suggestion.

But by the end of March even Admiral King (who was preoccupied with the desperate state of affairs in the Pacific war) was convinced that something drastic had to happen. The British were not going to like it, but he persuaded President Roosevelt to intervene and take back seventy OS2U 3 naval aircraft suitable for patrol from a shipment bound for England and give them to Admiral Andrews. The navy now had its first reasonable antisubmarine equipment.

Andrews also asked King for additional destroyers. The Atlantic fleet had seventy-three destroyers, only two of which were available to Admiral Andrews on a loan basis. They changed every week or two, and the destroyer captains were never drilled in anti–U-boat warfare. Andrews wanted permanent assignment of destroyers for convoy duty. Otherwise he agreed with Prime Minister Churchill: the sailing of tankers had to be stopped. He had already spoken to the British about changing the convoy cycle from one every six to one every seven days. That way the British could send two escort groups to America. But the British rejoined that to do this would cost Britain 30,000 tons of shipping supplies per month, and they could not afford to take that loss. Admiral King flatly refused to give Andrews additional destroyers. Andrews told him that if matters did not improve he would have to cancel the sailing of tankers until further notice.

At the end of March came the really bad news. The sinkings, including those from the southern areas, came to seventy-nine ships; tonnage sunk in the Americas in March was equal to that of January and February combined.

But on April 1 the first contingent of British trawlers arrived in New York harbor: 900 tons, 170 feet long, with a four-inch gun in the bow and a .30-caliber machine gun. They made only thirteen knots, carried 100 depth charges and could throw a pattern of 10 at a time. They were also equipped with asdic, and manned by crews experienced in using depth charges and asdic. The Royal Navy had stripped the ships of tools on the principle that the Americans had plenty of tools. This was true, if annoying on first blush. The Americans still did not understand the depths of Britain's difficulties.

The trawlers weren't much, but as Churchill said, "It was little enough, but the utmost we could spare." It also gave Admiral Andrews his first effective weapons against the U-boats.

Once the British trawlers arrived, Admiral King seemed to believe all Admiral Andrews' problems were solved. He ordered convoys to begin between Hampton Roads and Key West, and a convoy system was put into effect early in April. Ships coming north from the Caribbean and Florida would form up in columns in the Florida strait early in the morning (four ships to a column and 1,000 yards between columns), and start moving up the coast. Any ship that traveled slower than nine knots or faster than thirteen had to sail independently. During the daylight hours each convoy was escorted by one slow escort in front and three fast patrol escorts around the edges. The slow escorts were usually the trawlers; the fast ones were mostly eighty-three-foot Coast Guard cutters.

At the end of the first day they made Charleston harbor. There they lay overnight and the next morning formed up again at dawn. The second night they made Cape Lookout. The third night they were in Hampton Roads. The fourth night they were in the Delaware. The fifth night the convoy would make New York, and the sixth, Buzzard's Bay. They would then travel through the waters of the Cape Cod canal to Cape Cod Bay. There they would meet the Canadians, who had real escort service, bound for Halifax and other Canadian points, and from there they would join the big convoys bound for Britain.

In the first seven days of April the U-boats sank seven tankers, an alarming statistic. A few days later tanker sailings were canceled indefinitely.

* * *

The U-boat captains grew cocky. At first they had approached the American waters with the same respect they showed the British around the Western Approaches. But three months of constant success *without a single U-boat loss* had made them confident that the Americans were incapable of action. The U-boats surfaced in the daylight and shelled tankers and freighters. They ran on the surface and virtually ignored circling aircraft. They ventured into dangerously shallow water, knowing the American antisubmarine patrol was almost nonexistent. Every U-boat captain yearned for a North American patrol, certain that there he could make his reputation.

21

Recasting the Defenses

The first U-boat sinking by the USS *Roper* came as an enormous relief to the British naval establishment. The figures on merchant shipping sinkings remained grim; in three months Allied shipping losses had totalled 1,200,000 tons, half of which were tankers, but at least there was a 25 percent drop from 500,000 tons in March to 400,000 tons in April. For the third successive month, Doenitz had concentrated his attack on independent shipping in the Western Hemisphere, at the moment mostly in the south. Admiral Andrews' convoys and the increased anti–U-boat activity provided by the British trawlers helped keep sinkings down along the American coast. Around the middle of the month, Doenitz diverted several boats to an area northwest of Bermuda, and a number of ships were sunk there.

On April 16 Admiral Andrews enjoyed another minor victory: the British finally agreed to open the Halifax convoy cycle from six to seven days, which released two escort groups for use along the West Coast of the United States. Also, the British had sent Captain G.E. Creasy, the Admiralty director of antisubmarine warfare, to Washington to teach the Americans the tricks of the trade. Admiral Harold Stark was appointed to command American naval forces in Europe, and the Admiralty laid out for him a review of their antisubmarine warfare procedures. Belatedly the Americans were taking an interest in what they should have learned two years earlier. But the British gave them full credit for the fifty old destroyers and ten Coast Guard cruisers. Had the Americans retained them, they would have had sixty potential escorts, enough to run four or five convoys.

* * *

One day in April a ship reported sighting a "supply submarine" in the Caribbean area. Admiral Doenitz's "milch cows," the tanker submarines, could now enable the U-boats to extend their cruises, and the Type VII boats could now perform as long as the Type IX boats. In April the "milch cows" were moving around the Atlantic, and on April 20 the *U-459* arrived off Bermuda and began refueling fourteen U-boats. But even as Doenitz took advantage of his technical superiorities, the ratio of sinkings began to fall. There was no mystery about it: the moment the Americans adopted the convoy system up and down the U.S. coast the sinkings decreased. What was needed now was a convoy system for the Caribbean, but the shortage of escorts prevented that. So in April sinkings in the Caribbean remained high; losses would remain high until the small destroyer escorts began to emerge from the American shipyards.

One other U-boat was sunk that month by Commander Walker's escort group on the Gibraltar convoy run. There was little submarine activity against Atlantic convoys. The British, Canadians, and Americans had pooled their antisubmarine forces for convoy and now operated under an efficient single command. The British were working on several new antisubmarine devices and had developed the "hedgehog," a multiple tube launching device to throw depth charges from an escort in a pattern designed to give the maximum coverage of an area. The RDF (sonar) system was improving every month. The Americans were working on a lighter device called "the mousetrap," which was capable of throwing a group of hedge-hog charges directly ahead of a vessel. The advantage of the mousetrap was that it could be used by a small patrol craft that could not accomodate a Y gun or the hedgehog apparatus.

But as the British well knew, none of these devices could match the escorted convoy. During April, 474 ships arrived in

United Kingdom ports in 19 ocean convoys. Only 4 ships were lost, and a fifth from an outward bound convoy. Until the United States could convert its enormous productive capacity into the development of numbers of escorts, the sinkings would continue. But the British remained serene; events were heading in the proper direction.

Captain Creasy stated: "If the early months of 1942 have seen a deterioration in the Battle of the Atlantic the later months of 1941 have seen a steady and progressive improvement and, with the maturing of the plans of the United Nations, this stage will come again. As has been said, we have beaten the U-boats once. We will now beat them a second time." All one had to do was remember the story of Convoy HG 76. Beset as the British were again, such confidence was remarkable. For in addition to the slaughter on the East Coast of the United States which would continue for weeks to come, Germany's U-boat production was increasing and Doenitz now had nearly 300 boats available. A new "soft spot" was being worked. Following Hitler's attack on the USSR in June, Britain and America had begun sending supplies to the Russians, and the supply convoys to Murmansk were now under attack by about 15 U-boats. So far these attacks were not serious: the U-boats were having difficulties with weather and ice. And, the British noticed that the quality of the crews sent to the north was not as high as that of those in the Atlantic. But that would change as the new men gained experience.

Doenitz was indefatigable in searching for that "weak spot" in the Allied defenses. In May, with still more boats at his disposal, he renewed his assault on the Atlantic convoys, while not neglecting the American area. Despite bad winter conditions in the north, he sent a boat to the Gulf of Saint Lawrence, which sank two ships. The Canadians responded with intensive air and sea antisubmarine measures and added escorts to every convoy no matter how small. The sinkings ceased.

The U-boat operations in the Atlantic in the spring of 1942 took a different turn, as the attack on Convoy SL 109 indicated. Doenitz was looking for soft spots again and thought he had found one off the bulge of Africa, where the Freetown convoys moved.

*   *   *

The thirty-one-ship convoy was under the protection of the Fortieth Escort Group consisting of four escorts with the destroyer *Landguard* in command. The convoy was steaming north at 7.5 knots on the afternoon of May 11 when the escort *Lulworth* sighted a suspicious object almost dead ahead on the horizon. Three escorts hurried to check the object which was identified as the conning tower of a submarine. The U-boat was steering across the course of the convoy from port to starboard, apparently planning to move down the starboard side to attack. The convoy made an emergency turn to port and the escort *Bideford* took station on the starboard beam.

Meanwhile, the U-boat had made a high frequency radio transmission and then dived. The transmission was picked up by the *Bideford* and by a second escort, the *Landguard;* the triangulation gave them the point where the U-boat had dived. Two escorts then set out to sweep and drop depth charges. Unfortunately the charges knocked out the asdic set of the *Landguard.*

At 5:50 P.M. the escort *Hastings* obtained an asdic contact two miles from the U-boat's diving position. Three of the escorts attacked with depth charges. Three hours later another contact resulted in another depth charge. No signs of damage were apparent, but the area had a strong smell of oil. The escorts then rejoined the convoy, arriving on station at 3 A.M. No more signals were intercepted, and no other U-boat was sighted that night.

At 3:30 P.M. on May 12, the lookouts of the *Hastings* sighted a submarine ten miles west of the convoy. Two escorts gave chase, but the U-boat scurried off at high speed on the surface. At 5:30 P.M. another U-boat was sighted twelve miles ahead of the convoy and the escorts went after this one. A cat and mouse game began. The U-boat turned away, but after one escort started back toward the convoy, the U-boat followed. The cap-

tain of the escort knew that the U-boat was going to try to follow
him to the convoy, so he slowed down and tried to lure it
toward the other escort. The U-boat captain was as canny as the
destroyer captain, and the ruse failed. The U-boat dived and
disappeared. The destroyer altered course to the north, away
from the convoy, fired star shells, left a delayed action depth
charge as a booby trap, and then altered course in the dark to
rejoin the convoy.

While three of the four escorts were out chasing submarines,
a U-boat torpedoed the freighter *Denpark* on the port wing of
the convoy. She carried a cargo of manganese ore and sank
without time to fire a rocket or send a message. It was ten
minutes before another ship could fire a rocket; in the meantime the U-128 had fired on another ship and missed. The
convoy now made snowflake to illuminate the area and the
escorts moved around searching for the submarine. At 11 P.M.
the *Landguard* made contact with a U-boat 3,500 yards out on
the port beam. The U-boat had just surfaced, and the RDF contact was immediately followed by sighting. The destroyer captain set his course to ram and fired snowflake over the U-boat,
which blinded the U-boat captain and prevented him from
firing on the convoy. The U-boat was too close to fire on with
the five-inch gun, but the pompoms and machine guns were
turned on it and hits were scored. The U-boat dived and the
escort dropped a pattern of depth charges, set shallow, into the
swirl. Then contact was lost. Nothing more was heard from the
U-boat that night.

Early the following morning, the lookout in the masthead of
the *Landguard* sighted a U-boat 10 miles off the starboard bow.
The escort *Lulworth* was sent to chase. A high frequency
transmission was intercepted by escorts, the U-boat dived, and
the *Hastings* was sent to the spot and ordered to keep the U-
boat down. The escort began dropping depth charges, even
though there was no contact. But the technique was new: the
convoy was steering north, so *Hastings* steered northeast, dropping five single charges set at 150 feet at five-minute intervals.
The idea was to suggest that the convoy was steering forty

degrees at eight knots. Having done that the *Hastings* rejoined the convoy.

In the afternoon the *Landguard* sighted a U-boat again on the port bow at a range of twelve miles. The convoy altered course, thirty degrees to starboard. But the *Landguard* did not try to chase. Her captain reported:

At this stage it was considered that no good results could be obtained by attempting to chase this U-boat as there was every indication that there were several in the vicinity of the convoy and the experience of the previous night proved the importance of the escorts remaining with the convoy.

The convoy commander considered the possibility that the U-boat was shadowing the convoy because of the smoke coming from several ships. When the convoy altered course, the *Landguard* stayed on the old course and made smoke to lure the U-boat. But it did not work. The transmission was heard again, off the convoy, indicating that the U-boat was shadowing. The *Landguard* speeded up and rejoined, following an evasive course to throw off any other U-boats in the vicinity. She was back on station on the bow of the convoy by dusk. At 8:40 P.M. the convoy altered course to starboard. Fifteen minutes later the steamer *Ingria* sighted a U-boat on her port bow and fired snowflake. The convoy followed suit and the area was lit up like a football field on a Saturday night. The commodore's ship, the *Thomas Holt*, fired its Oerlikon guns at the U-boat and changed course to ram. With the Oerlikon tracers coming at it, a ship turning to ram, and the night as light as noon, the U-boat captain lost heart and beat a retreat without firing a torpedo. The *Lulworth*, on the other side of the convoy, came around and chased the U-boat. The U-boat dived and four minutes later the *Lulworth* had an RDF contact; she moved in and began dropping depth charges. The *Lulworth* then ran out 1,000 yards and reduced speed to twelve knots. The noise of the U-boat blowing its tanks was heard on the port bow and the course was altered. But no further contact was made and the Lulworth rejoined the convoy after midnight.

The Bideford remained and obtained a firm asdic contact on the submarine after the Lulworth left the scene, and dropped a ten-charge pattern. A few minutes later she fired snowflake and saw large air bubbles breaking the surface. They may have been pillenwerfer, which the Germans were now using regularly. No further contact was made, and the Bideford rejoined the convoy, which altered course to fifty degrees.

At 11:10 P.M. the hydrophone operators of Landguard heard torpedo noises, bearing 120 degrees. The ship altered course and went to full speed. The torpedo passed down the side 400 yards away. The area was illuminated but nothing was seen and no U-boat contact was made. It seemed evident that the U-boat had fired from a long distance, by periscope bearing.

At 11:40 P.M. the Landguard intercepted high frequency transmissions and obtained a fix ten miles astern of the convoy. The Bideford was sent back, but did not make contact. Huffduff bearings continued to indicate that the convoy was being shadowed, but the escorts had neither sightings nor any RDF or radar contacts. Nor did any asdic sounds disturb the tranquility of the convoy.

On May 14 the Fortieth Escort Group was weary. The escorts were reduced to 5 percent of their depth charges and the ships were short of fuel. On May 18 the Thirty-seventh Escort Group showed up, and the Fortieth Group then set course for Gibraltar to replenish. The Thirty-Seventh Group had no further difficulty and the convoy arrived on schedule with only one loss, although analysis later indicated the group had been in contact with at least five different submarines during the voyage.

Here was the lesson Captain Creasy was to teach the Americans: antisubmarine patrols were comparative failures, aircraft could be of enormous use in convoy protection, the convoy escorts must be properly trained and known to one another, and RDF (sonar) was enormously valuable.

As regards the comparative failure of antisubmarine hunting forces, this is one of the hardest of all the lessons of the war to swallow. To go to sea to hunt down and destroy the enemy makes a strong appeal to every naval officer. It gives a sense of the initiative and of the offensive that is lacking in the more humdrum business of convoy protection. But in this U-boat war of 1942 fought out in the oceans the limitations of antisubmarine hunting forces have made themselves very clear. . . . Where the position of the U-boat is accurately known and a number of antisubmarine craft are available in the immediate vicinity there is some small chance of locating the enemy. Even in these conditions, the difficulties of locating a U-boat intent on evasion are apt to be forgotten. It is mathematically calculable that four destroyers aware of the position of a U-boat only twenty miles distant have a 40 percent chance of gaining asdic contact.

The performance of the Fortieth Escort Group had certainly shown all these lessons learned. Trailed by five submarines for nearly a week, the escorts had concentrated on the essential but unglamorous job of guarding the convoy day and night. Only when three of the four had gone haring off on submarine chases was a single ship torpedoed. Not a single submarine was claimed as sunk, and there were no heroics involved. But the Fortieth Escort Group had done the job and—on the basis of past performance of the U-boat packs—saved at least a dozen ships from destruction.

22

Ebb Tide

At the end of May the inauguration of coastal convoys from Key West cut into the U-boat sinkings. Yet the totals grew higher; Doenitz had more boats out. The Coast Guard cutter *Icarus* sank the *U-352* and captured thirty-two prisoners. In May 601,000 tons of shipping were lost, 451,000 in American waters. In June the number of U-boats operating in the Atlantic rose to about sixty-five, and with the addition of "milch cow" U-boat tankers, the extended cruises made the situation even worse than it appeared on the surface; the greater part of shipping losses for the month were in the Caribbean and the Gulf of Mexico. Altogether the losses in American waters in June were 416,000 tons; the total loss was 627,000 tons, the highest yet.

But Admiral Doenitz was not satisfied. By June, 1942, Doenitz's statistical analysis showed that the United States could build 15 million tons of shipping in 1942 and 1943. To Doenitz this meant that if he was to keep pace with the enemy's shipbuilding, he had to sink 700,000 tons of ships a month. And he was not doing it.

July was much better for the Allies, the best month of the year so far. One reason was that the American defenses were beginning to shape up. Doenitz recognized that the introduction of American convoys meant the system was going to expand, and even as he kept his boats on the American station he planned for future operations and looked for weak spots. He would have to move his major operations elsewhere.

Doenitz decided to transfer the main attack back to the mid-Atlantic where the convoys were still beyond the range of land based air cover from Britain or Iceland. Beginning in July he was getting thirty new boats per month and was ready to return to the wolf packs.

23

North Atlantic Offensive

In the summer of 1942 Admiral Doenitz was preoccupied with the problem of sinking more than 700,000 tons of Allied shipping per month. The western Atlantic was no longer the happy hunting ground of easy prey, and distance took on a new importance. Doenitz could keep three U-boats on station in the Western Approaches for every one on the American shore. Thus, with his growing number of U-boats, he could send out ten to fifteen boats to attack a convoy in the eastern Atlantic, and had the further advantage of knowing that the sea routes were like a funnel, with the narrow end at the British side. Once again the U-boat war changed. Finally, Admiral Doenitz was beginning to get more than lukewarm support from the naval establishment. Three new classes of U-boats were coming out of the yards: a 1,600-ton minelayer and operational boat, a 1,600-ton supply boat, and a 1,200-ton, long range operational boat. The torpedo problems had been largely resolved with the development of new exploder devices. Technicians were working on the Metox radar search receiver, a device designed to detect British radar transmissions. It would become standard equipment in the U-boat force in the fall, giving the U-boats another advantage in the struggle. But the Germans' greatest advantage, once again, was a new breach of the British naval codes. B-Dienst, the German cryptographic service, had done it again. As August began, Doenitz knew the convoy routings and was able to read messages from the Admiralty to the convoys.

On July 27 Doenitz made an unusual broadcast to the German people, discussing the future of the U-boat war and preparing the Germans for heavy U-boat losses in the future. The British read in Doenitz's message a warning that he was about to begin a new offensive against the Western Approaches.

The British Admiralty braced itself for a new onslaught, but were not well equipped to withstand it. The removal of two escort groups to American waters and the dispatch of ten corvettes and the ninety trawlers left a gap in the eastern Atlantic that had not appeared important when the emphasis was in the west, but that now took on a new complexion. Escorts were badly needed to protect the Freetown convoys and those going in and out of Gibraltar. The comparison between the attacks on Commander Walker's convoy HG 84 and HG 79 were a good indication of things to come. With HG 79 Walker had an escort carrier and never less than nine escorts. With HG 84 there was no carrier and only four escorts. HG 79 sank at least four U-boats and lost only one merchant ship. HG 84 sank no U-boats and lost five merchant ships.

The shortage of escorts was, as usual, the most serious problem. The need for auxiliary carriers was seen and efforts were being made to convert large merchant ships to carriers capable of taking on four or five planes. The going was slow. Apart from the Leigh light the British had other improved weapons available that summer. The hedgehog multiple depth charge throwing device had been tested and proved, and H.M.S. *Westcott* had used it successfully to sink a U-boat earlier in the year. Long range depth charge throwers were now under development, as were developments in the asdic sets to make them more reliable and increase their range. Basing longer range aircraft in Iceland had helped cut down that broad gap in the mid-Atlantic over which there was no air cover. But there were still several hundred miles of water where the convoys were on their own.

In August Doenitz had an average of about a hundred boats out, about thirty in North and Central American waters, thirty to forty in the Western Approaches, half a dozen in the South

Atlantic along the African coast, a few in the Mediterranean, the rest scattered between Norwegian and Arctic waters, and the Central Atlantic. With his new fleet of supply submarines Doenitz planned a siege of Britain, with the U-boats staying out for what previously would have been two or even three patrols, moving from one wolf pack attack to the next.

24

The Long, Long Trail of Losses

The remainder of 1942 was a nightmare for Britain. Soon Admiral Doenitz was able to pit more than twenty submarines against a single convoy. In the beginning his U-boats had hunted like wolves; now they hunted like piranhas, summoned by the Admiral's voice from miles around the scene of blood.

The Admiral was canny; his force of attack when possible was exerted in those areas outside shore-based air cover. In August and September the convoys between Trinidad, Aruba, and Key West lost a large number of ships, but in September the emphasis shifted toward the North Atlantic. Convoy ON 127 suffered eighteen attacks in three days and lost only five ships; but three other vessels were seriously damaged and one escort was sunk. In October SC 100 was beset, as were five other major convoys. SC 107 lost fifteen ships.

This action coincided with the Allied invasion of North Africa; Doenitz sent U-boats to the African coast to work off Algiers, Oran, and Gibraltar. Others went to the waters around South Africa, where ships still sailed independently. November was a bad month for Britain, with 190 ships sunk, 729,000 tons of shipping.

In November, Doenitz had about a hundred boats out in the Atlantic and its side areas, plus others in the Mediterranean, the North Sea, and the Arctic. At the end of the month, Convoy

HX 217 was beset by twenty-two U-boats. Fortunately weather and air cover kept the loss down to two ships, with two U-boats sunk. It was one of the best records of a sad period for the British.

The most important result of the increase in U-boat losses was the establishment of a special anti–U-boat committee within the British war cabinet. The Admiralty had its special anti–U-boat section, which kept track of every activity of U-boats and anti–U-boat warfare everywhere; but the war cabinet unit was something new on the highest level. The first meeting was held in the Prime Minister's meeting room at Ten Downing Street on November 4. Churchill explained that he had decided to hold these meetings to give "the same impulse to anti–U-boat warfare as had been applied to the battle of the Atlantic. . . ." Britain had to expect to face a larger number of U-boats in 1943, he said, operating in all the oceans and moving from one area to another, as Doenitz manipulated them. "To meet this, we should have to provide much stronger escort for our convoys. Indeed, our fast ships might have to be convoyed. Air forces would have to be provided to protect the local areas, and also to assist in the protection of ocean routes. . . ."

Also needed were more planes, but not at the expense of the night bombing of Germany; and more American planes, converted to protect sea communications.

A. V. Alexander, the first lord of the Admiralty, expressed his concern about the rising ship losses. Furthermore, American ship production had lagged 50,000 tons in October as against September. But the sinkings were an even more serious problem. Doenitz now had 243 operational U-boats, with a monthly production of 20 to 30 new U-boats, and while the Allies had sunk 159 boats and had probably sunk another forty-four and damaged 353, it was not enough. "The inference was that we were not destroying more than one-third of the monthly output of new boats," said Lord Alexander:

The spreading out of U-boat activities was making evasive routing more and more difficult. The Germans were now thought to have in the North Atlantic three large U-boats which were each capable of giving supplies to ten other boats sufficient to last for one month. In other waters U-boats were supplied by surface ships, of which there were probably not less than two operating at any one time. We had, therefore, to meet a more sustained as well as an increased area. The air had been of great help in meeting the U-boat menace, but there was a blind spot in the center of the North Atlantic where no air cover was provided and it was here that our heaviest losses occurred. . . . Aircraft with an overall range of 2,500 miles would be needed to cover this area.

Soon Averill Harriman and Admiral Stark were attending the meetings of the new anti–U-boat committee. The prime minister did not miss a meeting, which emphasized the importance he gave to it. The conferees discussed everything from the way to save kerosene to the new acoustic torpedoes—GNAT—the Germans had perfected, which were costing many escorts. They homed on propeller noise. During one November convoy, the Germans had concentrated on attacking escorts and had sunk three. But the convoy commander believed the escorts had also sunk three submarines. The remedy against the acoustics: a new kind of degaussing technique that destroyed the electrical field attracting the acoustic torpedo or streaming paravanes.

Every kind of antisubmarine device was given consideration at these meetings. The conferees first turned to a report on shipping losses covering the period from January to November 8, 1942. The picture was bleak; the shipping situation had never looked worse, and shipbuilding was lagging. Although 159 U-boats had been sunk since the beginning of the war, it was simply not enough. Ways had to be found to control the U-boat. How about submarines to hunt U-boats? Yes, their record had been very good; they had sunk several in the North Sea and in the Mediterranean. The problem was that British submarines were fully occupied in the Mediterranean, where their record in destroying enemy shipping was superb. And that, not anti–U-boat warfare, was the submarine's natural activity. The discussion turned to aircraft, and it was agreed that more long range aircraft were needed and that heavier attacks on the Bay of Biscay bases were in order. Escort carriers were discussed. The British had become leery of carriers in support of convoys, after their sad experience with the *Audacity* and, of course, the bitter experience with the *Courageous* and the sinking of the *Ark Royal* while on fleet operations. The committee had the following comments:

It was pointed out that there was already a shortage of carriers of the United Nations and this type of ship would always be required for future operations. Moreover the auxiliary carrier on [Merchant Auxiliary Comm] M.A.C. was as vulnerable to attack as the merchant ships escorted, and aircraft could not be flown off in very bad weather. Again they had generally to operate outside the antisubmarine screen when flying off and on. It would clearly be a very long time before it would be possible to provide sufficient of these ships to enable one to be with every convoy.

What the committee was looking for then was a solution to the Atlantic gap. Forty planes with an operational range of 2,500 miles were needed to cover that area of the mid-Atlantic. There was a way: Liberator bombers could be modified, but only at the rate of ten a month.

The Bay of Biscay received considerable attention, as well it might. Possession of these bases gave the Germans an enormous leg up on their forays against British shipping in the Atlantic. Two squadrons of Wellingtons were working the Bay of Biscay bases with Leigh lights. Another two squadrons were to be equipped with the new high frequency radar sets to enable them to conduct more successful attacks against the U-boats on the bay. The Germans had got onto the old radar by this time. The stepped up plans were all the more important because of the coming invasion of Sicily, and then of Italy, and continued activity in Africa. That meant more convoys moving by the Bay of Biscay and the need to keep the U-boats down.

The anti–U-boat committee was not then aware of certain activity in America: the development of the new escort carriers, pioneered by Henry Kaiser, the engineer and shipbuilder. A contract had been signed in June, and the first of these escort carriers were under construction at a west coast yard. The Americans called them CVES. The sailors of the fleet called them "jeeps," and their crews called them "Kaiser coffins" because they were built on merchant ship bodies without naval compartmentation. Whatever they were called they were going to be a new type of escort carrier: 512 feet long and 7,800 tons; one 5-inch gun on the fantail; eight twin 40 millimeter and twenty twin 200 antiaircraft guns, and thirty or more aircraft on her flight deck for antisubmarine operations. There would be other uses for these escort carriers, but from the antisubmarine point of view, they were a great step forward. And Kaiser was going ahead full speed. The *Casablanca* was built in 241 days. In 1942 Kaiser had built the 7,000-ton Liberty cargo ship *Robert E. Peary* in seven days, fourteen hours, and twenty-nine minutes, and he figured he could use the same shipbuilding techniques to turn out escort carriers in a hurry.

There was other good news from America to match the bad news from the mid-Atlantic. American shipping losses in the fall of 1942 were encouraging; but only because Doenitz had pulled back when the convoys made the going difficult. It was also part of Doenitz's strategy to keep moving, keep the enemy guessing, so that he never got completely set in any area. The British story of shipping losses in October and November war dismal; in December there was less than a three-month supply of fuel oil in Britain, so effective had been the Doenitz war against tankers. As the year ended the Admiralty had to examine the woeful truth: the U-boats had sunk 1,160 ships totalling 6.25 million tons. Added to the other losses the total became 7.75 million tons, and only 7 million tons of new shipping had been built. A deficit of a million tons of shipping had been added in 1942; British imports had dropped to two-thirds of the 1939 figure, although the war economy was demanding more and more supplies. Doenitz had begun the year with 91 operational U-boats and by December had 212 boats operational. The British had always anticipated that when the United States entered the war, its naval resources would be pooled. But the war had come to America on an entirely different level; the major naval challenge to the United States was in the Pacific, where the Japanese were having a field day with American destroyers and carriers. American industrial resources were certainly at the disposal of the British now and shipbuilding was continuing as fast as could be managed. But the United States was definitely fighting a two-ocean war, and the British could not expect as much as they desired. The beginning of 1943 promised to be the crisis point in Britain's war for survival, and for the most part, the British would be on their own, at least at sea.

25

Victory Over the Escorts

As the Allies looked into 1943 they were agreed that escort carriers and more convoy escorts would have to be produced if the U-boat menace was to be met, and that the air gaps must be closed wherever they existed.

Britain would provide a dozen escort carriers in the spring, the United States had promised to deliver another thirty in the first half of 1943. The bottleneck was arrester gear; only a handful of manufacturers could produce it.

All these were details, but comfortable details, the sort of nitty gritty that the political leaders could seize upon with some confidence as they looked into the future of the war. And that was precisely what they had to do on January 14, 1943, when the Allied leaders met at Casablanca. There was highflown talk about "unconditional surrender" of the Axis powers, and many plans were laid. But not one of these plans would come to anything—and Winston Churchill knew it better than anyone—if the U-boat menace in the Atlantic could not be brought under control and conquered in the coming twelve months.

Doenitz shared precisely the same feeling in reverse. At the end of 1942 he looked back with concern. Despite the fine record of his U-boats in the last half of the year, he felt that the Allies had gained the upper hand with their countermeasures against his boats. Radar, RDF, sonar, asdic, huffduff, the Leigh light, all made the U-boat captain's life difficult. It was the problem of surface detection which had deprived the U-boat of its great advantages of surprise and concealment. The wolfpack could not function if the enemy could put twenty escorts around a convoy, forcing the U-boats down whenever they approached, preventing them from coming in at night on the surface and firing their destructive broadsides. What Doenitz needed desperately was a submarine that could go faster under water, and stay underwater for long periods of time. He was using the "submersible," a warship whose natural element was still the surface of the sea. What he wanted was a "submarine" which would restore the balance of 1939.

Such a machine did exist in the developmental stage: the Walter U-boat, propelled by an Ingolin (peroxide) engine. As Churchill convened his anti–U-boat committee to deal with the growing problem, so on the other side of the channel Admiral Doenitz went to his constituency, Adolf Hitler, this time with the support of Admiral Raeder. Doenitz laid out the charts showing the successes on the American side, how they had then dwindled, then showing how the area of unfettered operations of the U-boats had shrunk steadily until now it was only a small segment of the North Atlantic. Hitler interrupted as he always did. He did not believe the British would be able to close the North Atlantic air gap, so why worry? But then Doenitz mentioned the Walter submarine, and Hitler's lagging enthusiasm was revived. If there was anything designed to appeal to der Fuehrer it was a "superweapon" and the Walter boat gave all indications of being just that. Doenitz then discussed the need for finding counterchecks to the British location devices that were giving so much trouble. Again this was just the sort of idea that appealed to Hitler, who always felt that because his technical experts were letting him down the going was getting more difficult.

From this conference Doenitz emerged with the influence and support he had always craved. The Germans had been working on their radar and had installed in the U-boat the advanced Fu MB search receiver which let a captain know when he had been spotted by enemy radar. What happened now was the war of the radars, with the British developing more powerful sets and the Germans putting together more powerful countersets. Other U-boat devices included a new gun platform and more effective antiaircraft guns. U-boat doctrine had once been: see an aircraft and dive. But now the doctrine had been modified: see an aircraft and shoot it out if you are caught. Doenitz also had the idea of creating his own Q-ship, a converted submarine looking like a U-boat but armor plated, with enough antiaircraft fire to bring down a Flying Fortress.

Another idea of Doenitz's was not a part of the superweapon philosophy. He wanted his own fleet of aircraft, long range planes that could work with his U-boats and that were powerful enough to come to their aid in times of need. Fortunately for the Allies, Goering opposed the idea and OKW was so hardpressed to produce aircraft for the Eastern and African fronts that it came to nothing.

In the fall of 1942 several convoys had been sent to the USSR and virtually every one of them had had a fighting voyage from start to finish. It was hardly surprising with the Germans controlling Norway, with their long range aircraft flying from Norwegian fields, as well as their access to the northern waters from submarine bases in Norway, and battleship and battle cruiser bases there.

In September Convoy PQ 18 sailed into the face of 90 German torpedo bombers, 130 long range bombers based in Norway, and the capital ships *Scheer, Hipper, Koln,* and destroyers based at Altenfjord. The convoy went easily enough until it reached the waters northwest of Bear Island. An escort sank the *U-88* on September 12, but the next morning *U-405, U-589,* and *U-408* all attacked and sank the steamers *Stalingrad* and *Oliver Ellsworth.* JU 88s and torpedo planes attacked in the afternoon and sank 8 more ships. On the morning of September 14 the tanker *Atheltemplar* was damaged by *U-457* and had to be sunk. But then a combined destroyer and aircraft attack sank the *U-589.* In the afternoon the convoy fought off a powerful air attack and shot down 13 torpedo bombers. The enemy attacked one carrier, *Avenger*, but her Hurricanes shot down 9 bombers. From then on there were repeated air attacks but no more ships were lost, and on September 16 the destroyer *Impulsive* sank the *U-457*. The British left the convoy on the afternoon of the sixteenth to pick up a homeward bound convoy, and 4 Russian destroyers took over. One more ship was sunk in the White Sea, but that was all.

Other convoys came and went north, including QP 14, which lost three ships to *U-435* in a matter of minutes. But twelve of the fifteen merchant ships got home. On the last day a Catalina sank *U-253* just off the English shore.

But from the British point of view, the convoys sailing to the USSR cost dearly in terms of escorts demanded, and Churchill put his foot down that fall. There would be no more convoys to Russia. President Roosevelt was unhappy; it meant the lend-lease supplies he was sending to Russia had to go in ships sailing independently through infested waters. But Britain was desperately beset. The cost was high: of the thirteen ships that sailed independently for Russia in the fall of 1942, only five arrived. Convoy JW 51B sailed for Russia in December and was attacked by the *Hipper* and other German capital ships. But the *Hipper* was badly damaged in a fight with heavy British ships and the German attempt to stop the convoy proved fruitless. When the *Hipper* pulled into port, damaged and with little to show, Hitler was furious and demanded the abandonment of the major capital ships as an enormous waste of money. On this issue Admiral Raeder resigned and Admiral Doenitz was appointed commander in chief of the German navy. But if anyone thought that the appointment meant the scrapping of the battleships and a corresponding increase in the building U-boats he was wrong. Doenitz was a Junker, a Prussian officer first and a U-boat man second. When he took over the German navy, he took personal responsibility for every part of it, and instead of gaining a commander in chief with inordinate political influence, the U-boat commander instead lost part of its admiral's attention to the greater cause. The U-boat menace might have grown worse in 1943 if Admiral Carls, Hitler's second choice for commander in chief, had been appointed instead of Doenitz.

What was to be done in Britain to aid the Russians was another matter of concern. Whatever had to be done was going to demand the use of Britain's slender escort forces, an unwelcome idea in London in January, 1943.

On January 5 the war cabinet met to discuss the problem. Churchill considered the issue so important that he put himself in charge of the meeting. Some difficult decisions had to be made, and the United States was not being helpful in offering convoy assistance. These points were made in the presence of special ambassador Averill Harriman, and much of the discussion was really stage-managed for the benefit of the Americans. A convoy of twenty ships would be run on January 17, and a second thirty ships would be run on February 11. Another convoy of thirty ships would be run in the second week of March. There would be a fleet carrier plus an escort carrier, twenty-five destroyers, corvettes, and trawlers for each convoy. Only thus could the convoy survive against the heavy infestation of U-boats that Doenitz could mass in the north. This was, the Home Fleet noted, the equivalent of a destroyer striking force, and the effect on the overall British defenses was prodigious. If the United States was not going to help convoy these ships to Russia, then the cycle of convoys was going to have to open to at least thirty-six days, and the British might not be able to manage even that. This was given enormous importance in the London and Washington meetings, since the Russians were clamoring for assistance and a second front.

All very well, said Churchill, but Britain's first responsibility was at home. If the Americans would not help and destroyer losses continued high, then the convoy situation would have to be reassessed. Such was the edginess of the Churchill government, moving into this new and fateful year of the war at sea.

26

The Jaws of Victory

March, 1943, began for Admiral Doenitz with the successes his U-boats had enjoyed in the "happy times" of the past. Looking back, he could see as well as the British war cabinet that 64 percent of the sinkings of Allied ships in the past three months had occurred while in convoy. So much, then, for the vaunted British claim that the convoy was the answer to shipping losses.

With British need to increase their depleted imports, the number of ships sailing in a single convoy was augmented to as many as eighty. The Admiralty did not like it a bit: it was asking for trouble. The war cabinet had high hopes from a greatly increased campaign of bombing of the U-boat yards and the U-boat bases—no one yet realized that bombing U-boat pens was useless. The Germans certainly weren't going to tell them to stop wasting their bombs. The British now had twenty long range aircraft that covered the eastern side of the Atlantic as far as Iceland. The Americans should have had a lot more covering their side of the Atlantic—they certainly had the resources. But the Americans, overwhelmed by the demands of the bombing squadrons in Europe and the air forces in the Far East, had no long range air cover at all on their side. So there was still an air gap on the American side. With the cessation of Doenitz's Operation Paukenschlag in the spring of 1942, the Americans believed they had beaten the U-boats. And with a major offensive in progress in the South Pacific Navy and a new offensive in the Central Pacific to begin in the fall, the American attention to the Atlantic was lagging.

The first indication of what was in store began when the Lorient command post detailed two U-boat wolf packs to catch Convoy SC 121, bound eastward from America, laden with war materials for Britain. This was one of the last of the northern convoys in which the Americans would participate, and the commander of the escort group was the captain of the U.S.S. *Spencer*. As seemed normal in this period, the Germans knew SC 121 was coming. The trouble began at 2 A.M. on March 7 when *U-230* sank the 3,000-ton steamer *Egyptian*. Two more ships were lost that day. The worst problem was that the escorts did not know where the convoy was: the terrible weather had caused a number of ships to straggle, which meant easy prey for the enemy. The *Empire Impala*, the *Guido*, the *Fort Lamy*, the *Vovjoda Putnik*, the *Empire Lakeland*, the *Leadgate*, the *Lange*, all stragglers, all buffeted by the storm, were all sunk by U-boats outside the range of any effective help. By March 12 sixteen ships were missing from the convoy. The storm was so fierce that the escorts' detecting devices malfunctioned. Several ships suffered breakdowns in the gale, and even radio communication was unreliable. The Germans faced the same problem, of course, but with perhaps twenty submarines hounding the convoy, their chances of hitting were excellent. Eight ships were sunk by the evening of March 8, all of them stragglers. The attack on the convoy proper began on March 9 and when it came, the escorts were unready. U.S.S. *Greer*, the Huffduff ship, discovered its direction finding apparatus was out of order. One escort was lost and much radio time was spent bringing her back to the fold. H.M.C.S. *Rosthern* discovered a contact on the starboard beam of the convoy and expended forty-four depth charges to bring up a piece of wood from a wreck. Then on the night of March 9 the U-boats closed in. Five boats took six more ships, making fourteen lost ships in all. At the same time one single U-boat in the South Atlantic found Convoy BT 6, bound from Bahia to Trinidad, and sank three and damaged five ships. Convoy KG 123, bound from Key West to Guantanamo, lost two ships.

The sailing of Convoy HX 228, which left the North American coast on March 1, marked a new development: the first of the U.S. escort carriers, U.S.S. *Bogue*, sailed with it. She had an escort of two destroyers of her own, and was stationed right in the middle of the convoy, between the fifth and sixth columns, except when landing and launching planes, when she had to head into the wind and moved away from the convoy.

The convoy moved along for nine days before it was pinpointed: 300 miles at sea in the western Atlantic, in the precise area where the Neuland wolf pack was operating. The convoy was bound to run straight into the arms of the enemy. But Doenitz outguessed himself; he figured the convoy would change course to avoid the Neuland group and head north, so he ordered the wolf pack north. In fact the convoy remained on course, and most of the wolf pack passed it by and got out of position for an attack. No U-boats were sighted until March 10, when a plane from the *Bogue* found one; but the aircraft's depth charges jammed in the racks and the plane was slow to report so the U-boat got away. It was another step in the learning process.

The first attack on Convoy HX 228 came at twilight on March 29, delivered by one of the boats with the longest way to go. The *U-221* fired at three ships, sank two and damaged one. H.M.S. *Harvester* came up and carried out an attack on an asdic contact with fourteen charges. Then the *Harvester* lost contact with the U-boat, but instead of dropping the attack, Commander A. A. Tait adopted baiting tactics. He withdrew about six miles, then turned his ship to make another attack. When that proved unsuccessful, he moved to rejoin the convoy.

While all this was happening, another U-boat was stalking the convoy. Lieutenant Albert Langfeld was on his first war cruise as a captain and was eager to do well. Since dusk he had been trailing the convoy and had an American freighter in view, the *William M. Gorgas*. He was preparing to fire torpedoes when the *Harvester* appeared on the scene and the U-boat lookouts shouted. The destroyer was only 500 yards away. Langfeld fired his torpedoes but his aim was shaky and he merely damaged the *William M. Gorgas*. Then he dived. As the boat went down, Langfeld turned to the radio operator, who was ahead of him in the conning tower. "Herr Funkmaat, you might as well make your will," he said. Then the depth charges were on them. They were set to explode at 100 feet, but the boat had already reached 120 feet. The damage was serious and the boat began to take water. One by one pieces of equipment began to break down; the bilge pumps began to fail and the lights went out. Morale was high in the beginning but after an hour it began to suffer. Langfeld decided to surface and see about fighting it out. He came up and put on the Diesel engines. The boat began to run, but the *Harvester* was right after her and chased, shooting and finally ramming the *U-444*. The U-boat hung up on the stern of the destroyer and was dragged, with only the conning tower above water. Finally it broke loose. There were many survivors in the water, but the *Harvester* was more concerned with the damage the ship had suffered in the ramming, so only one man was picked up.

Harvester's propeller shaft was gone and she could only make eleven knots. Then the other shaft broke down and she went dead in the water. She was wallowing abaft the convoy when she was sighted simultaneously by the Free French escort *Aconit* and the *U-432*. The *Aconit* came boiling down to help, and the *U-432* hurried up to damage. The U-boat got there first and torpedoed the *Harvester*. She sank with heavy loss of life, including Commander Tait. The *Aconit* then depth charged the *U-432*, forced her to the surface and rammed her back down into the sea to sink. Convoy HX 228 then reached port, with six ships lost. The losses were hard to take, but there was one positive outcome: thereafter escorts were forbidden to ram submarines.

Convoy OS 44, United Kingdom to Freetown, lost 4 ships on March 13. Convoy GAT 49, Guantanamo to Trinidad, lost 2 ships on March 13. Convoy UGS 6 from the United States to Gibraltar lost 4 ships between March 13 and March 16. Then came the greatest convoy battle of the Atlantic war, three days and nights of unremitting fighting, involving two large convoys, HX 229 and SC 122. The two convoys (including HX 229A, an element of HX 229) comprised 141 ships. Their combined displacement was 860,000 tons and they carried 920,000 tons of cargo including meat, locomotives, ammunition, and invasion barges. Ten thousand men were aboard these ships.

On March 5, part of Convoy SC 122, fifty merchant ships with four escorts, sailed from New York at seven knots. The weather was foul and on the first night the ships scattered. In the morning eleven ships were missing, two had returned to New York, six put in at Halifax and three sailed after the convoy. Only two caught up.

Three days after SC 122 left New York, the forty ships of HX 229 also sailed, and on March 9, the twenty-seven ships of HX 122A sailed. Both of these convoys were lucky to miss the storm that dispersed Convoy SC 122, but they hit fog and snow. These two convoys lost three ships due to attrition, but all made it back to port.

All three convoys turned northeast toward Newfoundland, passed 150 miles east of Cape Cod, then passed by Cape Sable in Nova Scotia. The slow convoy, SC 122, was still making seven knots. The two fast convoys were making nine to ten knots and gradually overtook the other. Off Nova Scotia thirteen merchant ships and the rescue ship *Zamalek* joined up with SC-122 (the other two convoys had no rescue ship) along with another escort, making five in all for the convoy. Messages were sent from various points and B-Dienst intercepted; as the convoys moved out, the Germans knew they were coming. On March 10 Doenitz had seventy submarines within striking distance, plus two tankers to refuel his U-boats. The convoys were about to get their ocean escorts: three of the new groups formed under Admiral Horton. B5 group was under British Commander Richard C. Boyle in H.M.S. *Havelock*, with one other destroyer, one frigate, and five corvettes. B4 group would take over protection of HX 229. It consisted of Commander C. C. L. Day's H.M.S. *Highlander*, the old four-stack destroyer *Beverley*, and four corvettes. Convoy HX 229A would be guarded by the Fortieth Escort Group, based at Londonderry. The group under

Commander John S. Dallison consisted of three 900-ton sloops, two large U.S. Coast Guard cutters (of the ten given the British), and two frigates. Thus, to face seventy submarines, the Allies had twenty-one escorts. Three more were then added to the B4 group, making a total of twenty-four.

On the evening of March 12, U-boat command began sending out orders to the boats at sea to begin attacking HX 229. They were to form two skirmish lines sweeping west to find the convoy. More boats were coming out from Germany and France to replace those which had used up their torpedoes against SC 121 and HX 228. The skirmish lines were named *Stuermer* and *Draenger* (stormer and harrier). Another section of fourteen U-boats, *Gruppe Raubgraf* (robber baron), guarded the narrows between Greenland and Newfoundland. Thus it was apparent that Doenitz was putting his whole U-boat force in the Atlantic against Convoy HX 229, and he had the position, the course, and the speed.

The three convoys were lucky in one way: two other convoys were at sea moving across the Atlantic, ON 170 and ON 172, and *Gruppe Raubgraf* got itself involved intercepting ON 170 and thus was out of position to intercept the eastbound convoys when they came. But forty-two U-boats would become involved against the convoys. Thirty-seven were Type VIII C, five were the newer Type IX C. Almost all of the U-boats were less than a year old, and fifteen were on their first patrols.

On March 15 two ships dropped out of SC 122 in a gale: the Icelandic merchantman *Selfoss* and the British trawler H.M.S. *Campobello*. The merchant ships then sailed straight through the concentration of U-boats to reach Iceland safely. The *Campobello* had earlier been strained when caught in the ice. She was taking water, her crew had abandoned ship and she was sunk with one of her own depth charges.

The storm that day and night was ferocious, with heavy seas pooping some of the ships and huge stern waves rolling up from behind to break across the decks. The Liberty ship *Walter Q. Gresham* lost a lifeboat, torn off the deck by a wave.

On March 15 Lieutenant Gerhard Feiler's *U-653* was re-

leased from further patrol duty with *Gruppe Raubgraf;* she had
only one defective torpedo left, she was low on fuel, was having trouble with her engines, an officer and four men had been
washed off the bridge in a storm and lost, and another man was
sick. That was what it took in the winter of 1943 to get released
from U-boat patrol with even one torpedo left. She was homeward bound to Brest, traveling on the surface at 3 A.M. on March
16, when the bridge watch caught a light directly ahead. It was
a sailor aboard one of the ships of HX 229, out on deck, lighting
a cigarette. The bridge watch called the captain and he could
see they were right in the middle of a convoy, with twenty
ships around them. Feiler sent a high-speed transmission to U-
boat headquarters, took the boat down and dropped back to
shadow the convoy. At U-boat headquarters a pin was stuck in
the chart of the grid system at position BC 1491. That is where
HX 229 was early on the morning of March 16, traveling a
course of seventy degrees.

The U-boats lined up, the two attack groups on the east and
the *Raubgraf* group on the west, and prepared to attack the
convoys. Their attention at the moment was occupied by the
convoy in the western air gap, which was being shadowed by
U-653. Ten boats were detailed to attack and eleven boats were
ordered to make speed to the west, to be ready to attack on the
morning of March 17. One boat short of torpedoes was sent off
to the south of Greenland to give weather reports twice a day.
(A move that indicated one of the Germans' serious problems:
the occupation of Iceland and Greenland by the Allies had
deprived the Germans of weather stations formerly maintained
by the Danes. Since Atlantic weather flows from west to east,
this had already proved to be a serious difficulty.)

Within an hour after *U-653* had made its sighting report,
twenty-one U-boats were on the hunt with the position, course,
and speed in hand. By nightfall forty U-boats were moving to
operate against the convoys. Thirteeen more were either taking
supply from the "milch cows" or were heading out from German bases.

Convoy HX 229 got the word from the Admiralty early on

March 16 that it had been found by the enemy and was being shadowed. An hour later, *U-758* discovered the convoy and reported. Another hour passed and a third U-boat found the convoy. Forty minutes later the fourth boat came up. An hour after that the *U-91* sighted several stragglers.

At noon, on the advice of the convoy commander Lieutenant Commander G. J. Luther, the convoy made a course turn of ninety degrees to starboard. So many U-boat signals had been picked up that there was no further need for radio silence. Six U-boats were now shadowing the convoy, but none had yet been sighted by the escorts. The *U-84*, the last to come up, tried to make a submerged attack on one of the stragglers but the sea was running too high. The destroyer *Mansfield*, which had dropped astern to try to find shadowers, speeded up to rejoin the convoy without being informed of the course change. She would not reach the convoy until midnight. The convoy was now deep inside the air gap. No aircraft support could be expected, because of the navy's refusal to listen to British pleas.

At 4 P.M. Commander Luther asked the commodore to bring the convoy back to its base course. The rule was that the commander could move the convoy twenty miles to either side of its base line, but no further. They were coming close to that, and it was time to move back.

Late that afternoon the *U-653* moved off, its place as official shadow taken by *U-615*. The *U-600* lost contact; there were now four boats in contact. But two hours later another three boats came up. It was now 6 P.M. and Doenitz was waiting for dark. The Admiralty sensed it and knew the situation of the convoy. Orders came to take a course of fifty-five degrees and hold it, running straight for England. The next day air cover would be available as the convoy moved out of the air gap. The problem was to get through the night. Lieutenant Commander Luther replied to the Admiralty with position, course, and speed, and the information that the escort now numbered five ships; the *Witherington* had been forced to drop out. For defense against three groups of U-boats which, to quote Admiral Doenitz, "now hurled themselves like wolves" against the con-

voy, Luther had his own destroyer, H.M.S. *Volunteer*, two an-
cient, wheezing coal burner destroyers inherited from the
Americans, and two slow corvettes. Seven U-boats were then in
contact with the convoy. U-boat headquarters sent out the signal: attack.

Lieutenant Hans-Joachim Bertelsmann in the *U-603* moved
his U-boat on the surface through the darkening night and
heavy seas toward the convoy. He and his lookouts were
strapped to the bridge railings and gun platform. In the darkness and spindrift the submarine edged its way between two
escorts and inside the screen on the starboard side of the convoy. The U-boat was not seen by any lookout in the ghastly
weather, nor was it picked up by the ships' radar. He fired four
torpedoes, one of which struck the *Elin K*, a Norwegian motorship, which went down quickly. The last ship in the column
was supposed to stop and pick up survivors, but did not. The
escorts moved out to sweep the area, but found no submarine.
The escort *Pennywort* then stopped and picked up survivors
from the *Elin K* and the convoy went on. Nothing happened for
an hour, then the *U-758* got in on the starboard side, where
there was no escort. The U-boat fired four torpedoes in rapid
succession. They struck the Dutch ship *Zaanland* and the
American liberty ship *James Oglethorpe*. The Dutch abandoned
ship with skill, the Americans panicked. The American captain
wanted to save his ship but his men began rushing for the boats.
One boat was cut away and fell into the sea, dumping its men.
About half the crew abandoned without orders. The captain
and the remainder stayed with the ship; its rudder had been
pushed hard over and she was running in circles.

On the port quarter of the convoy the *Anemone* came upon a
surfaced U-boat 3,000 yards away. The U-boat bridge watch
failed to see the corvette and the captain held fire with his deck
gun. Finally when the corvette was only 300 yards off, the U-
boat dived. The *Anemone* dropped a depth charge pattern of
five at 50 feet. The U-boat surfaced almost immediately, ran,
then dived. The *Anemone* attacked again, using her hedgehog.
Only four of the charges fired and none hit the U-boat. After

another attack the *Anemone* moved away, certain of a kill. But *U-89* was actually only slightly damaged and did not bother the convoy again.

Several more U-boats had now joined up and the *U-435* torpedoed the American liberty ship *William Eustis*. The captain had to admit to the escort that picked him up that he had not destroyed his confidential papers; the escort sank the ship (which had been abandoned prematurely) with depth charges.

For the next hour and a half the convoy was fortunate. All the escorts were out, either picking up survivors or attacking U-boats, and the convoy was unprotected. But four perfectly sound U-boats failed to attack. Admiral Doenitz was reaping the harvest of his rapid expansion program; some of his captains were not up to snuff.

But after midnight more aggressive captains arrived on the scene in the *U-228* and *U-616*. The freighter *Harry Luckenbach* was torpedoed and went down, with eighty men killed. Ten torpedoes had been fired at that same time, but no other ship was hit. Not long afterward the escort *Beverly* nearly took a torpedo but evaded.

At 3 A.M. the *U-600* got into the convoy and torpedoed three ships, the *Irenée duPont*, the *Nariva*, and the *Southern Princess*, all of which sank. By dawn, when the attacks on the convoy ended, the U-boats had torpedoed eight merchant ships, and not one U-boat had been lost.

* * *

That night, while searching for Convoy HX 229, the *U-338* came upon convoy SC 122, 120 miles north, and fired four torpedoes. Four merchant ships were hit and sunk.

By morning on March 17 the convoys were coming close to the area of operations of the Very Long Distance Aircraft in Iceland. Unfortunately, the weather was so foul that the aircraft canceled all flight operations. There was no help from that source. That same morning the *U-439* was trailing Convoy SC 122 on the surface—this was the air gap—when suddenly a Liberator caused the captain to order a crash dive. It was one of the Very Long Range Aircraft stationed at Aldergrove in England that had taken off eight hours earlier to join SC 122. The U-boat escaped the depth charge attack, but the captain spent the rest of the day submerged, shaken by the news that British aircraft were where they were not supposed to be.

The Liberator also frustrated attacks by two other U-boats. But in Convoy SC 122 the freighter *Granville* was sunk, as well as the *Coracero* and the *Terkolei*. The attacks continued through the night of March 19. The Germans had the convoy surrounded and, like a school of piranhas, rushed in to finish off the fatted calves. Dawn on the nineteenth brought help in the form of escorts steaming out from British bases. Coastal Command had seven squadrons, and a Flying Fortress flying through a squall found a surfaced U-boat inside and attacked, dropping four depth charges before the U-boat had a chance to dive. Thus perished *U-384*, the sole boat to be lost in this most successful of all U-boat attacks on North Atlantic convoys. Two more U-boats were damaged, and a dozen kept down that day by aircraft.

Back in Berlin, Doenitz was thrilled with the success of his U-boats in the multi-convoy attack and decreed that it would continue on the night of March 19. But the picture the U-boats saw that night was different: Convoy HX 229 now had eight escorts, SC 122 had eight escorts and air cover after dark which frightened away several U-boats. There were no sinkings. As dawn approached the convoys had come within easy air access from the British shore; Berlin called the operation off. All U-boats were ordered to break off and start searching the convoy paths for stragglers. That day the British air force was out in strength, and any U-boat that ventured its conning tower above the surface was a brave one. Several U-boats were damaged by air attack but none were actually sunk.

When it was all over, the British Admiralty realized the enormity of the disaster the first twenty days of March had produced. The U-boats had sunk 141,000 tons of shipping in three convoys, with the loss of only one submarine.

The British cabinet railed against the Americans for failing to provide air cover on their side of the Atlantic. Averill Harriman got a taste of it, which was passed on to President Roosevelt. The complaints reached home, and even a preoccupied Admiral King had to recognize the extent of the disaster and what it meant to the entire war effort if it were allowed to continue. Steps were taken to provide more escorts and long range aircraft. And the British were aroused to even stronger action. They would not sit by and see their convoys ravaged by the wolf packs.

In retrospect there was one bright moment in the first three weeks in March for those engaged in the war at sea. On March 3, in the middle of the Atlantic opposite the African bulge, Lieutenant Hans Joachim Schwantke in the *U-46* radioed back to Berlin that he had sunk a 5,000-ton British merchant vessel traveling alone. The ship was in fact the German blockade runner *Doggerbank*, which had made its way safely around the British Isles, only to come to disaster at the hands of one of its own. Except for that little light, the picture seemed very black indeed.

27

The Big Switch

The next move was presaged in a meeting on March 24 of the British war cabinet's Anti–U-Boat Warfare Committee. It began at 6 P.M. at Ten Downing Street. Present were the prime minister; the first lord of the Admiralty; the first sea lord, Admiral Pound; the commander in chief, Western Approaches, Admiral Horton; Air Marshal Harris of Bomber Command; Air Marshal Slessor of Coastal Command, the secretary of state for air; the chief of the air staff; the minister of air production; and several other lesser lights. Also present were Averill Harriman, representing President Roosevelt, and Admiral Harold Stark, representing Admiral King. It was Stark's baptismal meeting.

Churchill first went over the appalling losses from Convoys SC 122 and HX 228 without flinching. Then admiral Horton reported on war games he had concocted, using the convoys at sea as representative, and three groups of escort carriers with attendant destroyers. The implication was that the system would have solved the problem of the convoys. Horton said they ought to operate independently of the convoys but with them.

Admiral Pound demurred. At the moment there was only the *Bogue* group, with five destroyers, operating out of Argentia. The Canadians were replacing some convoy corvettes with minesweepers, then would have the corvettes to form another group on the western shore. In England, Pound hoped to have two escort carrier groups operating by April 20. But with the convoys or independently? Churchill wanted them with, Horton wanted them outside, Stark said that only time would tell. Pound agreed. That was how it was left.

The talk turned to aircraft. In their about-face the Americans now said they could increase the number of Liberators to be delivered in the next three months. The bottleneck now might be the speed with which crews could be trained. In that case fifteen or twenty Liberators could be given to the Canadians to strengthen coverage of the old air gap on the western side.

Air Marshal Slessor noted that since the new, powerful radar had been added to one squadron of his aircraft the result had been disappointing. But they would have to wait and see; seventy aircraft were operating, with fifteen sorties a day over the Bay of Biscay. The big question at the moment was the comparative value of maintaining the Bay of Biscay patrols as opposed to strengthening air convoy protection. Churchill favored the latter.

Air Marshal Harris reported on Bomber Command's efforts against the U-boat bases. Saint-Nazaire was to be bombed again as soon as weather permitted. (The results would be nil.) The U-boat yards at Bremen and Hamburg also would be bombed (much more productive).

The first lord of the Admiralty suggested the expansion of the escort building program in Britain. But Churchill reminded them that this could be done only at the expense of merchant ship building, which could not be slackened in view of the sinkings. Indeed the building of merchant ships should be increased. The result of the meeting was the expectation that the Americans could turn over more ships. Ten thousand British merchant seamen were then unemployed because there were no ships for them to sail. Harriman, the aircraft production minister, and the minister of war transport were asked to prepare a letter to President Roosevelt from Churchill, calling for transfer of more American merchant ships; then Britain could expend more resources to build new escorts.

One of the hallmarks of Churchill's committee was that no item was too small for the prime minister's attention. The meet-

ing considered the need for 7 × 50 binoculars. Most merchant
ships carried the inferior 6 × 60 type. Twenty-three hundred
pairs were needed to supply the merchantmen, said Admiral
Pound. All right, said Churchill, for the next two months 750
pairs of 7 × 50 binoculars would be allocated to merchant
ships; the rest would be made up from army supplies.

Admiral Horton brought up the need for a weapon to sink
surfaced U-boats too close to the escort for the guns to bear.
Ramming was unsatisfactory because of the damage to the escorts. A corvette, in particular, might sink itself ramming a U-
boat. The prime minister turned to Admiral Pound. The Admiralty would have a report ready on this problem with a
solution in a week.

The following week a new set of problems would be pre-
sented, many of them to be resolved by action.

*   *   *

During the next few weeks much was done to strengthen the
war against the U-boats and the results began to show. Soon
ninety more Liberators were given to Britain and fifteen diverted to the Canadians, strengthening the western air defense.
A hundred and six vessels had been fitted out with mesh torpedo nets which worked. More vessels would get them.

The anti–U-boat committee recommended a series of attacks
on the U-boat bases at La Pallice, Bordeaux, and Brest. Air
Marshal Harris did not like it. He had just done Saint-Nazaire
and Lorient, and he was beginning to suspect that attacking the
pens was nonproductive. Rather, he urged, attack the U-boat
building yards as he had also been doing. Agents had reported
that the bombing was hurting production.

But others wanted the U-boat bases bombed and Churchill
agreed that they must be bombed if only to keep the Germans
off balance. So it was; the instructions that came so effortlessly
out of these meetings had the force of urgent orders. What was
really needed, said the prime minister, was a cooperative effort
between the American and British air forces to expand the patrols of the Bay of Biscay to get at the submarines leaving and

returning from patrols; that meant day and night air patrols, something that would take many considerable resources from both air forces. Averill Harriman offered to take any requests straight to the Joint Chiefs of Staff in Washington—that was how swiftly the red tape was cut.

*   *   *

At the end of March Churchill made his strongest statement to date. They had to get at the U-boats in a hurry, and they had to destroy three of every ten that put to sea. That meant a new offensive in the Bay of Biscay.

Sir Archibald Sinclair, the secretary of state for air, de-murred. He said this could be done only by sacrificing the bombing of Germany. Stalin had been promised that the bomb-ing of Germany would be unremitting. Besides, if Coastal Com-mand were given the aircraft and began the raids, then the Germans would produce fighter cover to take out their sub-marines.

Before this argument was settled, nothing could be done, said Admiral Stark, and unless the U-boat menace was stopped "we should be in a bad way." He agreed that the Bay of Biscay patrols should be increased "to carry out an all-out offensive against the U-boats."

The trouble was that in April no one yet knew how effective the new ten centimeter radar might be. The committee had high hopes, but it was too early to tell.

Not quite, said Admiral Pound. Between March 20 and 28 Coastal Command had carried out a special anti–U-boat attack. Twenty-seven boats had been sighted, sixteen attacked. The results, of course, were not yet known. The number of aircraft for the Bay of Biscay had to be increased. There should be no argument.

But there was. The chief of the air staff did not want to give up aircraft to Coastal Command for anti–U-boat work. And that was the real rub. The U-boat killers wanted fifty-five of his bombers. The Americans would supposedly have a surplus of planes in three months. Put the responsibility on them.

Churchill, despite his hatred of the U-boats, more or less took the RAF's side. The results of the Coastal Command experiment were inconclusive. Wait a while, said the prime minister.

The question of aircraft was put "over on the Americans." Admiral King turned the British down flat, but President Roosevelt intervened and agreed to give the British 135 Liberators from the United States.

At the anti–U-boat meeting on April 14, matters came to a head. The Americans had begun bombing the U-boat construction yards. Photographs taken after a raid at Vegesack showed that of fifteen U-boat hulls on the slips, seven were badly damaged, and six others seemed to have suffered some damage. The prime minister was delighted, and asked Admiral Stark to convey his congratulations to General Ira Eaker of the USAAF.

There was more good news. British figures indicated fourteen to sixteen U-boat sinkings in March, higher than expected. Admiral Horton had good news too: the U-boats had ganged up on Convoy HX 231 between March 30 and April 6. Of the sixty-one ships in the convoy, only three were lost. There were still four stragglers to be accounted for, but . . . good news indeed, and it could be laid to the feats of the new system: a trained escort group, working with a trained attack group, supported by aircraft. (It *was* good news, but not quite as good as Admiral Horton indicated. The four stragglers were all lost, making seven lost altogether, but still an improvement over the first twenty days of March.)

The Very Long Range Aircraft were now arriving. The United States would provide 135, the British 105 and the Canadians 15. The number of escorts would be increased; the Americans would provide more merchant ships and Britain would increase its escort production from 185 new vessels to 205 by the end of 1944.

By the middle of April desperate circumstances had altered the cooperation between America and Britain in the right direction and there was an immediate effect on the U-boat war. U-boats sank ninety-five merchant ships in March, but sixteen U-boats were sunk. U-boat sinkings for April were forty-seven ships with seventeen U-boats sunk. U-boat sinkings of merchantmen for May were forty-five ships—totalling less than 250,000 tons—but forty-seven U-boats sunk. In May, for the first time, more U-boats were lost than Allied merchant ships.

The support groups indeed were a part of the answer to the U-boats as the convoy records showed. Convoy ONS 6 sailed April 30, escorted by Escort Group B6, consisting of eight escorts and two rescue ships. U-boats came in contact at 9 A.M. on May 6. By 9 P.M. ten U-boat sightings had been made. The escorts darted to and fro, air cover was continuous and the convoy frequently changed course. The U-boats got lost. Two days later the U-boats tried to close the convoy again. The escort *Viscount* delivered a hedgehog attack on one U-boat and there were no attacks. Icebergs were more of a problem that night than U-boats. At 7 A.M. on May 9 the escort was joined by the Fourth Escort Group and no ships were attacked all the way across.

*   *   *

Convoy HX 237 sailed on May 6. The two escort groups numbered about fifteen warships. Nine stragglers were reported; two went back to America, four joined the convoy and three went on alone and were torpedoed. The British merchant carrier *Biter* joined up and provided air patrols. Several U-boats were sighted on May 8 and May 9 and Swordfish aircraft from *Biter* sank one U-boat on May 12. A Liberator sank another U-boat. The escorts *Broadway* and *Lagan* sank another U-boat with hedgehog attacks. At dawn on May 13 a Sunderland flying boat attacked a U-boat ten miles off the starboard side of the convoy, and the escorts *Lagan* and *Drumheller* finished it off with hedgehog attacks. *Biter*'s aircraft attacked another U-boat that day. Three days later the convoy arrived safely in the United Kingdom. Score: at least four U-boats sunk, one probable, three straggler merchantmen lost, four aircraft lost.

Convoy SAC 129 met her nine-ship escort on May 6. The first contact with the enemy came on May 11 when a U-boat found the convoy and reported to Doenitz. At 6 P.M. on May 11 two ships were torpedoed and sank. All escorts attacked although the senior officer said the U-boat attack had been made from long distance, outside the screen. The convoy altered course and no submarine contacts were made.

* * *

On May 7 Convoy ONS 7 sailed with eight escorts. Five days later the usual U-boat shadow appeared. Two escorts attacked and drove the U-boat away. The convoy changed course and lost the shadow. On May 14 the convoy commander had word of several U-boats in the south of the convoy. The convoy changed course and a Liberator attacked and may have sunk one U-boat.

After midnight on May 17 the steamer *Aymeric* took two torpedoes and blew up. Escorts attacked a contact on the port quarter with hedgehogs and sank the U-boat. No more U-boats appeared. Again icebergs were more trouble than U-boats.

* * *

Convoy ON 184 moved across the Atlantic with eight escorts and then picked up the U.S.S. *Bogue* and her five destroyers. The escort carrier moved inside the convoy. Bad weather prevented flights for two days and U-boats shadowed the convoy. But on May 21 the *Bogue* launched her planes and they began sighting and driving the U-boats under. On May 22 the planes found five U-boats and made four attacks, the last after picking up a Huffduff bearing astern of the convoy. The last attack brought up a U-boat which surrendered before it sank and H.M.C.S. *Saint Laurent* picked up twenty-five survivors. The convoy was then unmolested the rest of the way across.

* * *

Convoy HX 239 crossed the Atlantic with nine escorts for two days and then picked up another five, including the escort carrier *Archer*. A Swordfish from the *Archer* attacked a U-boat twenty miles ahead of the convoy. Within twenty-four hours other aircraft attacked four more U-boats and the last one was sunk.

* * *

The results of Convoy HX 239 were the clincher for Admiral Doenitz. Two months of decreasing results had followed after the assault of early March. The British combination of increased ocean escort, operating in conjunction with the "support groups" and escort carriers and long range aircraft were too much to bear. Each day had brought Doenitz additional discouraging information, such as the new radar's effectiveness, the potent hedgehog attacks. By May 22 Doenitz had already lost thirty-one U-boats in three weeks, almost as many as he had lost in the *entire years of 1939 and 1940*. On May 24 Doenitz recalled his U-boats from the North Atlantic. He had lost the battle he had been so confident of winning only ten weeks earlier.

In the halcyon years, when the U-boats had been frustrated in one area, they had moved around until a new weak spot was found. But in June, 1943, the weak spots had suddenly all been strengthened. The U-boats moved to the Arctic, the Southwest Approaches, the Western Atlantic, the Azores, the Freetown run, the South Atlantic, and the Indian Ocean. By the end of June, ninety-two U-boats were in operation over this vast area, but their sinking reports were dismal. The merchant tonnage lost in June was 101,000 tons, the best record for the Allies since November, 1941. The new tonnage produced that month was nearly 900,000 tons. And to make it worse for the Germans, even with fewer attacks the U-boat force still lost a dozen boats.

After all the storm and strife over Coastal Command, in the summer of 1943 the real needs were beginning to be met: between March 20 and April 6 sixty-six boats crossed the Bay of Biscay, Coastal Command sank two, surprising both with the Leigh light. Doenitz's answer was to order all U-boats submerged while crossing the bay. Thus they had to surface by day to charge their batteries. In the first week of May the British airmen sighted seventy-one submarines, attacked forty-three, sank three and damaged three others.

By midsummer more planes and new weapons were available, including a thirty-five pound depth bomb, which could be dropped easily at low level. This started a pattern of attack on the U-boats. Another development was the sonic radio buoy, developed by the Americans, which, when dropped, sent off a signal that guided aircraft to the precise point where a U-boat had dived.

In July Admiral Pound told the anti–U-boat committee that the number of Atlantic escorts had been decreased to six, because of lack of interest by the U-boats. Prime Minister Churchill warned that the British should not yet believe they had conquered the U-boat threat, that they had to be eternally vigilant and constantly improve their methods of attack. "Although encouraged by the growing success of our methods," he said, "we must redouble our efforts and our ingenuity."

But it was hard to feel gloomy when in June the committee reported a net gain of 1,119,000 tons of shipping over losses. In July, thirty-seven U-boats were sunk and thirty more damaged, eighteen in the approaches to the Bay of Biscay, sixteen by aircraft without any help from surface forces. The war against the U-boats had been revolutionized again.

28

The Aggressive Convoys

By autumn 1943, the British convoy system was in better shape than it had ever been, with plenty of escorts, plenty of long-range air cover, and plenty of escort carriers available. The British had or were soon to have eighteen escort carriers called MAC, which were converted grain ships and tankers, with the additional duty of carrying grain and fuel. On her first voyage, for example, the H.M.S. *Empire MacAlpine* protected a convoy and also delivered 7,339 tons of grain.

Virtually all vessels now had radar, even the merchantmen which were sometimes independently routed. Radar meant protection, virtually no sea lane was without air coverage, and forewarned was forearmed; and statistically the British could show that a merchantman knowing the whereabouts of a U-boat had a better than 50 percent chance of avoiding it altogether.

There were still fierce convoy battles, and in September Doenitz made a new attempt to destroy the North Atlantic convoy system. The U-boat men went out with new instructions: work in pairs. It was a risky concept, but the U-boat men followed their leader. They were to discover that the British convoy system had improved considerably since March.

* * *

Convoy ONS 18 sailed from Liverpool on September 13, bound for North America, twenty-seven ships in eight columns with ten escorts. These included the Escort Group B3 (five

ships), three French escorts, the MAC ship *Empire MacAlpine*
with its aircraft, and the rescue ship *Rathlin*.

Bad weather on September 15 and 16 kept the *Empire
MacAlpine* planes from flying, but the weather cleared on the
seventeenth and flight operations began. That day, the escorts
Keppel and *Escapade* fueled from the tanker *Beaconstreet*
while at sea; this was another development which had enormously increased the range of the corvettes, sloops, and frigates.

On the evening of September 18 the convoy changed course
to avoid a concentration of U-boats ahead. The convoy commander requested help, and the Ninth Support Group, which
had been covering Convoy HX 256, was told to move down and
join ONS 18. The following morning, too, air cover arrived from
Iceland in the form of three Liberators. During the afternoon,
Huffduff interceptions indicated that a concentration of U-
boats was moving in on the convoy. The convoy commander
instructed the Ninth Support Group to join up by a circuitous
route in order not to lead the enemy to the convoy. During the
afternoon, bearings began pouring in, and the H.M.S. *Escapade*,
on the convoy's starboard beam, investigated one close
transmission, but found nothing. Convoy HX 256 was also
routed to join up for mutual protection, thus doubling the number of ships and escorts. At 9:30 P.M., two U-boats tried to attack
the convoy. The *Escapade* made a quick attack on the first and
drove it down, then went after the second with its hedgehog
thrower. The battle was joined.

In a series of attacks by fifteen U-boats over five days on the
combined convoys, only three times did the Germans get in
close enough to the convoy to fire torpedoes. They managed to
sink six merchant ships and damage two more, and also sank
three and damaged four escorts, although they attacked at least
four more. The cost to Doenitz was two submarines sunk and
several damaged. The new onslaught against the Atlantic convoys was not a roaring success.

In October Doenitz had eighty U-boats out, thirty-five in the
Northwestern Approaches; air attacks took a heavy toll on

them. Several convoys passed through the area virtually unmolested. The total shipping loss was 69,000 tons, the lowest since November, 1941. Doenitz lost fifteen U-boats in this abortive attempt to bring back the happy days.

In November Doenitz again changed tactics. The U-boats were instructed to remain submerged by day to avoid air attack. As the British U-boat watchers noted, "Ubiquity of air cover, now that we have flying facilities in the Azores, has compelled the adoption by the U-boats of a mode of existence which favors their survival rather than their effective employment against shipping." After the first week, there was no U-boat activity at all in the Northwestern Approaches and little in the entire Atlantic. Another dozen U-boats were sunk and more damaged. In this month more U-boats were sunk than merchantmen. In December half a merchant ship was sunk in the North Atlantic—that is, the ship was torpedoed on December 31 and while struggling toward Iceland was torpedoed again on January 3, 1944, and sank. But that was all. The other eleven sinkings were scattered around the world, with the greatest success accomplished by the *U-515* and *U-516* off the West African coast. *U-515* sank three ships and *U-516* sank two. It was a long memory that could recall Otto Kretschmer's exploits of eight and ten ships on a patrol. The sinking tonnage rose a little, to 87,000 tons. Kretschmer once nearly sank that much shipping by himself in a couple of weeks. The British were now complaining about the "nuisance value" of the German activity in the North Atlantic, which tended to "force convoy routes to the westward with a resultant strain on escorts through increased sea time and reduced layover."

Admiral Doenitz remained indefatigable. At a conference of admirals on December 17 he spoke frankly of the heavy U-boat losses, but then promised a new navy, larger and stronger than anything the Germans or the world had ever seen. What Doenitz was talking about were the new Type XXI, XXIII, and XXVII U-boats. The Type XXI were already in production, with a target of 350 boats by 1945. Indeed they were something new: 1,600 tons, with a submerged speed of sixteen knots; an endur-

ance of ninety days; six forward firing torpedo tubes and a
capacity for fourteen extra torpedoes. Possessed of the new
schnorkel, or underwater breathing device, these U-boats need
never surface, which was a direct answer to the air threat posed
by the British. The schnorkel need be used only a few hours a
day to recharge the batteries and clear the air in the boat. Also,
the German radio technicians had developed the new Kurier
transmission method by which an entire message could be
cleared in a third of a second. This was supposed to make the
Huffduff useless. But all this had not happened yet. The first
Type XXI U-boat was not supposed to be delivered until October, 1944. For the moment, Doenitz had to make do with what
he had at hand, as he had done in the beginning. And at this
time, he was not doing so very well. A member of the Admiralty secret antisubmarine war staff went on leave during
December, 1943, and happened to run into an old friend who
asked him how the war was going. Since the officer was exceed-
ingly security conscious, he gave a noncommittal reply. "You
need not be so discreet," said his friend. "I can tell you how the
war at sea is going. My business is to assemble machines sent
over in parts from the States. At the beginning of the year I was
practically stopped; since early summer I've been like a man
caught in a flood."

These were words Admiral Doenitz could least bear to hear.

29

Doenitz Contracts

The U-boat operational force never again reached the height of March, 1943. About seventy boats were out, two thirds of them concentrated in the Atlantic. Their sinkings were minimal, in terms of Britain's ability to feed and supply herself. In January, only two merchant ships were sunk in the north Atlantic by submarine. The U-boats made more attacks on warships than against merchant ships; the warships and aircraft kept them away from the convoys. Virtually all the torpedoes fired that month were Gnats, and even these with all their fearsome homing device, were not successful. The U-boats attacked twelve escorts, sank one and damaged two others. As against that performance—submarines sinking thirteen ships in all theaters with 92,000 tons total—Doenitz lost fifteen U-boats. Another powerful sign of the war against the U-boats was the nature of the forces that sank the enemy submarines. They were as much American as Canadian and British, as much air as sea escorts. The Americans operated well in the area east of the Azores. The U.S. carrier *Block Island* sank one U-boat on January 11, encountered three more on January 14 and attacked them. That day she picked up forty-three survivors of one of the victims of the Leigh light on a Wellington which had caught a U-boat on the surface of the night before. On January 16 the U.S. carrier *Guadalcanal* reported sinking a U-boat northwest of Flores.

So it went. The Germans put more boats up north against the Russian convoys. On January 25 half a dozen submarines attacked Convoy JW 56A with twelve escorts. The attack began 200 miles northeast of North Cape and continued for two days. The Germans used a new technique, attacking from the bow onto the convoy, which gave a small silhouette and in the heavy seas prevented the radar from being very effective. They sank three merchantmen and damaged the escort *Obdurate* with a Gnat torpedo. On the twenty-seventh British and Russian destroyers joined the defense forces and the U-boat backed off.

By February the U-boat watchers of London were concentrating their attention on attacks in the Indian Ocean and off the coast of Africa. There was virtually no action in the North Atlantic; no pack appeared anywhere. The Allies were looking for a buildup of the U-boat force to meet the expected invasion of the continent. But in February there was no such sign. The total tonnage of merchant ships sunk was again 92,000, and even Radio Berlin with its propensity for wild exaggeration claimed only 144,000 tons sunk by submarines that month. In the North Atlantic only 12,000 tons were lost. The month marked one of the great events of the war against the U-boats: Captain John Walker's Second Support Group sank six U-boats between January 29 and February 24. Walker had become the supreme U-boat killer of Britain since his return to sea in H.M.S. *Starling*. He had hunted *U-202* for fourteen hours before finally sinking her. He had destroyed two U-boats in one morning in June and for this he had been knighted; later in the summer his force had combined with aircraft to destroy a small wolf pack of three U-boats and his group had sunk another handful of U-boats before the January–February triumph. By this time Walker had become a symbol of Britain's defiant success against the U-boat, and when his group put in to shore after that patrol, they were greeted by a band, the first lord of the Admiralty, Mr. Alexander, and Admiral Max Horton, both of whom had come to make speeches. These were duly recorded by the British press, and Captain Walker was the lion of the hour. Captain Walker was awarded a third bar to his Distinguished Service Order and given two years' seniority on his road to flag rank. Such a departure from the usual low key of British naval tradition was an indication of the value Churchill put on the efforts of these men to wipe out the U-boats.

In March, although the sinkings went up, most of the increase was due to activity in the Indian Ocean. The Germans were then operating six submarines out of Penang; they sank twelve ships, or 75,000 tons. In the North Atlantic seven ships were lost. Seven ships—that was what Doenitz used to expect out of a single convoy. But in March, despite a concentration of a dozen submarines against an outward bound convoy to Russia, not a single mechantman was lost, and the escort and aircraft sank five U-boats and damaged a number of others. Captain Walker was there again and his *Starling* got one U-boat and damaged several others.

When you are winning, the problem is to keep from slacking off, and this difficulty troubled the British in the spring of 1944: it was getting too easy. In March, when the total sinkings went up to twenty ships, or 130,000 tons, the Admiralty warned ". . . a timely reminder that the battle of the Atlantic is not over." Then convoy RA 57 from Archangel was attacked by U-boats, and aircraft of the Fleet Air Arm sank three U-boats. They could be permitted a small feeling of confidence. And what could the Admiralty say to the navy when in April shipping losses dropped to the lowest point in four years, with twice as many U-boats as merchant ships sunk? The British and American escort carriers were making all the difference, particularly in operations with the escorts, which were properly nicknamed "hunter-killer groups"; the aircraft hunted and the escorts killed, although often the aircraft did the killing themselves. H.M.S. *Biter* was out in the Bay of Biscay in April, patrolling with the seventh and ninth Escort Groups. The weather was foul and flying was reduced to a minimum, yet on April 14 the *Biter*'s presence brought about the sinking of a U-boat.

The escort *Pelican* had just taken on fuel from the *Biter* when the escort *Swansea* on the starboard side of the screen obtained a contract. The *U-448* had been attracted by the presence of the escort carrier and hoped to have a shot at her. The

Swansea averted by making a swift depth charge attack on the
running submarine. After three depth chargings the *U-448* went
deep and began changing course. The two escorts stuck with
the boat, and a final depth charging brought her to the surface
and surrender. Even when the escort carriers could not operate,
their presence as decoys sometimes resulted in a submarine
kill.

The American escort carriers had a fine month in April.
Planes from the U.S.S. *Croaten* destroyed a U-boat 250 miles
south of Halifax. Between April 8 and 10 the U.S. *Guadalcanal*
and her escorts sank two U-boat, rescuing crew members from
each. On April 26 *Croaten*'s planes and the U.S.S. *Frost* and
U.S.S. *Huse* sank another U-boat west of the Cape Verde islands.

The U-boats were on the defensive and it remained that way
in May. The area of action shifted to the Trondheim region and
the Shetlands; four U-boats were sunk there. Listeners in London were puzzled in May by the enormous traffic in what had
to be meteorological reports. They were quite right; Doenitz
was responding to the demands of OKW, which was expecting
the Allied invasion of France. Since the elimination of the
weather stations in Greenland and Iceland the Germans found
it difficult to secure constant weather reports from the northwest territorys where the English Channel weather originated,
and thus half a dozen of Doenitz's boats were relegated to this
apparently mundane task. There was little aggressive activity
during the month in the Atlantic region. It was a period of
waiting.

Then came June 6 and the invasion of Normandy. The Allied authorities had been concerned about the potential effectiveness of Doenitz's U-boats against the invasion fleet; the
nightmare of burning transports piled up on the beaches. It
didn't happen. The U-boats were conspicuously absent. Not
until June 15 did U-boats make any aggressive moves; on that
day the H.M.S. *Mourne* and H.M.S. *Blackwood* were sunk by
Gnats fired from U-boats. One reason for the paucity of U-boat
activity had to be the Allied force around the Western Ap-

proaches: ten escort groups, totalling thirty-seven frigates, fourteen destroyers, and three sloops, supported by three escort carriers, and an English Channel alive with a thousand ships, covered day after day by hundreds of aircraft. There was another reason, however, why the U-boat force was so quiescent. Admiral Doenitz was at last bringing in his new submarines, and many of the older ones were being equipped with schnorkel gear, to permit them to operate for days without surfacing. In the English Channel several schnorkels were recognized that month, and an American aircraft secured a particularly satisfactory photograph of a schnorkel. Little wonder that Doenitz would stop and take pause: in June he lost twenty-five submarines to Allied planes and ships, in July, twenty-three U-boats were sunk against twenty-five ships lost. It was not the kind of war for which Doenitz was prepared. And it grew worse for the Germans. In August the Americans captured Brest, Lorient, La Pallice. Then they learned how ineffective the air operations had been against the U-boat pens; it was the towns that had been destroyed. But now the U-boat menace in the Bay of Biscay was a thing of the past. Two dozen U-boats made the last dangerous passage out of the bay, heading for Norwegian bases. Eleven other U-boats did not make it, sunk by Allied hunter-killer teams in the bay.

Faced with such adversity, Doenitz did not give up. The schnorkel boats could now deliver an entirely new method of attack. Half a dozen boats operating in the English Channel did an irritatingly high amount of damage to shipping. Irritating is the operating word here, for in all only 120,000 tons of shipping were lost, twenty-five ships. To achieve that result the Germans sacrificed thirty-six submarines, a number of them scuttled or scrapped at Toulon, Lorient and other bases.

August marked a new development in British antisubmarine warfare, the perfection and blooding of the "squid," a lightweight, forward-throwing depth charge device. The hedgehog had never been completely satisfactory. Its charges had a tendency to explode prematurely, to the woe of the attacking ship, or not at all, to the delight of the U-boat men. The

American mousetrap was not very satisfactory either. Further-more, after so much difficulty with ramming, Admiral Horton had asked for the creation of a weapon that could sink sub-marines close to the sides of the attacking vessel. The squid met all these requirements, and was doubly valuable now, since one of the new techniques of the U-boats was to come in close to an escort and then fire their Gnat torpedoes. The British had developed the new device, which met its first success in the Bay of Biscay by the Second Escort Support Group, Captain Walker's outfit. Walker, alas, had died of a heart attack after the Normandy invasion, as brave a man and as much a victim of the sea war as a Schepke, crushed in his own conning tower. But the escort group and its tradition lived on, and on August 1 the Starling and the frigate Loch Killin sighted a periscope in the Bay of Biscay. The Loch Killin's asdic then picked up a sub-marine passing down the ship's starboard side. She altered course and slowed to six knots. The submarine was only 600 yards away, 80 feet down, preparing to fire a gnat. The Loch Killin fired a pattern of six squid charges, then went full stern. The charges exploded and blew up the gnat. They also blew up the U-736, which came up abreast the bridge of the Loch Killin, and caught on the port side of the ship. The Loch Killin's Oerli-kon gunners began firing on the conning tower, but it was al-ready a twisted mass of wreckage. Survivors came pouring out and climbed onto the decks of the Loch Killin to surrender. The boat hung there for five minutes, then slipped off and down by the stern. The Loch Killin moved away quickly, in case the boat or its torpedoes blew up. The Starling dropped twenty depth charges for insurance.

The U-boats tried to operate in the English Channel during August. On August 4 the U-671 was twenty miles south of Beachy Head when she was detected by H.M.S. Stayner, which made an attack with depth charges and hedgehogs. She called for help and three other escorts came up at midnight. H.M.S. Wensleydale made a depth charge attack, and shortly afterwards found six men in the water, the only survivors.

Two days later, forty miles southeast of Saint Catherine's

Point, the *U-741* torpedoed a LST (Landing Ship Tank) in cross channel convoy. This was observed by a ship from another convoy, and H.M.S. *Orchis* rushed to the scene. The U-boat had gone to the bottom and stopped, to avoid attention, but the *Orchis* made contact with her asdic and dropped two patterns of depth charges. She then made two hedgehog attacks. Quantities of oil and debris came up, and finally two oil-soaked men emerged in a pool of fuel oil.

On August 20, off Beachy Head again, the *U-413* was discovered by H.M.S. *Forester* and two other escorts. They attacked with depth charges and hedgehogs, and after forty-five minutes one man surfaced. Although the U-boat was streaming oil, it was still moving and was attacked again. This time wooden wreckage and clothing came to the surface. Following the loss of the *U-413*, Doenitz pulled all his boats out of the English Channel.

Most of the boats moved to Norwegian bases, where Doenitz had ordered concrete U-boat pens built at Trondheim and Bergen. The Allies watched and on October 1 sent a massive bombing raid to plaster Bergen. A good deal of damage was done to the unfinished pens, but some were finished and considered safe. Several other air raids did more damage. The Germans had begun building the Type XXI and Type XXIII U-boat, and a number of these were destroyed.

That summer and fall Doentiz was hard at work restructuring his U-boat force. The idea was to replace the old Type VII and the newer Type IX C boats with still newer weapons. By October the Germans had completed about fifty of the new U-boats and were preparing the fleet for sea in Norwegian waters. The U-boat men had to learn how to take the fullest advantage of the schnorkel, particularly against shipping close inshore. For now they could creep almost into a harbor.

Because Doenitz's efforts were concentrated on the changeover, U-boat activity slipped almost to zero. In September, 1944, only 2 convoys were attacked by U-boats, 44,000 tons of shipping lost altogether. The Germans lost 21 U-boats that month. The next month only 1 ship was sunk by a submarine—

a Japanese submarine operating off San Francisco. The Germans lost 12 U-boats in October. But if these figures would seem discouraging to Admiral Doenitz, the situation was not quite so desperate as it looked. Doenitz then had a total of 400 U-boats in service, 141 operational, 260 undergoing training and trials. Despite the bombing and enemy activity, he was still receiving U-boats at the rate of 15 to 20 per month. True, he was losing far more, but by U-boat command standards that was to be expected during this transitional phase of the U-boat war.

30

Until the Bitter End

By the time winter set in around the North Atlantic and the North Sea, Admiral Doenitz was ready to launch a renewed attack against his enemies. The schnorkel and winter weather combined to make it a formidable one. The first stirrings came in November when, after a lull of months that had made many forget Admiral Pound's warning that the war was not yet won, U-boat activity picked up. Nine ships were sunk in November and another twenty-six in December, and the tonnage sunk climbed up over the 100,000 mark for the first time since August. The reason was the serious difficulty aircraft and escorts were having with the schnorkel. A boat underwater was not easily detected by radar.

By mid-December the anti–U-boat warfare committee was seriously concerned. Sir Andrew Cunningham, the new first sea lord, expounded on the subject of the U-boat war. Cunningham had succeeded to the post after Admiral Pound suffered a stroke late in the year and had been studying the problem since August. The new German techniques were proving effective. It was not yet the new U-boat war that Doenitz had promised a year earlier, yet the hunter-killer teams were not having success in finding schnorkel boats. Thus the kills were decreasing and the buildup of Doenitz's force was increasing. Doenitz's immediate aim was to interfere as much as possible with supplies crossing the channel to the continent and the U-boats were having some success here. They were working in so close to shore that one boat had run aground and foundered. The U-boats were not then attacking convoys in mid-Atlantic sea, but were working in closed water. At least 3 boats were known to be in the Gulf of Saint Lawrence, and at least 25 in North Atlantic and British waters, close to shore. A hundred and twenty boats were believed ready for operations, apart from the 40 working the Baltic and 150 in the Arctic harrying the Russians.

Two new types of U-boats were known to be ready for action, the Type XXI, and the small (250-ton) Type XXIII. The Type XXI was a giant boat, built in two levels, with a huge battery in the lower level. On one charging it could supply a submerged speed of five knots for four days, or sixteen knots for an hour. The schnorkeling was necessary only once every four days and the boat need never surface. It had a rubber skin, which deflected radar, and a new search receiver, on the principle of the tuned dipole, which reacted to the 10-centimeter waves of the British radar and warned the crew that the boat was in the beam. The acoustic torpedo was standard. The British escorts had learned to avoid the acoustic torpedoes by streaming energized paravanes, but these in turn virtually destroyed the effectiveness of their asdic. Now the Type XXI boats would have a new torpedo, the Lut. The old torpedoes had to be fired at an angle not more than ninety degrees from the target. The Lut could be fired from any point on the compass and could set its own course in a series of wide, sweeping turns that were almost impossible to track. A Type XXI boat could fire six of these torpedoes in one salvo, from as deep as 160 feet below the surface homing in on the target.

The antithesis of the big boat, the Type XXIII carried a crew of only seventeen men, but had the same capabilities on a miniature scale as the Type XXI. The Type XXIII was designed to work the waters in the British Isles, the Type XXI for long voyages overseas to the American shore.

The British expected to encounter them soon in battle. Forty Type XXI had been manufactured; twenty Type XXIII, and ninety Type XXI were being built as well as thirty-five Type XXIII. Admiral Cunningham declared that Doenitz was waiting until he had enough of these new U-boats to launch a really telling attack. That meant the Allies had about two months in which to prepare themselves for boats that could make at least fifteen knots underwater, that were fitted with radar almost as effective as British radar, and that had new and strengthened double hulls, with almost silent engines and redoubled underwater endurance. One U-boat was reported to have spent thirty days submerged.

Sir Sholto Douglas, commander of the Coastal Command, confirmed all the gloomy statements of Admiral Cunningham. He reported that the old style Type VII and Type IX U-boats, fitted with schnorkels and the new German radar, were proving to be very elusive and that sightings were extremely rare. When they did occur, there were only swirls or puffs of smoke from the schnorkels.

What were they going to do about this?, Churchill asked. Bomb the production facilities, again and again, said the navy. Air Marshal Sir Charles Portal, chief of the air staff, warned against diverting bombers from the Rumanian oil fields and German oil refineries. Admiral Max Horton then gave a bleak view from the standpoint of protection. With the new submarines, the Germans could come inshore near the roads, bay entrances, and outer harbors. On the bottom in shallow water they were protected from radar, and from asdic by cold layers of water. Like prehistoric monsters they would burrow in the mud and wait there for a convoy, then rise up to eighty feet, attack, then go down again, undetected from the surface or the air.

Admiral Horton reported on experiments to modify a submarine to cruise at twelve knots. Cunningham reported he had increased his antisubmarine surface forces to twenty-one groups but was unconvinced that the increased surveillance would solve the problem. Ideas were exchanged from Admiral Stark's suggestion that blimps be brought in to suggestions from several scientists that new IFF (Identification Friend or Foe) be put to use and coastal radar stations be increased. (ASV radar was effective on schnorkel at six miles.)

Churchill expressed himself as unalarmed, which was the

proper thing to do since others were so alarmed. He did lean toward bombing, but was cautious about asking the RAF to lay off the oil refineries at a time when Germany's air forces and Panzer divisions were at a standstill.

The navy was adamant about bombing. Why should the British handicap themselves and let the U-boats come out at all?, Admiral Cunningham asked. His paper on the subject went into technical detail as to how, where and why the bombing should be done. "To sum up, it cannot be denied that the new enemy technique is going to so handicap our countermeasures at sea that we cannot expect fully to repeat our successes of the past. The most effective countermeasures at present are those which will prevent the enemy boats from putting to sea. We have been warned by good intelligence of the danger, and the sands of time are running out. It would be a real catastrophe if we did not heed." For an admiral, speaking in a meeting dominated by politicians, that was a pretty strong statement.

But bomber command was adamant, and when the new year arrived the bombing campaign did not. Cunningham went back to the war cabinet committee again on January 3, full of trepidation. He reported:

> Since 20 December, fifteen merchant ships have been lost as a result of U-boat activity. Of the merchant ships twelve have been sunk in the English Channel and the Irish Sea. Our successes compared unfavorably with our losses . . . three U-boats were known to have been sunk, two probably sunk and there had been only one promising attack. . . . With their growing experience in the use of the schnorkel and comparative immunity from attack by bottoming tactics, the enemy have shown a much more offensive spirit. About twelve U-boats have been operating in coastal waters around the United Kingdom, two or three in the Halifax area, and one in the Western Approaches to the Straits of Gibralter. . . . The extent of the U-boat offensive depended a great deal on the spirit of the U-boat commanders which will no doubt be in-

fluenced by the success or failure of land operations, upon our ability to destroy U-boats, and also upon the degree to which bombing of U-boat construction slips, repair yards and bases can be pursued. . . . By mid-February the enemy should be able to maintain a total of sixty increasing during the spring to ninety boats on patrol. . . ."

Cunningham went on to warn again that the enemy was achieving new success with the old style boats, and that he had to expect their successes to be much greater with the Type XXI and Type XXIII.

Admiral Horton spoke of the deep mine fields in the inner waters of the United Kingdom. But the rub was that to mine your own waters was a chancy business, and the complicated system would take more resources than he possessed.

Sir Sholto Douglas reiterated his previous statement about the difficulty Coastal Command was having finding schnorkel boats.

It was a redundant performance, not usually welcomed at cabinet sessions, but it did emphasize the fact that the finest minds concerned with the U-boat menace were virtually stumped. Doenitz's new blitz radio technique—of sending a whole message in a fraction of a second—as well as schnorkel and the burrowing device, had the admirals and the air marshals grasping for straws. Sir Charles Portal of the RAF offered the only positive view that day: at least the bombing had been effective; it had interfered with the German training program and sunk and damaged a number of boats at Hamburg.

All well and good, said Admiral Cunningham, and he would not ask that bombing of U-boat yards be given priority over bombing of oil resources—but the new U-boats wouldn't use oil and therefore would not have fuel problems.

Churchill refused to get into the argument on the operational level. He expressed confidence that the RAF and the navy would come to an accomodation. By the end of January the debate was still raging at the highest levels. The navy pressed constantly for bombing but offered no solutions of its own.

And in fact no solutions were found. Admiral Doenitz was correct: he was about to bring to the British a whole new submarine war, one they were not yet able to cope with successfully. His real limitation was not to be found at sea, as in the past. But there was a limitation: at the end of January, 1945, instead of the thirty or forty Type XXI boats that Admiral Cunningham feared were about to be launched against England, only two were nearly ready, and they would not be prepared to operate until February. Two boats were being tested in the Baltic, one by Lieutenant Commander Emmermann, the other by Commander Topp. The redoubtable Lueth had now been made a full captain—Kapitan zur See—and his responsibility included preparation of a new training course for officers and men, based on a life of many days to be spent undersea. But the program had been slowed. The reason, unknown to the RAF, was the success of their bombing as well as the American bombing of communications inside Germany. In November, Bomber Command had severely damaged a number of canals, including the Dortmund-Ems canal and the Mitelland Canal. The Type XXI boats were built in eight separate sections and then transported to an assembly point in a shipyard for rapid assembly. But the prefabricated parts were too large to carry on railways or by road to Hamburg and Bremen; thus, virtually none of the new U-boats were being completed. The Germans were so near and yet so far. Their new U-boat war was being hampered by events beyond Doenitz's control. Admiral Cunningham was being proved right, although the RAF, which he criticized, was really doing the job he wanted in its own fashion.

The navy, having been caught napping at the beginning of the war, was now insisting on bombings. Cunningham was determined not to be caught again; even so the navy position was somewhat hysterical. The fact was that the figures did not justify the fears: in January, 83,000 tons, or eighteen ships sunk. To accomplish this the Germans lost fourteen submarines, a number of them destroyed in the yards at Hamburg by American bombing raids.

* * *

Fourteen U-boats were sunk in January but still the Admiralty worried. First Lord Alexander went before the House of Commons during the budget debate to give the navy estimates for 1945 and laid out the picture as the admirals saw it:

> Despite the continued and encouraging successes, however, it must certainly not be assumed that the war against the U-boat is over. The enemy is employing new equipment and new types of U-boats may be used at any time. With this new equipment we may be sure they will develop new tactics. In recent months, after a long period of comparative quiet, U-boats have appeared in the coastal waters around the United Kingdom. So far their successes have been small, but we believe the enemy has been making great efforts to renew the U-boat war on a big scale. It is highly significant that, after the trouncing which the U-boats suffered in 1943, he should consider it worthwhile to continue to devote so large a part of his resources to this form of warfare. This shows that he still considers it to be his best hope of averting defeat against a nation which lives by seaborne supplies. This is a highly important fact which will, I trust, never be forgotten by future First Lords, future Boards of Admiralty, or future Governments, or by the people of this country.

Alexander was right in his assessment of Doenitz's thinking. And the reason, known to the Admiralty, was the radical improvements in German submarine weapons. The ultimate Doenitz weapon was to be the Walter boat, a 600-ton submarine, driven by a radically new engine that worked on peroxide, thus solving the fuel problem. It would have a speed of twenty-four knots underwater, which was faster than more than half the British escorts. Besides the main engines it carried a diesel, an electric motor for emergency use and a noiseless motor. The Walter boat would be the ultimate boat for attacking Britain even within her harbors. It was, however, still some months from operational production even as the British admirals looked into the future and found it blacker and blacker.

But for the present these were the results (see Table 3).

——————————— TABLE 3 ———————————			
Month	Ships	Tonnage Sunk	U-boats Sunk
February	15	65,000	22
March	13	65,000	32
April	13	72,000	55

These figures largely represent the destruction of U-boats in the yards at Hamburg and Bremen, but not all by far. Despite the handwringing in London, the schnorkel boats were not having it all their own way, as in the case of the *U-300*.

Her captain was Lieutenant Fritz Hein. In the fall of 1944 she was equipped with a schnorkel, then sent to the mid-Atlantic, off Iceland. She torpedoed two of the four ships the British lost in that area during November. She spent sixty-one of her sixty-five-day cruise at schnorkel depth, then returned to base at Trondheim in December. She went out again on January 20 into the North Atlantic, to patrol around the Scilly Isles. But she found so little activity there that Commander Hein asked for permission to move south toward Gibraltar. It took him several days to get the word; he had to surface six times before he caught the transmission from Berlin giving him permission (one of the disadvantages of the schnorkel). Then he headed for Cape Finisterre, hugging the coast to escape aircraft and hunter-killer groups. Off Cape Saint Vincent Hein had a message from Berlin that an American convoy was about to enter the Strait of Gibraltar.

He found the convoy west of Tarifa, attacked and torpedoed two merchantmen. But now the escorts came in, found him and damaged the U-boat, causing several leaks. They were closed up with wooden plugs and bacon fat. *U-300* went into Tangier bay, where the plugs were replaced by welding, and then the *U-*

300 crossed the straits to the area between Cadiz and Cape Saint Vincent, where she burrowed into the mud. On February 2 she rose to schnorkel depth to receive messages from Berlin and sighted a convoy of LSTs. She fired a Gnat torpedo at an escort but the escort stopped its engines, and the Gnat, which homed on propeller noises, missed altogether. The commander decided to attack the transports, but then saw two more escorts coming in on him; he surfaced and surrendered the boat.

One important aspect of this tale was its implications about the morale of the U-boat men. All the rosy promises of the future, all the talk about Doenitz's marvelous new weapons, was going stale with the U-boat force. They had been pushed out of the Bay of Biscay up to the frigid Norwegian coast. Their lives were those of hunted creatures, not hunters. They tended to refer to their boats now as iron coffins. And when they got back to Germany or heard from friends at home, the story was always the same: losses, losses, losses. Despite all the brave words of the Lueths and the Topps and the other celebrated captains, the morale of the U-boat force had never been lower than it was in the spring of 1945.

* * *

As for the British, the seamen were learning what the admirals had forgotten: where there is an action there will be a reaction. Having recovered from the shock of the schnorkel, the men at sea set about dealing with it. They began sinking schnorkel boats as the Anti-U-Boat Committed indicated: ". . . the result of detection by the Asdic makes manifest its effectiveness in inshore water now that more experience has been gained. . . . In view of the anticipated expansion of the enemy of what is already a considerable effort, these successes come at a crucial time to give our forces renewed confidence in their ability to sap the still increasing boldness of German captains, who have so often seen initial successes turn into failure or disaster by the essential soundness of our tactics and devices."

There was nothing wrong with the morale of the British bulldog, on the operational level.

31

The Last U-Boat

The new U-boat war that Admiral Doenitz had promised Churchill and that severely worried the British admirals never came about, but not through any failure by Doenitz or his brilliant staff. They had it all worked out in detail; the Type XXI boats were as perfect as they could be, given the speed with which they were assembled. By May, 140 Type XXI boats had been launched and were ready for service, 20 in Norwegian harbors, 120 in Germany. Sixty-one Type XXIII boats had also been completed and a number of the "canoes" were on service in the inshore waters of Britain. So were several dozen two-man midget submarines, which had first come into use after the Allies invaded France, and thereafter worked the eastern British coastal waters and the channel. They did considerable damage to coastal shipping and the Allied war effort since they were so hard to detect. But in the last months of the war 50 "canoes" were sunk by coastal craft and another 15 by aircraft. As with all the new developments it was a question of finding the antidote, which took time, but which the British did not fail to do.

Although the Germans had their Type XXI boats ready for action, the necessary support was not forthcoming. Fuel transportation and manning could not be arranged as quickly as submarine technology. Also, because the RAF and American strategic bombers were not doing what the navy wanted, General Eisenhower was persuaded to make a special effort to capture the U-boat yards and factories. In the summer of 1944 a large contingent of American troops had rushed down to the coast of the Bay of Biscay although the German armies were retreating eastward, and Montgomery's forces along the Belgian and Dutch coasts gave special emphasis to capturing shipyards. Their prime mission was to force the U-boat operations back to Norway and Germany.

In the beginning of May the first Type XXI boat went out to raid British shipping. She was the *U-2511*, commanded by Lieutenant Commander Adelbert Schnee, who had gained his fame in the *U-60* and the *U-201*. He was instructed to take the boat into the Caribbean, which was about as far as he could go, and attack shipping, testing the boat to its maximum. Schnee had reached the Faroe Islands on May 4 when Grand Admiral Doenitz ordered all his U-boats to cease hostilities and return to their bases. He issued an order of the day explaining that the war had come to a point where there was no future for the U-boat and paid homage to the men of his command for waging "a heroic fight which knows no equal".

Lieutenant Commander Schnee was just then taking sight on a British cruiser on the edge of the North Atlantic. Having satisfied himself that he could have sunk the ship with a homing torpedo, Schnee snapped down his periscope shears and pointed the boat back east. That was the last patrol of the U-boat campaign. It ended in the North Atlantic, where it had started, where the most important battles had been fought and where Britain had won the war against the U-boats.

Afterword

The capitulation of Germany was signed by the high command (including Admiral Doenitz, who was the last fuehrer of Germany as well as commander of the navy and the U-boat corps). The Admiralty arranged with the Germans to give surrender orders to their U-boats at sea. They were to surface and report in plain language their position and number, then proceed to designated ports and anchorages. The first U-boat to comply was the *U-249*, which surfaced off the British coast and was escorted into Portland by H.M.S. *Magpie* and H.M.S. *Amethyst*. By May 31, forty-nine boats had surrendered at sea, leaving a dozen unaccounted for. The difficulty here was that the Allies had destroyed the high-powered radio transmission stations, which alone could reach the U-boats. As time passed more boats straggled in, some of which must have been lost earlier or were not accounted for. The last boat to reach port was the *U-977*, whose captain, Lieutenant Heinz Schaeffer, was an ardent nationalist out on his first patrol, with no sinkings to his credit. At first he refused to believe the surrender, then he persuaded his crew to sail with him for Argentina. They arrived on August 17, were interned, and Schaeffer and his U-boat were turned over to the Americans, who at first tended to believe the *U-977* had been the instrument for Hitler's escape to the Argentine. Later it was suggested that since Hitler was dead at the time of the surrender, it had been Martin Bormann who had escaped in the submarine. But the fact was that the escape was simply the misdirection of a loyal German who could not stand the thought of defeat.

And there was no question about the defeat, on land or at sea. The Admiralty's fears were the result of too much information about technicalities, and not enough about the state of the German economy in the last months of the war. On the surface the U-boats seemed bound to grow more formidable each week. By the end of the war the Germans had launched 1,900 submarines, of which 1,150 were commissioned. Thirteen major shipyards had built U-boats at Hamburg, Bremen, Vegesack, Danzig, Kiel, Lubeck, and Flensburg. But the Allied planes hit them day after day in the spring of 1945. On March 30, for example, United States Army Air Force bombers destroyed 13 U-boats in the yards at Bremen and Hamburg. To be sure, the Germans had the most advanced submarine technology in the world, with plans for no fewer than 45 types of submarines. They had actually gone into production on 12 types, ranging from the ocean-going Type XXI down to the Type XXVII, the two-man midget boats. They were working on a one-man midget boat, the Dolphin, and had two prototypes in testing. If Admiral Doenitz had been able to complete his U-boat building program and man his U-boats at sea, Britain would have had to start all over again in the U-boat war, as she did in the winter of 1943. But that did not happen, and given the way the war was going it could not have happened.

Admiral Doenitz never gave up his belief that if he had been given in 1939 the materials of war he needed, he could have defeated Britain with his U-boats by 1943. Certainly Churchill worried enough to make the point ceaselessly in his communications with President Roosevelt. At least a little of his anxiety had to be propagandistic. Had the U-boat menace grown worse sooner than it did, the British would have had to make a further shift of British resources to the U-boat war in the Atlantic, which would have cost the Allies the Mediterranean in all probability, and thus cost the Americans more dearly in the long run. And, had the situation been more grave than it was in 1940 and 1941, America's entry into the European war would undoubtedly have been accelerated; as noted, the United States was in fact at war with Germany on the high seas early in 1941.

From Doenitz's point of view his argument seems logical. But always in the war against the U-boat the British were in position to respond to attack. Every challenge that Doenitz put to the Allies was met and overcome—807 of the 1,150 commissioned boats had been destroyed. Doenitz had achieved an operational force of about 350 boats by 1943, where it remained. Sometimes the Allies sank more than the Germans produced; sometimes they sank less, but despite the massive German building program during the last two years of the war, the Allies sank enough boats to keep the U-boat threat under control while the Allied armies moved steadily towards Berlin.

Certainly the German U-boat force was the most dedicated and most tragic of all military forces of either side in World War II. Of a total of 39,000 men in the U-boat crews, 28,000 were killed in action and 5,000 were captured: a casualty rate of 85 percent. One can not call the U-boat war a gallant effort, for it was much too cruel for that after the early days of 1939 when the U-boat captains were observing the London Submarine Agreement of 1936. But it was a struggle of heroes against heroes, deadly enemies all the way. In the end, British perseverance and American productivity overcame German aggression and technological skill. That is the real story of the war against the U-boats.

Chapter Notes

CHAPTER 1

Page
1   "In the winter of . . . " ADM 199/1 54621 letters and reports regarding convoys.
2   "The convoy system . . ." see Edwin P. Hoyt's *The Last Cruise of the Emden, Defeat at the Falklands, Disaster at the Dardanelles.*
3   "And across the channel . . ." *The Gathering Storm,* page 147 ff, page 405 ff.
4   "When the war actually began . . ." ADM 199/1 documents relative to convoy.
5   "There were still not enough . . ." *The Gathering Storm,* page 422 f.
7   "Churchill not only had . . ." *The Gathering Storm,* page 433; ADM 199/ papers relative to the *Ark Royal.*
8   "On September 17 . . ." ADM/199/2130 54621 Report of interview with J. Busby, master of S. S. *Kafiristan.*
9   "Once again the Germans . . ." Doenitz, page 57 ff.
10   "The British had lost . . ." ADM 199/2057 54758 monthly report for September 1939 of the Admiralty Anti-U-Boat committee

CHAPTER 2

11   "At 6:45 A.M. on October 13 . . . " Log of the *U-47. The Sea Wolves,* page 58 ff.

CHAPTER 3

CHAPTER 4

CHAPTER 5

CHAPTER 6

CHAPTER 7

CHAPTER 8

44   "As 1939 drew to an end . . ." unpublished manuscript by author, *Hitler's War*.

CHAPTER 10

53   "The spring of 1940 . . ." Bekker, page 96 ff; Doenitz page 78 ff; Roskill, Volume 1, page 148 ff.
55   "More important, in the first week of the campaign . . ." Doenitz, page 84.

CHAPTER 11

58   "On May 15 Doenitz dispatched . . ." Doenitz, page 101 ff; Rohwer, pages 17–18.
61   "If even two days passed . . ." Doenitz, page 102.
62   "British and neutral ship losses in August . . ." ADM 199/2054 45478 August, 1940 monthly report of the anti-submarine warfare section.
62   "Admiral Doenitz was well aware of the British . . ." A comparison of Doenitz' statements that the Italians did not do well and the statistics compiled by Rohwer for this period indicates that Doenitz was indulging in master race chauvinism in his criticism of the Italian submarine force.
63   "But in September . . ." ADM 199/142 54758, various accounts of the encounters of units of SC 2 with U-boats.

CHAPTER 12

67   "After the attack on Convoy SC 2 . . ." Doenitz, page 105 ff; ADM 199/142 54758 accounts of convoy HX 72 and various ships within the convoy.
74   "If September was a dreadful month . . ." ADM 199/142 54758, various convoy accounts; Doenitz, page 105 ff; Rohwer, pages 27–35.
76   "Not a bad haul for eight submarines . . ." ADM 19/142 54758, detailed account of Convoy HX 79 in October report of the Admiralty anti-submarine warfare section.

CHAPTER 21

CHAPTER 22

CHAPTER 23

CHAPTER 24

CHAPTER 25

172   "Such a machine did exist . . ." Doenitz, page 265ff.

173   "In the fall of 1942 . . ." ADM 199/2059 Report of Convoy PQ 18; Rohwer, page 200.

CHAPTER 26

176   "With the British need to increase . . ." USN ESF War Diary, 1943.

177   "The first indication . . ." ADM 199/2059, account of Convoy SC 121, Convoy HX 228.

180   "On March 5 . . ." Martin Middlebrook has devoted an entire book to the stories of Convoy SC 122 and HX 229. I also used the anti-submarine section's reports on these convoys (ADM 199/2059). Doenitz also has an account in his memoirs in the chapter called "The Collapse of the U-boat War."

CHAPTER 27

188   "The next move . . ." CAB 86/2 54512 Minutes of March 24 meeting of the War Cabinet's Anti-U-boat committee.

190   "The anti U-boat committee . . ." CAB 86/2 54512 Minutes of April meetings.

192   "There was more good news . . ." ADM 199/2059 account of convoy HX 231.

193   "Convoy ONS 6 sailed . . ." ADM 199/2052 Account of attacks on convoy ONS 6, May issue of anti-submarine section reports.

193   "Convoy HX 237 sailed . . ." ADM 199/2059 Monthly reports of the anti-submarine section for May and June, 1943.

194   "On May 7 Convoy ONS 7 . . ." IBID.

194   "Convoy ON 184 . . ." IBID.

194   "Convoy HX 239 . . ." IBID.

CHAPTER 28

197   "By Autumn, 1943 . . ." ADM 199/2059 Monthly reports of anti-U-boat section. . .

197   "Convoy ONS 18 . . ." ADM 199/2061 Convoy reports.

Bibliography

In the preparation of *The U-Boat Wars* I used a number of sources in the United States and the United Kingdom. Primary were the records of the United States Navy Historical section, particularly the Operational Archives, over which Dr. Dean Allard presides. I used the war diary and other papers of the Eastern Sea Frontier. I also used Vice Admiral Eberhard Weichold's unpublished manuscript, *German Surface Ships, Policy, and Operations in World War II*, prepared for the U.S. Navy. In England I consulted records and works in the Imperial War Museum and the British Museum. But the major source of materials was the Office of Public Records at Kew. There the Admiralty records were invaluable, particularly the CAB series and the ADM series, which contain the proceedings of the War Cabinet and its subsidiary bodies, the Admiralty and all the elements of the Royal Navy. I am indebted to many archivists and librarians in this establishment.

Arnold-Forster, Mark, *The World At War*. New York: Stein and Day, 1973.

Bekker, Cajus, *Verdammte See*, English translation by Frank Ziegler, *Hitler's Naval War*. London: MacDonald and Jane's, 1974.

Bloomfield, Howard V. L., *The Compact History of the United States Coast Guard*. New York: Hawthorn Books, 1966.

Bryant, Ben, Rear Admiral, *One Man Band*, The Memoirs of a Submarine C.O. London: Kimber and Company, 1958.

Buchheim, Lothar-Guenther, *The Boat*, translated from the German by Denver and Helen Lindley. New York: Alfred A. Knopf, 1975.

Busch, Harald, *So War der UN-Boot Krieg*, English translation by L. P. R. Wilson. Published by Ballantine Books, New York, under the title *U-boats at War*, 1965.

Churchill, Winston S., *The Second World War*, Vols. 1–6. Boston: Houghton Mifflin Company, 1948–53.

Doenitz, Karl, *Zehn Jahre und Swanzig Tage*. Bonn: Athenaeum-Verlag Junker und Duennhaupt, K. G., 1958.

———."The Conduct of the War At Sea," Division of Naval Intelligence, Washington, 1946.

Frank, Wolfgang, *The Sea Wolves*,English translation by Lieutenant Commander R. O. B. Long, RNVR. New York: Rinehart and Company, 1955.

Gallery, Daniel V., Rear Admiral, *Twenty Million Tons Under the Sea (U-505)*. New York: Warner Books, 1956.

Goebbels, Joseph, *The Goebbels Diaries*, translated and edited by Fred Taylor. New York: G. P. Putnam's Sons, 1983.

Halstead, Ivor, *Heroes of the Atlantic*. New York: E. P. Dutton and Company, 1942.

Hezlet, Vice Admiral Sir Arthur, *The Submarine and Sea Power*. New York: Stein and Day, 1967.

Hinsley, F. H., *Hitler's Strategy*. New York: Cambridge University Press, 1951.

His Majesty's Stationery Office, *The Battle of the Atlantic, Official Account of the Fight against U-Boats*. London: HMSO, 1946.

Hoyt, Edwin P., *The Sea Wolves*. New York: Lancer Books, 1972.

———.*Submarines at War*. New York: Stein and Day, 1982.

Jones, R. V., *The Wizard War*. New York: Coward McCann & Geoghegan, 1978.

Lund, Paul, and Ludlum, Harry, *Night of the U-Boats*. London: W. Foulshamand Company Ltd., 1973.

MacIntyre, Donald, Captain, *U-Boat Killer*. Annapolis Naval Institute Press, 1976.

Mason, David, *U-boat: The Secret Menace*. London: MacDonald & Company, 1968.

Middlebrook, Martin, *Convoy*. London: Allen Lane, Penguin Books, 1976.

Morison, Samuel Eliot, *History of United States Naval Operations in World War II*, fifteen volumes. Boston: Atantic-Little Brown, 1948–62.

Noli, Jean, *Les Loups de l'Amiral*. Paris: Libraire Fayard, 1970; translated by J. F. Bernard and published by Doubleday Inc., Garden City, N.Y., as *The Admiral's Wolf Pack*, 1974.

Raeder, Erich, Grand Admiral, *Struggle for the Sea*, translated by Edward Fitzgerald. London: William Kimber Limited, 1959.

Reisenberg, Felix, *Sea War*. New York: Rinehart and Company, 1956.

Rogge, Bernhard, with Freank, Wolfgang, *Schiff 16*. Oldenburg: Gerhard Stalling Verlag, 1955.

Rohwer, Juergen, *Die U-boat Erfolge Der Achsenmachte 1939–1945*. Bibliothek fuer Aeitgeschichte, Munich: J. F. Lehmanns Verlag, 1968; English, translation by John A. Broadwin, Naval Institute Press, Annapolis, 1983.

Roscoe, Theodore, *United States Submarine Operations in World War II*. Annapolis: Naval Institute Press, 1949.

Roskill, S. W. Captain, DSC RN, *History of the Second World War, United Kingdom Military Series, The War at Sea, 1939-45*, (four volumes). London: Her Majesty's Stationery Office, 1954.

Ruge, Friedrich, Admiral, *Der Seekrieg*, Translation into English, *The German Navy's Story*, by Commander M. G. Saunders, RN. Annapolis: Naval Institute Press, 1957.

Schaefer, Heinz, *U-Boat 977*. New York: W. W. Norton and Company, 1952.

Shirer, William L., *The Rise and Fall of the Third Reich*. New York: Simon and Schuster, 1959.

Stevenson, William, *A Man Called Intrepid*. New York: Harcourt Brace Jovanovich, 1976.

Waters, John M. *Bloody Winter*. Princeton: Van Nostrand Company, 1967.

Watts, Anthony J., *The U-boat Hunters*. London: MacDonald and Janes, 1976.

Werner, Herbert A., *Iron Coffins*. New York: Rinehart and Winston, 1969.

West, Nigel, *MI-5*. New York: Stein and Day, 1982.

Index